Japan and East Asian Regionalism

In the post-war period, Japanese foreign policy was structured around the preservation of good relations with the United States. Japan's relations with regional countries and involvement in regional issues were relatively underdeveloped even though Japan was the biggest regional economic power. In recent years, there is discernible evidence that the Japanese government is looking to play a larger role within its region, and this is an increasingly topical issue. In the light of this, *Japan and East Asian Regionalism* looks at Japanese regional foreign policy, not in terms of Japan's relations with specific countries but rather in terms of specific regional issues and problems.

After an introductory overview of Japanese foreign policy – which also traces issues of regional leadership and foreign policy activism – the book explores recent political developments within Japan, and how these might impact on future foreign policy priorities and objectives. Further chapters consider issues such as: the nexus between domestic politics and foreign policy; environmental aid and management; human rights and democracy; and conflict management.

The book concludes that whilst it is unlikely Japan will unilaterally exert its economic power and influence to secure a political leadership role within the Asia Pacific region, Japanese foreign policy is increasingly marked by greater activism and responsibility, even in the difficult issue area of conflict management. Much more however will remain to be done to change the negative perceptions of Japan, including its image as an environmental vandal.

S. Javed Maswood is a Senior Lecturer in the School of International Business, Griffith University. His many publications include *International Political Economy and Globalization, East Asian Crisis and Japanese Political Economy,* and *Japan and Protection: The Rise of Protectionist Sentiment and the Japanese Response* (also published by Routledge).

The Nissan Institute/Routledge Japanese Studies Series

Other titles in the series:

Industrial Harmony in Modern Japan: The Intervention of a Tradition
W. Dean Kinzley

Japanese Science Fiction: A View of a Changing Society
Robert Matthew

The Japanese Numbers Game: The Use and Understanding of Numbers in Modern Japan
Thomas Crump

Ideology and Practice in Modern Japan
Edited by Roger Goodman and Kirsten Refsing

Technology and Industrial Development in Pre-war Japan: Mitsubishi Nagasaki Shipyard, 1884–1934
Yukiko Fukasaku

Japan's Early Parliaments, 1890–1905: Structure, Issues and Trends
Andrew Fraser, R.H.P. Mason and Philip Mitchell

Japan's Foreign Aid Challenge: Policy Reform and Aid Leadership
Alan Rix

Emperor Hirohito and Shōwa Japan: A Political Biography
Stephen S. Large

Japan: Beyond the End of History
David Williams

Ceremony and Ritual in Japan: Religious Practices in an Industrialized Society
Edited by Jan van Bremen and D.P. Martinez

Understanding Japanese Society: Second Edition
Joy Hendry

The Fantastic in Modern Japanese Literature: The Subversion of Modernity
Susan J. Napier

Militarization and Demilitarization in Contemporary Japan
Glenn D. Hook

Growing a Japanese Science City: Communication in Scientific Research
James W. Dearing

Architecture and Authority in Japan
William H. Coaldrake

Women's *Gidayū* and the Japanese Theatre Tradition
A. Kimi Coaldrake

Democracy in Post-war Japan: Maruyama Masao and the Search for Autonomy
Rikki Kersten

Treacherous Women of Imperial Japan: Patriarchal Fictions, Patricidal Fantasies
Hélène Bowen Raddeker

Japan and East Asian Regionalism

Edited by S. Javed Maswood

London and New York

First published 2001
by Routledge
11 New Fetter Lane, London EC4P 4EE

Simultaneously published in the USA and Canada
by Routledge
29 West 35th Street, New York, NY 10001

Routledge is an imprint of the Taylor & Francis Group

Typeset in Baskerville by
HWA Text and Data Management, Tunbridge Wells
Printed and bound in Great Britain by
University Press, Cambridge

British Library Cataloguing in Publication Data
A catalogue record for this book is available from the British Library

Library of Congress Cataloging in Publication Data
Japan and East Asian regionalism / edited by S. Javed Maswood.
    p. cm. – (The Nissan Institute/Routledge Japanese studies series)
    Includes bibliographical references and index.
    1. East Asia – Foreign relations – Japan. 2. Japan – Foreign
relations – East Asia. 3. Asia, Southeastern – Foreign relations –
Japan. 4. Japan – Foreign relations – Asia, Southeastern. 5. Japan –
Foreign relations – 1989–. I. Maswood, Syed Javed. II. Series

DS518.45 .J363 2001   00–058262
327.5205´09´049–dc21

ISBN 0-415-23747-5

Contents

Contributors

Peter Dauvergne is Senior Lecturer in the Department of Government, Sydney University, Sydney, Australia.

Hirata Keiko is Professor of Politics at the University of Hawaii at Manoa, Hawaii, USA.

S. Javed Maswood is Senior Lecturer in the School of International Business, Griffith University, Brisbane, Australia.

T.J. Pempel is the Boeing Professor of Politics in the Jackson School of International Studies, University of Washington, Seattle, USA.

Lam Peng Er is Research Fellow at the East Asian Institute, National University of Singapore, Singapore.

Watanabe Akio is Professor of International Relations at the School of International Politics, Business and Economics and Aoyama Gakuin University, Tokyo, and President of the Research Institute for Peace and Security, Tokyo, Japan.

Abbreviations

AMF	Asian Monetary Fund
APEC	Asia Pacific Economic Corporation
ARF	ASEAN Regional Forum
ASEM	Asia Europe Meeting
ASEAN	Association of South East Asian Nations
ASEAN–ISIS	Association of South East Asian Nations–Institute of Strategic and International Studies
ASPAC	Asia and Pacific Council
CBMs	confidence building measures
CGDK	Coalition Government of Democratic Kampuchea
CGP	Clean Government Party
CMEA	Council for Mutual Economic Assistance
CoCom	Coordinating Committee for Export Control
CPP	Cambodian People's Party
DAC	Development Assistance Committee
DK	Democratic Kampuchea
DRV	Democratic Republic of Vietnam
DSP	Democratic Socialist Party
EAEC	East Asian Economic Caucas
ESCAP	Economic Commission for Asia and the Far East
EU	European Union
EXIM	export-import
FDI	foreign direct investment
FUNCINPEC	*Front Uni National pour Cambodge Indépendent, Neutre, Pacifique et Coopératif* (National United Front for an Independent, Peaceful, Neutral and Co-operative Cambodia)
FY	financial year
G-5	Group of Five
G-7	Group of Seven
G-8	Group of Eight
HDTV	high definition television
ICCPR	International Covenant on Civil and Political Rights
ICETT	International Centre for Environmental Technology Transfer

ICORC	International Committee on the Reconstruction of Cambodia
ICSECR	International Covenant on Social, Economic and Cultural Rights
IEA	International Energy Association
IMF	International Monetary Fund
ITTO	International Tropical Timber Organisation
JBIC	Japan Bank for International Cooperation
JCP	Japanese Communist Party
JDA	Japan Defense Agency
JETRO	Japan External Trade Organisation
JICA	Japan International Cooperation Agency
JNP	Japan New Party
JNR	Japan National Railways
JRP	Japan Renewal Party
JSP	Japanese Socialist Party
JUTA	Japan-Vietnam Trading Association
KPNL	Kampuchean People's National Liberation
KPRP	Kampuchean People's Revolutionary Party
LDP	Liberal Democratic Party
MC	Mekong Committee
MFA	Ministry of Foreign Affairs
MFN	most favoured nation
MHW	Ministry of Health and Welfare
MIA	missing in action
MITI	Ministry of International Trade and Industry
MOE	Ministry of Environment
MOF	Ministry of Finance
MOFA	Ministry of Foreign Affairs
MPT	Ministry of Post and Telecommunications
MRC	Mekong River Commission
NAFTA	North American Free Trade Area
NFP	New Frontier Party
NGO	non-governmental organisation
NLD	National League for Democracy
NPS	New Party Sakigake
NTT	Nippon Telephone and Telegraph
OAS	Organisation of American States
ODA	Official Development Assistance
OECD	Organisation for Economic Cooperation and Development
OECF	Overseas Economic Cooperation Fund
PAVN	People's Army of Vietnam
PDD	Partnership for Democratic Development
PDK	Party of Democratic Kampuchea
PKO	peacekeeping operations
PRC	People's Republic of China
PRK	People's Republic of Kampuchea

RITE	Research Institute of Innovative Technology for the Earth
SDF	(Japanese) Self Defense Forces
SDPJ	Social Democratic Party of Japan
SEANWFZ	Southeast Asia Nuclear Weapon Free Zone
SEATO	Southeast Asian Treaty Organisation
SLORC	State Law and Order Restoration Council
SNC	Supreme National Council
SOV	State of Vietnam
SPDC	State Peace and Development Council
SRV	Socialist Republic of Vietnam
UNGA	United Nations General Assembly
UNSC	United Nations Security Council
UNTAC	United Nations Transitional Authority in Cambodia
USAID	United States Agency for International Development

Series editor's preface

At the beginning of the new century Japan, widely seen as a 'miracle country' between the late 1950s and early 1990s, was struggling out of its 1990s recession, which became particularly acute between 1997 and 1999. The 1990s were a time of turbulence in Japanese politics as in the economy, and pressure for restructuring has been strong. Grave weaknesses in the banking system were revealed in the form of a massive overhang of bad debt inherited from the boom period of the late 1980s and subsequent collapse. An ambitious programme of reform of the political system was announced by the Hosokawa coalition Government that replaced single-party rule by the Liberal Democratic Party (LDP) in 1993, but the path towards implementing reform proved far from smooth. Indeed, after a brief period out of office, the LDP was soon back in power as part of a succession of coalition arrangements, during which it gradually clawed back its dominant political position. Even at the start of the new century, however, the LDP was still unable to run the country without help from other parties, and curiously enough this help was beginning to bring about results in the form of the implementation of a reformist agenda. In particular the dominant role of government bureaucracy over policy-making was now being challenged through parliamentary legislation. Even the 1946 Constitution, which had inhibited Japan from acting as a 'normal nation' in defence matters, was now to be the subject of scrutiny by parliamentary commissions. Nevertheless, uncertainties remained and were being compounded. The removal of Prime Minister Obuchi from his post having suffered a severe stroke in April 2000 coincided with the withdrawal of a large section of one of the smaller parties in the coalition. Obuchi's successor, Mori, seemed unlikely to steer a conspicuously different course from his predecessor, but his leadership qualities were widely questioned.

The Nissan Institute/Routledge Japanese Studies Series seeks to foster an informed and balanced, but not uncritical, understanding of Japan. One aim of the series is to show the depth and variety of Japanese institutions, practices and ideas. Another is, by using comparisons, to see what lessons, positive or negative, can be drawn for the other countries. The tendency in commentary on Japan to resort to out-dated, ill-informed or sensational stereotypes still remains, and needs to be combated.

For most of the past half-century, the principal pillar of Japanese foreign policy has been the relationship – both economic and defence-related – with the United States. Japan was generally seen as a global, rather than a regional player in international affairs, though the focus of her foreign policy was far more economic than political or strategic. Over the past decade or more, however, a rather more regional focus has become evident in the orientation of Japan's external relations. This trend has not – as some observers thought in the early 1990s – led to a breakdown in the time-honoured structures of the Japan–US relationship. But in a post-Cold War world where the East Asian region still maintains something of a Cold War residue, Japan's attention has necessarily come to shift focus towards regional problems and linkages.

This book, ably edited and part written by S. Javed Maswood, tackles the often confusing and multi-faceted character of Japanese relations with its region. The authors here brought together are leaders in their respective fields of expertise. Between them they analyse the relationship of regionalism to Japanese foreign policy, the domestic political aspects of it, region-wide issues of environmental protection and human rights, and more specific relations with Vietnam and other parts of Southeast Asia.

J.A.A. Stockwin

1 Introduction

S. Javed Maswood

The papers in this volume were, with one exception, first presented at a workshop on Japan and Regionalism in Brisbane in January 1998. The Faculty of International Business and Politics, Griffith University provided funding for the workshop and it provided participants an opportunity to present and discuss their papers so that comments and suggestions could be incorporated into revised papers. These have been collected together in this volume. I am grateful to contributors to this volume for their diligence and for completing the revisions promptly.

The papers collected here do not necessarily present a consistent view of Japanese foreign policy but this is a reflection of Japan studies in general. Japan's international role and responsibility have been debated since the early 1970s and we continue that debate not with a view to bring closure but rather to ascertain policy initiatives and effectiveness in several areas of regional significance. The participants who presented papers at the workshop were selected for their expertise rather than for consistency of views. Hirata Keiko was a late entrant but her paper on the reactive nature of Japanese foreign policy is useful both as a complement to the others and in rethinking the basic essentials of Japanese foreign policy. Her paper is an expanded and revised version of one that appeared in *Japanese Studies* in 1998.

The papers deal with Japan's political involvement in the Asian region. One option would have been to try and understand Japan's regional diplomacy through a bilateral approach. That would, no doubt, have yielded many interesting insights but we have avoided a country focus, opting instead to analyse Japanese foreign policy through a thematic approach. An advantage of focusing on issues rather than on bilateral relations was that it allowed us to highlight the nature of Japanese involvement in some of the key areas of contemporary concern, such as environmental protection and human rights. The issues looked at are certainly not exhaustive of the possibilities but important enough to warrant closer analysis and scrutiny.

In the post-war period, Japan's regional involvement was not extensive but this is now in a process of transition. Besides regional initiatives to engage Japan as an active player, Japanese foreign policy also displays attempts to play a constructive regional role. This transition can be attributed to several factors, including the end of the Cold War, domestic political reforms within Japan and regional developments. There have been important developments in domestic politics within Japan, such as the decimation of the socialist left and resurgence of conservative political parties. Electoral and administrative reform agendas have also realigned the powers of the administrative elite and political leaders in Japan. Pempel looks at domestic political changes to trace the potential impact on foreign policy. He argues that the changes reflect a 'regime shift' in Japan but while he does not anticipate a major shift in foreign policy patterns, he does expect Japan to play an increased role in Asia subject to the constraints of global interests.

Pempel begins his chapter by outlining the basic features of 'embedded mercantilism', the dominant post-war policy orientation of successive Japanese governments. He argues that, beginning in the 1990s, regime stability was eroded by a series of shocks that resulted in changes to domestic political structures and institutions, such as electoral reforms, bureaucratic reforms and political realignment, including the demise of the traditional left in Japanese politics. Moreover, according to Pempel, progressive reforms and economic liberalisation have also eroded the mercantilist orientation of the Japanese government. All these changes lead him to conclude that Japan is in the middle of a regime shift and that the shape of the future regime, while still uncertain, can be gleaned from an examination of probable socio-economic cleavages, political and economic institutions, and public policy profile. In terms of foreign policy, it would be unlikely for Japan to continue its relatively passive international role but he also argues that we should not expect a dramatically more activist foreign policy role. In general the shape of Japanese foreign policy will be decided by outcomes in the three central tensions facing the Japanese government: that between regionalism and internationalism; between domestic and international forces; and between economic orientation and a military/diplomatic focus.

The currency and financial crisis that affected several East Asian countries in 1997 has hastened the process of Japan becoming a more active foreign policy player. The crisis was a result of several factors, such as economic mismanagement in East Asia, cronyism and corruption, and misallocation of foreign capital inflows. The crisis generated considerable regional and extra-regional expectations that Japan would play a constructive role in assisting the countries burdened by the debt crisis and help avert severe regional and global economic downturn. It was an important opportunity for Japan to demonstrate its leadership qualities and while the Japanese government was, indeed, generous in providing financial assistance, there is a growing perception that Japan has, again, failed to grasp the moment and establish leadership credentials. The expectation that the Japanese government would move quickly to reflate its depressed economy in order to generate economic growth in the region has not been translated into policy. A common explanation for this failure is that Japan, as before, had neglected its international responsibilities in the interest of good domestic housekeeping. In his study of the Depression of the 1930, Charles Kindleberger criticised the US for displaying international irresponsibility by not taking steps to liberalise its economy. In the contemporary crisis, similar criticisms might be hurled at Japan for not reflating domestic demand and not liberalising its economy quickly enough to allow regional countries to export their way out of the financial crisis.

Such an assessment of the Japanese response to the crisis is not altogether wrong except that the crisis has, in fact, had a serious impact on the paradigm of Japan's post-war diplomatic relationship. Japanese foreign policy was structured around its relations with the United States and minimal regional involvement. Now Japan is being asked to provide regional leadership and assume a position of responsibility for the region. This, in itself is nothing radical except that there is also a possibility that it may not be easy for Japan, in future, to balance its regional links with the interests of its trans-Pacific alliance. This is a theme I explore in my paper. I argue that Japan is unlikely to pursue a course that might jeopardise its relationship with the United States. Instead, Japan's regional involvement has to be understood as not only a delicate balancing act but also as an exercise in preventative diplomacy against that brand of insular regionalism that could harm the prospects of maintaining foreign policy on an even keel between competing American and regional interests.

The issue of Japan's regional diplomacy and future directions is also taken up by two other papers in this volume. Japanese foreign policy has been characterised as being 'reactive' to highlight the absence of initiatives and assertiveness even though it has the capacity to act in a more proactive manner. A reactive state, thus, chooses not to take initiatives and in the case of Japan, produces a situation where it has to be compelled to act. The compelling pressure is externally derived, in particular from the United States. There is an extensive literature on various aspects of the reactive nature of Japanese foreign policy and the role of 'gaiatsu' or foreign pressure.[1]

Lam Peng Er argues that the end of the Cold War and the Gulf War were the catalysts for Japanese activism in its regional diplomacy. In the Gulf War, Japan's involvement was only financial, which even if not insignificant failed to measure up to western expectations that Japanese defence personnel would stand shoulder to shoulder with troops from other countries. The extent of western criticisms finally forced a recognition within Japan that it could not appease western sentiments with chequebook diplomacy. But before Japan could become more actively involved, the internal legislative framework had to be established to permit Japanese participation in foreign operations under UN command. Following the passage of the Peacekeeping Operations Bill in 1992, the Japanese government decided to participate in UN peacekeeping operations in Cambodia. Tokyo, he says was also instrumental in establishing the ASEAN Regional Forum (ARF) to provide a forum for discussion of regional political and security issues. Alongside these successes, there are also failures of Japanese diplomacy, one being the Japanese offer to help resolve the Spratlys dispute. The Spratly Islands in the South China Sea are claimed by several countries and the Japanese offer was made with a view to prevent any possibility of armed conflict that might disrupt sea lanes of communication and trade. The Japanese offer, however, made little impression on the Chinese government, which simply reiterated its standing policy that the Spratlys were Chinese territory and that outside intervention was unwelcome. The paper shows that while Japan has increased its foreign policy profile, its efforts have not been uniformly rewarded.

In her paper, Hirata first expands on the reactive state thesis and argues that Japanese foreign policy cannot be understood as either exclusively reactive or exclusively proactive, even in dealings with one target country. Japanese foreign policy, she says, is a hybrid and that even in those instances of foreign policy activism, there is a clear desire not to be seen as aggressive. The hybrid nature of Japanese foreign policy is a result of two competing demands: becoming a regional leader and maintaining links with the United States. Because of the latter concerns, Hirata says that Japanese activism is evident particularly in issues that do not directly engage American interests.

Moreover, she argues that the Japanese pattern of pro-activism is not aggressive but cautious. She applies this model to explain Japanese relations with Vietnam. Even before the Vietnam War ended in 1975, Japan had normalised diplomatic relations with North Vietnam but the fall of Saigon encouraged Japan to become more politically active. The Fukuda Doctrine (1977), she says, was evidence of Japan trying to act as a bridge between Indochina and ASEAN and bring the two blocs together in a relationship of peaceful co-existence. However, before anything could materialise, the outbreak of hostilities between Vietnam and Cambodia (1978) and between Vietnam and China (1979) put an end to any Japanese vision to work for a more peaceful Southeast Asia. Japan did not become more actively engaged until 1989 when Vietnam withdrew from Cambodia. This new period of activism coincided with the end of the Cold War and declining US interest in Indochina. There was thus, less at stake for Japan in the context of its relations with the United States.

Peter Dauvergne looks at Japan's involvement in combating regional environmental damage through the provision of environmental aid. Environmental damage has reached epic proportions and is evidenced by the continued destruction of rain forests, pollution in the Sea of Japan, and acid rain across the region. In recent years, Japan has tried to project an image of environmental leader and has had some limited success, for instance in getting nine East Asian countries to agree, in early 1998, on the need to establish a regional network to monitor sulphur emissions and the incidence of acid rain. Japanese initiatives in establishing such a network had to battle regional suspicions of Japanese motives.[2] In general, this regional suspicion was an important obstacle to Japan emerging as an environmental leader, as described by Dauvergne. He also identifies some of the domestic political and economic problems that have reduced the effectiveness of Japanese environmental aid and compromised its ability to act as a leader. It is important to note however, that Japan allows recipient countries more control over aid projects than do other donor countries and this may be another factor limiting the effectiveness of Japanese aid.

Official Development Assistance (ODA) is the principal tool of environmental diplomacy and it is also the main instrument in Japan's human rights diplomacy. Human rights and democracy are key issues in the Asia Pacific region, especially in the period following the currency crisis. It had been common for Southeast Asian countries to contain democratic impulses and limit human rights using self-serving arguments of Asian values and Asian democracy. Asian values have been used also to explain rapid economic growth in the region but the financial crisis exposed the tenuous links, if any, between values and economic outcomes. The collapse of the Suharto regime in Indonesia in 1998 was a direct consequence of the Asian crisis. It exposed the lie that liberal democracy is inconsistent with Asian values although it is by no means certain that Indonesia will emerge as a liberal democracy. There is no denying, however, that there is considerable underlying support for political openness and freedom. The West and the United States have been strong supporters of democratic reforms in Asia, and elsewhere, and it is arguable that the IMF conditions imposed on Indonesia following the crisis were partly motivated by a desire to advance the democratic cause. Watanabe Akio observes that Japan has used its ODA to encourage regional countries to observe and promote human rights, but in a non-confrontational way. He also points out that Japanese human rights diplomacy incorporates both principles and pragmatism, perhaps more of the latter. The Japanese approach to human rights and democracy is in sharp contrast to the more confrontational stand of the US and western governments. The West has emphasised political and civil rights while Asian countries have emphasised economic and social rights. Japan, according to Watanabe, has walked a tightrope between these two position and formulated a 'solution' in the shape of a "comprehensive approach", which emphasises the need for an integralist approach. Other important aspects of Japanese human rights diplomacy, according to Watanabe, are pragmatism and multilateralism.

Finally, by way of acknowledgement, I would like to register my thanks to Professors David Lim, William Shepherd and Colin Mackerras for support and help in organising the workshop. Thanks are due also to all workshop participants, those who presented papers and those who participated as discussants and commentators. This was a collective exercise and would not have been successful without their commitment to see it through to completion. Although it is not possible to individually thank all those who contributed to the workshop and to this volume I must acknowledge my debt of gratitude to Professors Hayden Lesbirel (James Cook University), Purnendra Jain (University of Adelaide) and Amitav Acharya (York University). I would also like to thank Selina Tang for her administrative assistance.

Notes

1 See for example, Calder, K., 'Japanese Foreign Economic Policy Formation: Explaining the Reactive State', *World Politics*, vol. 40, July 1988 ; Rosenbluth, F.M., *Financial Politics in Contemporary Japan*, Cornel University Press, Ithaca, 1989; Encarnation, D.J. and Mark Mason, 'Neither MITI Nor America: The Political Economy of Capital Liberalization in Japan', *International Organization*, vol. 44, no. 1, Winter 1990.
2 See 'Asian States Take 'First Step' on Acid Rain', *Nature*, vol. 392, 2 April 1998, p. 426.

2 Japanese foreign policy and regionalism

S. Javed Maswood

The US–Japan relationship has been the mainstay of Japanese foreign policy in the post-war period. The importance and endurance of this relationship is underpinned by the US–Japan Security Treaty and by their economic linkages. It is remarkable also that political bonds have remained firm despite sustained trade imbalance and periodic economic and political crises. By contrast, apart from a generous aid programme, official pronouncements and rhetorical assertions of common identity, Japan remained relatively uninvolved in East Asian political, security or economic relations. The West had more to offer to Japan and, in any event, there was little goodwill towards Japan in the region as a result of wartime experiences.

Over time, as memories faded and as the Japanese economy rebounded from its wartime destruction, some East Asian countries began to emulate the Japanese growth model and recreated their own economic miracles. The Malaysian government, for example, encouraged a 'Look East' policy in the early 1980s to learn from the Japanese economic experience. Like Japan, these countries also relied on the American market as a destination for their manufactured exports. Consequently, regional trade interdependence remained low until the mid-1980s, when Japanese firms began to invest in production facilities in East Asia. The catalyst for a growing division of labour within the region was the revaluation of the Yen in late 1985. This eroded the competitiveness of Japanese exporters and led to their foreign investment activities. Between 1988 and 1990, Japanese foreign direct investment in Taiwan, Hong Kong, Thailand, Malaysia, Singapore and Indonesia totalled US$17.6 billion compared to US$4.6 billion invested by American firms in these countries.[1] Japan also became more involved in regional security and co-operation, proposing or playing a leading role in the establishment of the ASEAN Regional Forum (ARF) and Asia Pacific Economic Cooperation (APEC).

This simplified depiction of post-war Japanese foreign policy approximates developments in the post-Meiji period when relations with Asia, initially, were subordinate to westernisation and modernisation. Driven by a desire to catch up with the West, Japan turned a blind eye to the region. Later, when Japan did shift its gaze to Asia, it was as a target of imperial conquest. This last aspect of early Japanese foreign policy is unlikely to repeat itself and the process of regional engagement will be peaceful. The logical end-point of this involvement might be regional integration and, indeed, this can be identified as the ultimate objective of some regional countries, like Malaysia. For meaningful regional integration, it is inevitable that Japan be persuaded to take on a more active and assertive political role. However, even as Japan interacts more extensively with East Asian countries, Japanese foreign policy objectives are not served by policies that instigate institutionalised regionalism. This may jeopardise Japan's relations with the United States and it is unlikely that Japan will abandon its western orientation for regionalism. Japanese interests are not to initiate policies that culminate in a tightly organised regional structure or an economic bloc. Instead, Japan can be expected to pursue a form of regionalism that dampens regional identity and is consistent with the current directions of US–Japan relations. However, given the potential for conflict between US and East Asian countries, Japanese foreign policy must seek to envelop and subsume this potential for conflict within a broader framework for cooperation in the interest of preserving congenial relations across the Pacific. Not surprisingly, the Japanese government has established a new post of Ambassador for Asia Pacific Cooperation within the Ministry of Foreign Affairs to reflect these developments and to facilitate further regional cooperation through the Asia Pacific Economic Cooperation (APEC) process. The challenge for Japanese foreign policy is also to develop policies that will allow it to effectively manage conflicts within the broadly defined Asia–Pacific region.

East Asian regionalism

Binding the region together is intra-regional trade, commerce and investment linkages that have expanded rapidly since the mid 1980s. In 1990, East Asian economies accounted for less than 30 per cent of all Japanese exports but by 1995 their share had increased to 42 per cent. This was a significant shift in market orientation away from the US. In the same period, however, Japan, along with the US, became a less important export destination for East Asian countries. Instead, intra-regional trade expanded from 31.6 per cent to 38.3 per cent.[2] This can be attributed, at least partially, to the nature of Japanese manufacturing FDI that is targeted not only at host country demand but demand also in third countries, particularly regional markets. The growth in East Asian economic interdependence was achieved without the benefit of any institutional framework to co-ordinate or manage economic relations. According to Edward Lincoln, the failure to evolve regional institutions was due to the absence of regional leadership. The question then is whether Japan is now in a position to assume a leadership role in creating regional integration and whether that role is at all in the Japanese interest.

The best example of regional integration today is the European Union. The process of European integration began after the Second World War following a couple of earlier attempts to create unity through force. In East Asia, too, the first attempt at regional integration involved the application of force. Japan's stated goal of creating a Greater East Asia Co-Prosperity Sphere ended in disaster for Japan but not before inflicting tragic consequences on other East Asian countries. The result was Japan's alienation from its regional neighbours. Regional hostility toward Japan has lingered in the absence of a formal apology from the government of Japan for wartime atrocities. In late 1998, when the Chinese President visited Japan for an official visit, the two governments issued a Joint Declaration but the Chinese President refused to take part in a signing ceremony on grounds of a Japanese refusal to include a written apology in the Joint Declaration. Japan's difficulties in the region arise not only from the issue of an apology but also from criticisms that Japanese educators do not present a full and accurate portrayal of Japanese atrocities during the war in history text books.

Nonetheless, in the fifty years since the end of the war, misgivings about Japan have abated considerably and not simply because of the passage of time. Trade and financial interdependence have progressively expunged the emotional content in Japan's regional relations. In 1998, as mentioned above, the Chinese refused to sign their Joint Declaration but this did not prevent them reaching agreement on other issues to deepen levels of economic cooperation. Still, the Japanese government, aware of regional sensitivities, has resisted US pressures to significantly expand its defence capabilities. It has, instead, sought to reassure regional countries of its peaceful intentions. Japanese defence spending remains low as a percentage of its GNP and the government has sought also to reassure regional countries of its peaceful intentions by adopting the three non-nuclear principles, which forbid the possesion, introduction or deployment of nuclear weapons in Japan. At the same time, the level of economic cooperation and exchange is also a source of assurance that Japan will not revert to the militarism of the past.

The idea of East Asian regionalism was advanced in the 1980s in order to consolidate growth and prosperity and to enhance the region's collective influence in international affairs. The Malaysian government was particularly vocal in advocating exclusive regionalism to maximise the global impact of the region's economic achievements and success. Later, in 1997, amid difficulties surrounding the Asian currency crisis, the Malaysian government reiterated the need for regional unity to enhance internal resilience and to safeguard growth prospects from externally generated disturbances.[3] ASEAN leaders at a summit meeting in December 1997 reiterated this message. Prime Minister Mahathir of Malaysia has also tried to recruit the Japanese government into a leadership role. In 1992, while visiting Japan, he invited Japan to become a regional leader. Again, in late March 1997, Prime Minister Mahathir, in a speech at Waseda University in Tokyo, urged the Japanese government to provide leadership in order to realise a united East Asia that might play a larger international role in the twenty-first century. The Japanese response has remained non-committal and unenthusiastic.

The Malaysian proposal of an East Asian Economic Caucus (EAEC) can, at least partially, be attributed to deeply held suspicions in Malaysia, about the US regional agenda and American support for human rights and democracy. To unite the East Asian countries and to give it negotiating strength vis-à-vis external actors, the proposed East Asian Economic Caucus excluded not only the United States but also Australia and New Zealand. While progress was slow, the Eighth ASEAN Ministerial Meeting in 1996 reiterated its commitment to the realisation of the EAEC. Further progress toward the EAEC was made at the December 1997

ASEAN summit with the support of China, which had warmed to the idea of an EAEC. The Chinese Government, in meetings with ASEAN leaders, paved the way for the de facto formation of EAEC by supporting the idea of another meeting of Northeast and Southeast Asian leaders within twelve months. There are other processes, as well, such as the Asia–Europe Meeting (ASEM) that enhance the prospect and credibility of East Asian regionalism. The first Asia–Europe Meeting (ASEM), in March 1996, brought together fifteen European and ten East Asian countries for inter-regional dialogue. The ASEM also strengthened East Asian exclusivity by excluding, at Malaysia's insistence, Australia and New Zealand. On this occasion Noordin Soopie, Director of the Malaysian Center for Strategic and International Studies and a long time spokesperson for Prime Minister Mahathir remarked that this was the beginning of a new world order not dominated by the US.[4]

Japan, however, has not been an active supporter of East Asian regionalism. Noda argues East Asian regionalism could potentially unleash developments paralleling the pre-war period when the Japanese government tried to exclude the US in order to realise the Co-Prosperity Sphere. He writes that, 'If we hope not to repeat this tragic blunder, we must do everything we can to stop the rising tide of Asianism …' especially if it leads to anti-American sentiments.[5] Even discounting the probability of this particular scenario, there remains a possibility that East Asian regionalism will impede Japan's primary foreign policy objective of maintaining good relations with the US. Instead of a narrowly conceived East Asian regionalism, Yoichi Funabashi argues that Japan, because of its global economic interests, should play a global political role rather than a regional role. He writes that 'Japan's reluctance and resistance to formulating a regional strategy and the heavy dependence of its economic expansion on the United States and world trade have made Japan one of the few countries in the modern world with truly global interests'.[6] Nonetheless, as indicated above, the Malaysian government is avidly pursuing East Asian regionalism and there appears to be some support for it from the Chinese government. The challenge for the Japanese government is to counter this drive for regionalism.

For the moment, the East Asian currency crisis has relegated the issue of regional integration to the backburner. Malaysia, Indonesia, Thailand and other East Asian countries are preoccupied with managing the crisis and with minimising the adverse consequences of drastic economic slowdown and its political fallout. The crisis, as should be expected, has focused attention on more pressing economic and social problems but the issue of regionalism cannot be assumed to have disappeared altogether. As a consequence, Japan has more time to develop a strategy to deal with it when it resurfaces. However, a more active political role will be required if Japan is to successfully channel regionalism in ways that do not jeopardise its primary links with the United States.

Foreign policy activism and leadership can be variously interpreted. At one level, international leadership involves the provision of public goods through, for example, an open economy to absorb surplus production. Just as the decision by the United States, to rescind pre-war protectionism, was critical to the establishment of global liberal trade after the war, Japan might be expected to use its economic strength and capacity to facilitate further liberalisation, at least within the region. To some extent, as observed by Richard Rosecrance and Jennifer Taw, Japan is already emerging as a systemic leader to supplement the US. Like those of other international leaders before it, they point out that Japanese policies reflect the importance of helping to maintain the international trading and financial system.[7] Japanese government policies however, do not even suggest the possibility of Japan supplanting the US as the international leader. Wary of antagonising the United States, Japan has assiduously steered away from any course of action that is not supported by the United States. Following the Asian currency crises, the Japanese government proposed the establishment of an Asian Fund. However, it abandoned the idea of formal institutionalism when it became apparent that the US would not support an Asian Fund, if it meant any weakening of IMF conditionality. For similar reasons, Japan has also not used its economic strength to raise the region's international profile or champion regional interests.

Leadership requires policy activism and initiatives to shape the international environment and create a climate within which to pursue national objectives. As mentioned, however, Japanese foreign policy has, in the past, not been known for activism. Even as Japan has assumed greater responsibility for system support, Japan, according to Calder, has rarely taken any independent initiative of it own.[8] Failure to utilise its economic potential for political objectives might be because of missing preconditions to international leadership and activism. Structurally, Japan's foreign policy establishment is bureaucratic and, as mentioned above, there remain some reservations within the region about Japan in a leadership role. For Japan to emerge as a regional leader, it will have to overcome both these structural constraints.

Japan's foreign policy options

The western orientation of Japanese foreign policy was established early in the post-war period. This was the result of several factors, including regional antipathy towards Japan and the need for western capital and technology to rebuild a war-torn economy. Later, as Japan emerged as a regional economic superpower, there were suggestions that Japan's foreign policy should reflect the changed circumstances and that Japanese government should seek to balance its relationship with the regional countries. The opportunities for Japan to play a regional role increased considerably in the post Cold War period given perceived US retrenchment from the region and rise of Asian nationalism, both within Japan and several Asian countries. Lincoln, for example, argued that the region required leadership and that Japan was well placed to fill that role given its economic size and influence and, indeed, that Japan was beginning to exercise leadership in order to bring regionalism to fruition.[9] He argued that earlier constraints were no longer applicable because of changed regional circumstances and that the 'newness and radicalness of this situation means that predicting the future on the basis of past behaviour (was) risky'.[10] By asserting the newness of the situation, Lincoln distanced himself from many other similar, but failed, predictions made years, even decades, earlier.

Alongside the push for regional integration and coherence and the attendant requirement for a leadership role, there are indications that the Japanese government is also searching for a more prominent role through, for instance, securing permanent representation in the United Nations Security Council. While reaffirming the centrality of its relations with the United States, the Japanese government cannot ignore the competing regional demands and considerations. There are, of course, some regional countries, which see the US–Japan relationship as a guarantee against Japanese unilateralism and adventurism. The United States, in this perspective, is seen as a constraining influence on the Japanese government. At the same time, other regional countries have been critical of US foreign policy and interpret the US–Japan alliance as working to American advantage and detrimental to regional concerns. The Chinese government, for example, voiced its concerns that the 1996 US–Japan Joint Declaration to strengthen the security alliance was a poorly disguised strategy by the two countries to implement a policy of 'containment' against China. The Chinese government, according to Garrett and Glaser, had reached the conclusion that the US–Japan security relationship was no longer a mechanism to contain Japanese ambitions but that it had been turned around to contain China.[11]

Based on the Joint Declaration, the two countries revised their Security Guideline in September 1997, which committed Japan to provide operational support and assistance to the US military in the event of an emergency in the region around Japan. The earlier Guideline formulated in 1978, by contrast, made no mention of Japanese security cooperation with the US in maintaining regional peace and stability. From the Chinese perspective, the possibility that Japan might become involved in a crisis involving China and Taiwan can only be described as an extremely negative development. Chinese concerns are understandable also in view of the fact that the Japanese 1996 Defense White Paper, for example, expressed for the first time concern about China's growing military might and expressed a need 'to keep a close watch on China'.[12] This was in the context of nuclear tests and live testing of missiles in the East China Sea in 1995. The Chinese government has also played up American criticisms of Chinese human rights record and denial of membership in the World Trade Organization as evidence of a policy of containment.

While the Japanese government has reassured the Chinese that the intent of the Japan–US Joint Declaration is not to contain China, the potential for damage to China–Japan relations is obvious. According to Chalmers Johnson, the 1997 Guideline ignored recent regional developments, such as the commercial reorientation of China and the 1997 policy decision to privatise state owned enterprises and scale back the size of the armed forces, the diminished threat from North Korea, peaceful elections in Taiwan and South Korea and ASEAN's contribution to stability in Indo–China. Contrasting these to the expanded military alliance between Japan and the US, he argued that '… the primary threat to stability and peace in East Asia today comes from a belligerent and anachronist military stance towards the region of the US and Japanese governments'.[13] While the potential for regional instability over the Taiwan issue cannot be ignored particularly if the independence movement in Taiwan gains momentum, one counter-balancing factor is the close economic interdependence between China and Taiwan. In 1994, for example, the cumulative total of Taiwanese FDI in China was US$8.4 billion, more than either American or Japanese FDI in China. Trade relations are also growing rapidly and Yabuki Susumu observed that China and Taiwan are 'in the process of creating a very good complementary relationship'.[14]

The suggested alternatives for Japanese foreign policy include a re-orientation to reflect Japan's geographic position; preparedness to act as a bridge between Asia and the US; continuation of a US centred foreign policy; or rejection of bilateralism and the American connection altogether in favour of a foreign policy grounded in multilateral initiatives and centred on APEC[15]. In the context of increased support for East Asian regionalism, these suggestions are understandable.

The peace clause of the Japanese Constitution suggested that Japan would rely on the United Nations to guarantee its international security. However, the Cold War security structure meant that reliance on multilateral institutions was impracticable as state policy. However, the original intentions have been revived in the post-Cold War environment and follow an assessment that the utility of bilateral alliances have diminished and new opportunities have arisen for multilateral institutions to become more active. Some Japanese scholars even question the viability of the US–Japan alliance and point to the 1995 US–Japan auto dispute as the harbinger of a more troublesome bilateral relationship. Nonetheless, it should be noted that there is no mutual exclusivity between multilateralism and the other scenarios and is therefore the least demanding of all options. In a regional context, the multilateral future might be the pursuit of open regionalism through the APEC process.

The option of continuing the main principles of post-war Japanese diplomacy might be regarded as the default setting for Japanese foreign policy. Japan acknowledges the United States as the cornerstone of its foreign policy even as it attempts to establish better relations with Asian countries. Essentially, in this scenario, we can expect Japan to continue to define its foreign policy objectives primarily in terms of its security and economic relations with the United States, as it did previously. In recent years, however, US–Japan relations have been buffeted by economic frictions. The 1995 auto dispute was particularly acrimonious but since then relations have returned to a more sound footing especially with a renewed focus on the security relations in the second term of the Clinton administration. While likening this to a default setting it is unlikely that Japan can continue with the established precedent and ignore regional developments and challenges. The Asia Pacific region is rapidly evolving and there are numerous challenges and potential conflicts that could exacerbate economic interactions and Japan's economic linkages with the regional countries. The viability of this option depends also on the continued relevance of the San Francisco system which, according to Stuart Douglas, is the mainstay of American foreign and defence policy in the region since 1953. He argues however that the San Francisco system cannot continue because new mechanisms have to be found to accommodate three new and potential developments: the growth of Chinese power, the inevitable collapse of North Korea and unification of the peninsula; and emergence of Japan as a 'normal' country.[16] The US will continue to be important to Japan but it would be unwise for Japan not to define its foreign policy objectives independently of the US. The hazards of dependency, suggested by American abandonment of Japan over China and Russia in the early 1970s and the early 1990s respectively, confirm that Japan must define and pursue its own interests in a realistic way that avoids excessive dependence on the US.

The option of an Asian identity is not as far fetched at it sounds. The regional countries, particularly China, are becoming increasingly important for Japan. Japan's total trade with China in 1996 was US$60 billion, second only to the United States. Asia, in general, has emerged as an important production centre for Japanese firms especially after currency revaluation following the Plaza accord of September 1995. Public interest in regional issues has increased substantially and is reflected in the more extensive coverage given to Asian news in the Japanese media. The Asahi Shinbun in 1985, for instance, carried 1,000 news items dealing with Asia but in 1994 the same newspaper carried 6,000 items on Asian affairs.[17] Similarly, a Sankei Shinbun survey in 1994 found that sixty four per cent of Japanese business leaders supported a shift in Japan's foreign policy away from the US and toward Asia.[18] This was admittedly at a time when US–Japan trade conflicts were arousing considerable passion on both sides of the Pacific and may help explain why only twenty five per cent of respondents were in favour of a strengthened relationship with the US. While opinion polls and surveys can be accepted neither as a guide to national interest nor as a guide to diplomatic stance, it is clear that Japan can no longer play down its relations with regional countries.

The second option can mean any one of the following three outcomes:

1 Japan as Asia's voice in global fora;
2 Japan as an active participant in regional security arrangements, and;
3 Japan as the hub of an Asian regional economic grouping.[19]

The first of these assumes that we can identify an Asian voice, that this voice is unheard in international fora, and that Japan is best able to articulate Asian concerns. Whether or not these assumptions can be validated Japan has occasionally acted to represent Asia in global talks. At the 1975 summit of industrialised countries, Prime Minister Miki assumed the role of representing Asia but later, under Prime Minister Nakasone, the Japanese government abandoned any pretence of acting to protect Asian interests. However, Japan has represented individual Asian countries in international gatherings as for example when Japan 'spoke up' for China after the Tienanmen massacre and in justification of its own policy to resume aid.[20] Japan also broke ranks with western countries over its decision not to use aid as a tool for defending the democratic principle in Cambodia following the ousting of First Prime Minister Prince Norodom Ranariddh by Second Prime Minister Hun Sen in July 1997. In this case, as with the earlier defence of China, Japan's main concern was to '… continue business as usual'[21] rather than assume a principled political stance.

In recent years, Japan has been more involved in regional security and political considerations. This is reflected in its participation in the Cambodia peace keeping force of the United Nations and the earlier suggestion that the ASEAN countries initiate a security and political dialogue with other regional countries to promote regional understanding and stability subsequently formalised as the ASEAN Regional Forum (ARF). The advantage of Japan as a regional economic hub would be that Japan's own developmental pattern resembled that of other East Asian countries, many of which emphasise strong governments and limited human rights in the interest of economic growth and prosperity. Leaving aside the issue of whether these are mutually exclusive goals or whether post-war Japanese history suggests a neglect of human rights, regional countries feel that Japan is likely to be more sympathetic to their style of government, unlike the US which advocates respect for human rights and democratisation. This assumption is not without merit and evident in Japan's refusal to impose sanctions on Cambodia following the coup d'etat led by Hun Sen.

None the less, while making common cause with regional countries over some issues, Japan is unlikely to abandon its security alliance with the US or become a fully autonomous regional actor. The perception within Japan has been clearly that maintaining the structure of US–Japan relations is important despite periodic shocks administered by the US to the Japanese foreign policy establishment, such as the sudden announcement of American rapprochement with China in the early 1970s. Prior to this the Japanese government, under American pressure, had steadfastly rejected domestic demands for normal relations with China. History repeated itself again in the early post-Cold War period with respect to Japan's relations with the Soviet Union. During the Cold War, the US had encouraged Japan to reject any compromise resolution of its territorial dispute with the USSR. After the Cold War, however, Japan found itself painted into a corner and isolated as the rest of the international community, led by the US, rushed to embrace the reconstituted Russia. Worse still, Japan was subject to diplomatic pressure to grant large scale financial assistance to Russia and set aside the territorial dispute. In the end, the Japanese government was obliged to sever the issue of aid to Russia from the territorial dispute and extend financial assistance for the Russian economic transition. For Japan, according to Mike Millard, the end of the Cold War was, for these reasons, a 'bittersweet triumph', because it weakened earlier US support on the territorial dispute.[22] At the same time, the American government, too, has had occasion to feel disenchanted with aspects of its relationship with Japan, especially in so far as defence and trade relations are concerned.

The US–Japan relationship has not been free of difficulties in the past and the future may be even more problematic. According to Barry Stokes, the United States and Japan are on divergent tracks. Without implying the inevitability of a collision course, Stokes argued that the 1995 US–Japan auto dispute which resulted in Japan's steadfast resistance of US demands and pressure and the divergent roles assumed by the two countries within the APEC framework, compounded by anti-US sentiments in Okinawa, were harbingers of future difficulties.[23]

The pessimism, however, is unwarranted. Following the auto dispute of 1995, trade relations between the two countries have reflected a greater sensitivity to each other's concerns. This is not surprising given the magnitude of their bilateral trade. For example, while Japan's exports to and imports from East Asian countries has increased substantially in recent years and while China is Japan's second largest trading partner, total Japan–China bilateral trade is still only about a third of US–Japan trade. In 1995, for example, Japan–China trade amounted to Y5,443 billion whereas Japan–US trade was Y18,409 billion.

Japan and the United States have also underscored the importance of their security relationship through the Japan–US Joint Declaration on Security Alliance for the Twenty-first Century signed on 17 April 1996. This was followed up by the Security Guideline Agreement that was signed in September 1997. David Asher correctly argued that the US government now had a better understanding of the significance of the US–Japan bilateral relations and had stopped the 'alliance drift' to reemphasise the security interdependence.[24] Japan's rejection of the East Asian Economic Caucus (EAEC) also suggests that the Japanese government had decided against inserting itself and supplanting the US in the region. Instead, Japan, along with the US, has lent support to the Asia Pacific Economic Cooperation and was also its primary instigator. It is unlikely that Japan will reject this in the future to pursue a more radical vision of itself as a regional political and economic hub. Given the overall significance of the US–Japan relationship, it is important to explore the nature of future Japanese links with East Asian countries. The rise of East Asian countries, despite recent economic setbacks and pessimism about their growth prospects, means that Japan will have to devise a formula for reconciling its trans-Pacific interests with the issue of regional identity.

Consideration of this important issue brings us to the final option of Japan as a transpacific *torii*, a bridge between the US, on the one hand, and Asian countries, on the other. Pempel writes that the most appropriate role for Japan would be as the lintel supported on two massive columns and acting as a bridge across the Pacific. Japan, according to Pempel, is ideally placed economically and culturally to be the bridge between the East and the West, between the US and Asia.[25] Continuing this theme, Yong Deng pointed out that officials and intellectuals in Japan, too, have often portrayed Japan as an intermediary or as a bridge between the US and East Asia.[26] The notion of a bridge assumes a divide and a separation, and for Japan to bridge that divide assumes, in turn, that the Japanese government is capable of pursuing an autonomous foreign policy and of mediating differences between Asian countries and the United States.

Equidistance is a familiar concept in the analysis of Japanese foreign policy but it was never taken seriously, least of all by the countries toward which Japan was supposedly equidistant. And recent developments confirm that Japanese foreign policy remains centred on its alliance with the US. Critics of a future Japanese policy of a bridge between the West and the East, like Funabashi Yoichi, argue that Japan cannot afford to remain an arbiter of conflicting interests but must define and act upon its own interests.[27] Funabashi makes the argument that the East–West dichotomy is immaterial within the APEC context and that there is, therefore, no question of Japan acting as a bridge. This, as Funabashi mentions, was also the view put forward by an American official spokesperson.

Leaving official assertions aside, the idea of a separation between the East and the West is not implausible. Relations across the Pacific have been strained as a result of conflicts over issues of human rights and democracy, perceptions of an American policy of containment of China, or American pursuit of results-oriented trade with its Asian trading partners. American attempts to manage relations with China and Indonesia, for example, have been patchy and less than salutary. If this opens up opportunities for Japan to act as a mediator, we have to consider also the constraints that make it difficult for Japan to be an active player and which have led in the past to depictions of Japanese foreign policy as reactive or cautious.

For the Japanese government, East–West separation and tension has been the source of an awkward dilemma because in this triangular relationship, shifts in US–Japan relations have tended to correlate inversely with Japan's relations with East Asian countries. Given the broader context of strained US relations with East Asian countries, each period of deterioration in US–Japan relations has provoked regional support for Japan against American demands and, conversely, improvements in US–Japan relations have impaired, or threatened to impair, Japan's relations with its regional neighbours. In 1994–95, for example, when economic friction and American demands for quantitative import targets buffeted US–Japan relations, the regional countries offered strong verbal support for the Japanese position. Not without selfish interests they encouraged Japan to stand firm and reject American demands because they, too, had been subject to the American policy of 'aggressive unilateralism'.[28] During this period, there emerged some convergence of interests between Japan and other export oriented East Asian economies. The Chinese government, according to Gaye Christofferson, has also tried to exploit periods of US–Japan friction to its own advantage by moving closer to Japan, when prospects of a 'Nichibei' hegemony seem remote.[29]

In 1996, however, American and Japanese efforts to enhance their security cooperation and improve their bilateral relationship produced considerable disquiet within the region. The Chinese government strongly denounced the proposed strengthening of the US–Japan security relations as an unfriendly act and as a devise to contain China. When Japan and the US signed the Guideline Agreement in 1997, China, again, criticised Japan for entering into an agreement that could potentially involve it in a crisis over Taiwan. Moreover, continuing US support for human rights has the potential for creating a sharp divide between Japan and other Asian countries if Japan were to be seen as following American policy directions. The Southeast Asian countries, especially Malaysia and Singapore, see liberalism and democracy as antithetical to their invented tradition of 'Asian values'. American advocacy of liberalism and criticisms of, for example, human rights in Indonesia were important considerations in the decision of the Indonesian government to cancel its order for the purchase of American fighter aircraft. The Chinese government, too, rejects liberalism in favour of the official policy of establishing 'market socialism' as the basis for the Chinese state.

Some Japanese scholars have suggested that it is essential for Japan to engage in a 'global partnership' with the US and West in the promotion of liberal values as the best defence for international peace.[30] Thus far, however, Japan's foreign policy has been based on pragmatism and it has resisted the temptation to follow the American lead in subscribing to the democratic peace theory, which has provided the moral underpinning of its contemporary foreign policy objectives. Japan, will probably continue that policy direction and refuse to make common cause with the US over issues of human rights. Prime Minister Hashimoto, in late August 1997, stated that, '… we have to ask whether liberalism is necessarily superior to other sets of values and whether it is right to ask other nations to uniformly accept that'.[31] This statement, however, should not be interpreted as suggestive of a significantly autonomous foreign policy. Indeed, the strengthening of the US–Japan security alliance suggests the importance, to Japan, of its relations with the US and, in that context, Japanese interests are better served by a weak sense of regional identity. The Japanese government cannot be too enthusiastic about a well-developed Asian identity or a regional bloc because of its potential to jeopardise its relations with the United States, still the primary external referent of Japanese foreign policy. It is ironic that 'aggressive (trade) unilateralism' on the part of the US and toward East Asia is, according to Bowles and MacLean, one of the most likely reasons for bloc formation.[32]

If we accept that East–West relations will continue to be problematic, then Japanese regional interests must be to contain the spread of Pan–Asian nationalism and regionalism, and to create political acceptance for Japan's own regional agenda. The Japanese vision of loose East Asian regionalism, of course, also includes a more prominent role for Japan. This aspect of Japan's regional objective could be upset by potential, or real, challenges from China for regional dominance. China has its own visions of regionalism in which it, and not Japan, is the central player.[33] The prospect for Chinese regional dominance is premised on continued economic growth and emergence as a sizeable economy early in the twenty-first century.

In keeping with its own regional agenda, the Chinese government has raised objections to developments that might enhance Japan's regional role. This was evident in events following the recent Asian currency turmoil. The Asian currency crisis was the result of a rapid outflow of capital from several countries of East Asia after investors were spooked by large, and presumably unsustainable, levels of private sector foreign debt. Capital flight produced rapid currency depreciation, which brought the crisis countries to an economic standstill after years of high growth. The crisis is variously attributed either to domestic factors such as weak financial structures or to external factors such as speculative capital flows. The Prime Minister of Malaysia, speaking at the World Bank/International Monetary fund meeting in Hong Kong in September 1997, blamed the crisis on currency specula-tors, like George Soros, bent on undermining economic performance of regional countries for their own gains and also to 'punish' regional countries for refusing to introduce democratic reforms. The position of the Malaysian government was ridiculed as uninformed and biased but, interestingly, the Chinese Prime Minister Li Peng also seconded Mahathir's criticisms of global currency speculators.[34]

In the rescue attempt that followed, the Japanese government played the leading role and committed over US$40 billion in financial aid and trade assistance to several regional countries. In addition, in September 1997, the Japanese government proposed a US$100 billion regional assistance fund to defend local currencies against speculative attacks and capital flight. In all previous crises, the Japanese government had been subject to western criticisms that it was slow to react and that its responses were deficient. In the Asian currency crisis the Japanese proposal for an Asian Fund was, in hindsight, an appropriate response to the crisis of confidence in regional countries. However, western governments, led by the United States, rejected it because of a concern that such a plan would compete with and dilute the effects of IMF conditionality. Instead, western governments insisted that Japan had to reflate its economy quickly in order to provide regional countries with a large market so that they could export their way out of economic difficulties. The plan for an Asian Fund was rejected also by the Chinese government because it would give Japan a dominant regional role at the expense of Chinese influence.

Indeed, if successful, the Japanese plan for an Asian Fund would have enhanced Japan's regional standing and, given Japan's membership of the western bloc, weakened arguments for anti-western brands of regionalism in East Asia. It should be noted also that there is no evidence that Japan is pushing for East Asian regionalism even under its own tutelage. Instead, Japanese interests are best served by 'soft regionalism'[35] in the form of APEC as an open and Pan–Pacific regional grouping, and sub-regional engagement focused on ASEAN and China, respectively. The advantage of Pan–Pacific regionalism is not only that it might help contain the more virulent forms of Asian nationalism but also that it may limit the possibility of a Chinese regional domination. APEC brings together countries surrounding the Pacific and a large forum may dampen Asian nationalism but the concept of open regionalism, the main principle of APEC, still has to demonstrate its practical viability. Beyond rhetorical statements of support and grand visions of non-discriminatory trade liberalism, APEC, however, has yet to produce concrete results. The success of the APEC process will depend on the level of commitment to the Bogor Declaration to achieve free trade by the year 2020 and on achieving consensus on the concept of open regionalism.[36] While Japan, understandably, has advocated trade openness on a Most Favoured Nation basis, the US position has been to require reciprocity from non-APEC member countries. The APEC agenda is in some disarray as a result of the Asian crisis and understandably the crisis countries are more concerned with restoring economic growth than with pursuing liberalisation, especially as liberalisation of capital account transactions have been blamed as one of the factors behind the crisis. It would be wrong, however, to be dismissive of APEC although progress is likely to be slower than initially anticipated.

Japanese interests are best served by a broad Pan–Pacific regional structure but we cannot expect Japan to pursue those interests in an assertive manner. Yong Deng looks for signs of assertive leadership and, not surprisingly, is disappointed by a diplomacy '… devoid of self-assertiveness and leadership'.[37] The difficulty for Japan has been that even APEC has been transformed into a venue for conflict between the US, which has pushed for co-ordinated and balanced liberalisation, and the other countries, which favour a concerted unilateral approach. Conflicts, such as this, have pushed Japan into a mediatory role, which it has performed without distinction. This lacklustre record of achievement is testimony to Japan's diplomatic style, which is both passive and uncreative – qualities that, as mentioned above, do not lend themselves to successful mediation.

In the meantime, as the second prong of its policy to limit the potential for Pan–Asian regionalism, the Japanese government has emphasised sub-regional engagement in order to contain comprehensive East Asian regionalism. Here, ASEAN has been the main focus in Southeast Asia and China in Northeast Asia. The Japanese government initiated a number of measures to elevate the role and profile of ASEAN, comfortable in the knowledge that ASEAN cannot extend itself into a Pan–Asian institution. In so far as China is concerned, the objectives of the Japanese government are to integrate it into the wider international community and avoid being caught up in a competitive struggle with China for influence in the region. Japan has led international efforts to integrate China into the World Trade Organization, despite western misgivings that economic regulations in China are neither sufficiently liberalised nor transparent to warrant inclusion into the world body. In 1999 however, the American and Chinese governments reached a landmark trade agreement that should facilitate Chinese entry into the WTO in the near future. For its part, the Japanese government has consistently argued against the isolation of China. After the initial wave of sanctions against China following the Tiananmen incident of 1989, Japan urged the G-7 countries to support renewal of World Bank lending to China and also supported its participation in the Uruguay Round negotiations as an observer.[38] Despite this, Japan–China relations have not been very smooth. As two large neighbouring countries, it is perhaps inevitable that each will view the other with some suspicion. But bilateral relations worsened following the strengthening of the US–Japan defence alliance and also following comments, in August 1997, by Kajiyama Seiroku, the Chief Cabinet Secretary, that Japan would help the US in any emergency in the Taiwan Straits. The Prime Minister, however, hastened to reassure the Chinese government that Japan had not altered its policy recognising Taiwan as an integral part of China.

Japan's regional diplomacy and leadership can, therefore, be understood as serving to channel East Asian regionalism in the direction of subdued identity and consistency with the US–Japan security linkage. In some ways therefore, Japanese leadership may be at odds with regional aspirations and this feature underscores the importance of building relations of trust within the region to eliminate the remaining pockets of hostility and resentment. Because Japanese objectives within the region are not necessarily shared by other regional countries, Japanese foreign policy will have to be more proactive and committed in order to lead regional countries toward a regional order that is consistent with its primary objective of maintaining its relations with the United States. The difficulty for Japan is that considering its foreign policy establishment is not ideally situated to act as a bridge or a mediator between the East and the West, it must be considered even less appropriate to the task of creating a regional order based on soft regionalism. It is necessary now to consider the obstacles to Japanese foreign policy activism and the extent to which we might anticipate changes in the future.

Japan and foreign policy leadership

The analysis of Japanese foreign policy usually begins with the paradoxical reality of low international profile and major power status. Japan is the second largest economic power after the United States, has the highest per capita GNP of western industrial countries, and is also the world's largest creditor nation. Although its military spending is a minuscule proportion of GNP, it nonetheless has a very potent military force. We might expect that Japan would use its economic power potential to generate political influence but Japan has failed to deploy its structural power to secure international advantages or exercise foreign policy leadership. This is inconsistent with international norms. Of course structural power does not always lead to influence and must be married with purpose to form the basis for international leadership. Japanese foreign policy, in the post-war period, however is characterised by an all-encompassing sense of pragmatism that de-emphasises the role of purposive international behaviour. The alleged lack of purpose is at the base of failure to take initiatives in the foreign policy arena.

It is important, here, to relate Japanese foreign policy and expectations of activism, even leadership, to the relevant prerequisites. In *The Business of the Japanese State*, Richard Samuels used the notion of 'reciprocal consent' to examine the interactions of states and markets.[39] The politics of reciprocal consent captures the spirit of mutual accommodation of state and market and of market players and public officials. Similarly, foreign policy leadership can also be understood as a process of mutual accommodation. The Japanese government can neither exercise regional leadership in the absence of acquiescence by the regional countries nor in the absence of prior domestic consensus. The discussion above alludes to some of the difficulties surrounding leadership; the lingering mistrust of Japan within the region. Japan cannot expect to assume a leadership position if it is likely to be met with resistance within the region and this emphasises the importance of building a level of trust and confidence that will tolerate a more politically active Japan. In the post-war period, US leadership in creating a liberal and open economic regime was made possible by a general acceptance that leadership was essential to create a more peaceful international environment. It is not certain that there is a similar acceptance within the region of a Japanese leadership role. Of course, it is important to note that not all the regional countries share the same ambivalence towards Japan. Senior Thai military officials have, for example, encouraged the Japanese government to be more active in regional affairs whereas South Korean official and public opinion remains relatively hostile toward Japan. Thai sentiments may not mirror those in other Asian countries but there is no longer a consistent or unified Asian stance against Japan and, consequently, Asian rejection of it cannot be used as an excuse for Japan's foreign policy inactivism and indecision. In 1996, Japan and the United States signed a Joint Declaration on Security Alliance for the Twenty First Century, which reoriented the US–Japan defence treaty to the peace and stability of the Asia–Pacific region. This broadening of the alliance from narrowly a defined security of Japan would, indeed, not have been possible with a prior assessment that such a redefinition would be acceptable to most regional countries.

Apart from the question of trust in foreign policy leadership, Japanese leadership will also have to contend with potential challengers. In the region, the most likely challenger is China which has tried to enhance its regional profile and credibility by withdrawing support for local communist groups, supporting the proposal for an East Asian Economic Caucus, and promising not to capitalise on the ASEAN currency crisis by engaging in competitive devaluation. The Chinese government has been wary of Japanese leadership drives, as mentioned in the section above and expressed concern at the strengthening of the alliance, criticising it as an unnecessary relic of the Cold War and detrimental to regional order and stability. The Chinese government appears to be, very cleverly, maximising its own profile in the region by using ASEAN as a platform. China may still be an unlikely regional leader at this stage given different economic structures but Chinese activism in support for regional integration must be a source of some concern for the Japanese government, which cannot be too pleased about a grouping that excludes not only Australia and New Zealand but also Japan's western ally.

Finally, conceptualising leadership as reciprocal consent forces us, also, to consider the problem of internal constraints to Japanese foreign policy activism.[40] It is assumed, for instance, that Japanese foreign policy inactivism is the result of a bureaucratic policy making structure.[41] Bureaucracies are perfectly adapted to the task of policy implementation but are by nature conservative and averse to activism and risk taking enterprises. They are ideally situated to deal with routine issues but not with exercising leadership and initiative. Leadership demands activism and, at times, risk taking behaviour. Bureaucratic dominance, however, is a contested concept. Some scholars have questioned the validity of the assumed bureaucratic dominance in Japan. For example, Rosenbluth argued that the early understanding of Japanese politics vastly exaggerated bureaucratic dominance in policy making in Japan. Instead, according to Rosenbluth, bureaucracies have operated within clearly defined and delineated parameters established by the ruling politicians. In this view, bureaucratic autonomy and bureaucratic dominance belong in the realm of political myths and are unsubstantiated by empirical evidence.[42] Similarly, in taking issue with notions of strong state, Margaret McKean also plays down the dominance of the bureaucracy. The strong state thesis assumes that policies are driven by bureaucracy and big business but McKean questions the usefulness of a concept that includes private societal actors as part of the state apparatus. She also emphasised that there is sufficient empirical evidence to refute assumptions of strong state, especially in the last two decades with the emergence of professional politicians as well as *zoku* politicians who have eroded the powers of the bureaucracy.

Kent Calder, however, argued that bureaucrats retained considerable influence and power, even in the late 1980s. According to him,

> In some important areas, such as industrial policy, the bureaucracy even in the late 1980s remained pre-eminent in the formulation of overall policy agendas, even where politics had some impact on the choice of tools for achieving those goals – for example, orienting the bureaucracy toward regional dispersal of high-technology industrial plants and research facilities.[43]

In a similar way, Blaker suggested that Japanese foreign policy is marked by a dominant pattern of coping with international pressures and strains. The principle of bureaucratic dominance led Calder to define Japanese foreign policy as 'reactive' and Japan as a 'reactive state', which chose inactivism in spite of available capabilities to pursue a more active foreign policy.

A reactive state compares poorly with other states since it is assumed that such a state fails to act on its national interest. Other analysts have suggested that the term leadership, as understood in the West, does not apply to Japan because Japanese society and value structures do not value such leadership. Alan Rix, for example suggested that Japanese leadership should be understood as leading from behind, rather than as forceful assertive action. Such a notion of consensual leadership has been suggested also by Japanese politicians. Former Prime Minister Takeshita observed that, 'It is the role of the leader today not to pull people along, it is to get the consensus of the people'.[44] Yet, there are also several examples of Japanese prime ministers who have done more than simply aim for a consensus, such as Kishi, Sato, and Nakasone.

The 'reactive state' and 'consensual leadership' models have a similar emphasis on low-key diplomacy but are substantially different. The bases of Japan's reactive diplomacy can be found in the bureaucratic structure of policy making while the consensual leadership model tries to develop a completely new understanding of leadership that is more applicable to Japan. Thus, while the former finds the reasons for passivity in structural features, the latter opts for a more cultural understanding of Japan, which also places Japan in a unique category of states. It has its origins in the group model of Japanese society but the group model has been criticised for emphasising the differences and for ignoring the essential commonalties. It is easy to say that Japanese understanding of leadership is different from the west but it is better to try and explain Japanese foreign policy using acceptable categories of social science rather than to invent new ones. Besides, activism is not absent from Japanese foreign policy and any difference is only a difference of degrees, not of kind. The Japanese government may be more reactive but other comparable states also display reactive behaviour. The reactive state model can even be applied to American foreign policy in post-Cold War Asia. According to Donald Hellmann, the United States had no fresh, coherent, long-term strategy to deal with Asia but rather

> moved from one specific issue to another on an agenda set not by policy initiatives emanating from Washington, but as dictated by regional crises (e.g., North Korea, the Philippine bases), America's *domestic* political, economic, and budgetary considerations, or initiatives by other Asia–Pacific countries to create new arrangements for international cooperation.[45]

Where evidence of reactive behaviour can be found in American foreign policy, there are also examples of Japanese initiatives.

In the age of globalisation, Japanese politicians are cognisant of the new demands on policy making and the inadequacies of bureaucratic policy making.

The Japanese government has, consequently, embarked on large-scale administrative reforms. In the past, administrative reform was carried out in the early 1960s and again in the early 1980s with the objective of limiting both the size and influence of the bureaucracy in policy making. Success in reforming the bureaucratic structure of government is dependent largely on prime ministerial leadership and the success of the reform agenda in the early 1980s, such as privatisation of government monopolies, might be attributed to Prime Minister Nakasone who, '... unequivocally expressed his determination to carry out administrative reform'.[46] The latest reform project has yet to produce real results, apart from a reduction in the number of ministries and agencies. Administrative reform, however, is not the only available avenue for altering the balance of power between bureaucrats and politicians. The process of realignment has continued through the emergence of the *zoku* politicians and through changes brought about by the electoral reforms of 1994, which encourages a greater emphasis on policies by the politicians than has been the case in the past. Under the old electoral system, resolution of political contests were largely achieved through monetary rewards and pork-barrel politics. Elections rarely, if ever, excited much policy interest. If, as a consequence of electoral reforms, the prevalence of money politics diminishes and if elections become policy contests, political leaders can be expected to assume greater responsibility in formulating, articulating and communicating a coherent policy agenda which might fulfil a basic condition of foreign policy activism. Indeed, according to Jain and Todhunter, the result of the 1996 election suggest that policies have become more important in determining electoral outcomes. They suggest that the setback for the Shinshinto (New Frontier Party) was due to its failure to formulate and to communicate to the electorate a coherent set of policies.[47] If true, this may be an early indication of the enhanced role of policy platforms to electoral success and of the primacy of political input into the policy process.

Conclusion

In the context of regionalism, as already indicated, the primacy of relations with the United States and the potential adverse consequences of East Asian regionalism, give clear indication of Japanese policy objectives. The Japanese government is unlikely to offer support to any moves to establish regional institutions and promote regionalism. For the moment, however, regionalism is not a pressing concern as there are more pressing concerns as a consequence of the currency and economic crisis that engulfed the region in 1997. A potential irony, for Japan, is that a resolution of the crisis will involve considerable Japanese economic support through demand expansion and market opening measures to enable regional countries to export their way out of the crisis. This will, inevitably, deepen regional integration and, over time, add to the demands for creating appropriate regional institutions that will steer the region away from any lingering anti-western bias. The Japanese proposal for an Asian Fund could have played a critical role but this, ironically enough, was rejected by the United States.

Notes

1 Brown, E., 'The Debate Over Japan's Strategic Future: Bilateralism versus Regionalism', *Asian Survey*, vol. 33, no. 6, June 1993, p. 547.

2 Kitahara, M., 'Economists fear baht's anemia may spread across region, cutting into growth', *The Nikkei Weekly*, 21 July 1997, p. 24.

3 'Mahathir Airs Asian Financial Unity', *The Australian*, 17 October 1997, p. 9.

4 See Kamiya, F., 'Amerika ga Okinawa o suteru hi' (The Day America Abandons Okinawa), *Bungei shunju*, November 1996, p. 265.

5 Noda, N., 'The Dangerous Rise of Asianism', *Japan Echo*, vol. 22, no. 1, Spring 1995, p. 11.

6 Funabashi, Y., 'Introduction: Japan's International Agenda for the 1990s', in Yoichi Funabashi (ed.), *Japan's International Agenda*, New York University Press, New York, 1994, p. 9.

7 Rosecrance, R. and Jennifer Taw, 'Japan and the Theory of International Leadership', *World Politics*, January 1990, pp. 195–6.

8 Calder, K.E., 'Domestic Constraints and Japan's Emerging International Role', in Clesse, A. et al. (eds), *The Vitality of Japan: Sources of National Strength and Weakness*, Macmillan Press Ltd, Houndmills, 1997, pp. 193–4.

9 Lincoln, E.J., *Japan's New Global Role*, The Brookings Institution, Washington, DC, 1993, pp. 171–2.

10 Lincoln, E.J., 1993, p. 17.

11 Garrett, B. and Bonnie Glaser, 'Chinese Apprehensions About Revitalization of the U.S.–Japan Alliance', *Asian Survey*, vol. 37, no. 4, April 1997.

12 See, Johnson, C., 'Containing China: U.S. and Japan Drift Toward Disaster', *Japan Quarterly*, vol. 43, no. 4, October–December 1996, p. 15.

13 Johnson, C., 'China vs US and Japan: Two Contrasting Visions of the Future', *The Straits Times* (Singapore), 29 September 1997, p. 36.

14 Yabuki, S., 'Reading Beijing's Foreign Policy', *Japan Echo*, vol. 23, no. 1, Spring 1996, p. 35

15 See Takenaka, H., 'Can Japan Glue Together Asia and the Pacific?', *Japan Echo*, vol. 22, no. 4, Winter 1995.

16 Douglas, S., 'Japan's Place in the New Asian Concert', *Japan Quarterly*, vol. 44, no. 3, July–September 1997, p.62.

17 Funabashi, Y., *Ajia Taiheiyo Fyujon: APEC to Nihon* (Asia Pacific Fusion: Japan's Role in APEC), Chuo Koron sha, Tokyo, 1995, p. 334.

18 Wang, Q.K., 'Toward Political Partnership: Japan's China Policy', *The Pacific Review*, vol. 7, 1994, p. 174.

19 Brown, E., 1993, p. 548.

20 Brown, E., 1993, p. 549.

21 This was stated by Nobuaki Tanaka, a Japanese foreign ministry official. See *The Japan Times* (Weekly International Edition), 4–10 August 1997, p. 5.

22 Millard, M., 'Reforming Japan: A Puzzle with No Solution', *Japan Quarterly*, January–March 1996, p. 38.

23 In the auto dispute US demands for quantitative import targets was rejected by Japan and within APEC Japan has championed a gradualist approach resulting ultimately in MFN liberalisation whereas the American approach has been to press ahead quickly but only on a reciprocal basis. Stokes says that the Japanese approach reflects Asian interests and concerns. See Stokes, B., 'Divergent Paths: US–Japan Relations Towards the Twenty-First Century', *International Affairs*, vol. 72, no. 2, April 1996.

24 Asher, D. L., 'A U.S.–Japan Alliance for the Next Century', *Orbis*, vol. 41, no. 3, Summer 1997.

25 Pempel, T.J., 'Transpacific Torii: Japan and the Emerging Asian Regionalism', in Peter J. Katzenstein and Takashi Shiraishi (eds), *Network Power: Japan and Asia*, Cornell University Press, Ithaca, New York, 1997, p. 51.

26 Deng, Y., 'Japan in APEC: The Problematic Leadership Role', *Asian Survey*, vol. 37, no. 4, April 1997, pp. 358–9.

27 Funabashi, Y., 1995, pp. 377ff.

28 Bowles, P. and Brian MacLean, 'Regional Blocs: Can Japan be the Leader?', in Boyer, R. and Daniel Drache (eds), *States Against Markets: The Limits of Globalization*, Routledge, London, 1996, p. 166.

29 Christofferson, G., 'China and the Asia–Pacific: Need for a Grand Strategy', *Asian Survey*, vol. 36, no. 11, November 1996, p. 1074.

30 See, for example, 'Kokusai Seiji no doko to nihon gaiko', *Kokusai Mondai*, no. 432, March 1996, p. 12ff.

31 Garran, R., 'Hashimoto sends China all right signals on Taiwan', *The Australian*, 30–31 August 1997, p. 13.

32 Bowles, and MacLean, 1996, p. 167.

33 Emulating the title of the controversial book *The Japan That Can Say No* by Ishihara Shintaro, a group of Chinese writers published a book titled *The China That Can say No* in 1996. It was directed against Japan and the United States and called specifically for a policy of containing Japan. The writers suggested that Japan's greatest contribution to world peace would be to remain passive on the international stage and do nothing. The book proved extremely popular in China and sold about 3 million copies. The level of anti-Japanese sentiment within China can be gauged also by a survey of Chinese popular opinion in 1997 that showed Japan to be the least liked (47 per cent) country. See Chan Tsuan Tsuan and Ishihara Shintaro, 'Nitchu gekitotsu: 'No' to ieru no wa dotchi da', *Bungei shunju*, November 1997, pp. 107 and 111.

34 *The Australian*, 24 September 1997, p. 8.

35 I am grateful to Amitar Acharya for this term.

36 The Bogor Declaration is not a legally binding document and there are no sanctions attached to non-compliance.

37 Deng, Y., 1997, p. 359.

38 Faust, J.R. and Judith F. Kornberg, *China in World Politics*, Lynne Rienner Publishers, Boulder, CO, 1995, p. 191.

39 Samuels, R.J., The Business of the Japanese State: Energy Markets in Comparative and Historical Perspective, Cornell University Press, Ithaca and London, 1987, pp. 8–9.

40 Kenneth Pyle, on the other hand, argues that Japanese foreign policy is not constrained but that its inactivism is the result of a conscious policy choice made first by Yoshida Shigeru, Prime Minister of Japan through much of the occupation period, and continued thereafter by his successors. See, Pyle, K., *The Japanese Question: Power and Purpose in a New Era*, The AEI Press, Washington, 1992.

41 It is worth noting here that the public sector in Japan is relatively small. In 1994, there were 40 government workers for every 1,000 persons in Japan compared to 68 in Germany, 83 in Britain, 86 in the US, and 104 in France. See Hamano, T., 'Is Administrative Reform Feasible?', *Journal of Japanese Trade & Industry*, no. 1, 1 January 1997, p. 25.

42 For a review of the literature on bureaucratic dominance see Margaret McKean, 'State Strength and the Public Interest', in Gary D. Allinson and Yasunori Sone (eds), *Political Dynamics in Contemporary Japan*, Cornell University Press, Ithaca, New York, 1993.

43 Calder, K.E., *Crisis and Compensation: Public Policy and Political Stability in Japan, 1949–1986*, Princeton University Press, Princeton, NJ, 1988, p. 445.

44 Hayao, K., *The Japanese Prime Minister and Public Policy*, University of Pittsburgh Press, Pittsburgh, 1993, p. 7.

45 Hellmann, D.C., 'America, APEC, and the Road Not Taken: International Leadership in the Post-Cold War Interregnum in Asia–Pacific', in Hellmann, D. C. and K.B. Pyle (eds), *From APEC to Xanadu: Creating a Viable Community in the Post-Cold War Pacific*, M.E. Sharpe, New York, 1997, p. 86.

46 Ito, M., 'Administrative Reform in Japan: Semi-autonomous Bureaucracy under the Pressure toward a Small Government', in Muramatsu, M. and Frieder Naschold (eds), *State and Administration in Japan and Germany: A Comparative Perspective on Continuity and Change*, Walter de Gruyter, Berlin and New York, 1997, p. 74.

47 Jain, P.C. and Maureen Todhunter, 'The 1996 General Election: Status Quo or Step Forward?', in Jain, P.C. and Takashi Inoguchi (eds), *Japanese Politics Today: Beyond Karaoke Democracy*, Macmillan Education Australia Pty Ltd, Melbourne, 1997, p. 236.

3 Japanese domestic politics and Asian regionalism

T.J. Pempel

For virtually the entire post-war period, Japan's international relations could best be described as deliberately low posture, closely linked to co-operation with the United States, and driven by economic rather than military ends and means.[1] Meanwhile, the Japanese domestic political economy was heavily insulated from most international pressures, resting as it did on a broad orientation among all key political actors in favour of what I have previously labelled 'embedded mercantilism'.[2] A host of institutional barriers insulated the Japanese domestic market from any massive penetration by foreign capital, plant transfer, or manufactured imports. Other measures provided the Japanese government with a comprehensive array of tools with which to provide central orchestration of national economic policies; whole sectors of the economy were protected from international competition through a complex mixture of government regulation and corporate practices. The result was nearly forty years of exceptional economic transformation, extensively improved productivity by numerous Japanese firms, increased shares of world exports to Japanese-owned firms, and economic growth that was substantially higher than that for any other OECD country.

In foreign relations, Japan's close bilateral ties to the United States generated both strategic and economic benefits. By maintaining the industrial world's lowest per capita ratio of defence spending, Japan freed up public monies for domestic investment while keeping a very low profile in international relations. Simultaneously, easy access to US markets was a boon to Japanese exporters of automobiles, consumer electronics, machine tools, and the like. Within Asia, meanwhile, Japan developed a regional predominance through extensive and regionally concentrated foreign aid, foreign direct investment, and eventually the regionalisation of many of Japan's once exclusively national production networks.[3] Yet such economic predominance rarely led to any heavy-handed exertion of diplomatic or political leadership in the region.

Simultaneously, and closely connected to all of these, thirty-eight years of single party conservative dominance saw the Liberal Democratic Party (LDP) consistently outdrawing its closest electoral opponent (the Japan Socialist Party–JSP, later SDPJ) by margins of two to one in national elections and even greater margins at the local level. Conservative domestic politics, tranquil international affairs, and high growth economics were locked in a long-term 'virtuous cycle', or what Kozo Yamamura once called a 'marriage made in heaven'.[4]

Both Japan's domestic political economy and the international conditions shaping Japanese foreign policy shifted dramatically between the end of the 1980s and the mid- to late-1990s. Japan's economic success foundered with the bursting of its asset bubble in the early 1990s; electoral dominance by the long-ruling LDP terminated with the party's internal split in 1993. Meanwhile, the end of the Cold War drastically reduced the likelihood of nuclear war and superpower confrontation, eliminating much of the logic behind Japan's tight military alliance with the US as well as for Japanese hostility toward Russia and China. As guns receded in their ability to shape international relations, and the economic issues of 'butter' gained priority, the entire Asian region initially benefited. Despite housing many of the world's most geopolitically nettlesome trouble spots, the region also came to enjoy remarkable economic growth and catapulted into enhanced international significance. Of particular importance was China's increased attention to its own economic transformation, carried out through a welcoming of foreign direct investment and a tentative embrace of various 'capitalist' market mechanisms. Of course, the increased predominance of economics subsequently came to haunt the Asian region. In the latter half of 1997 currency collapses and financial failures reversed the fortunes of numerous prior success stories, including Thailand, Malaysia, Indonesia, and most importantly South Korea. 'Rescue packages' were trotted out by the International Monetary Fund (IMF), and suddenly, headlines that once touted Asian regional economic miracles gave way to dire warnings about the 'Asian contagion'.

The central question that Japan poses for international and regional relations at the turn of the century is the extent to which these new domestic and international conditions will propel Japan to alter its previous foreign policies in fundamental ways. And more particularly, to what extent will domestic transformations in the Japanese political economy bear on, and perhaps alter, Japanese policies toward Asia and Asian regionalism? Three key threads of domestic change seem critical to answering these questions – most notably changes in the electoral and party systems; pressures for deregulation; and finally, the likelihood of financial overhaul. Shifts within these three areas are most likely to be the key contributors to any domestically-driven alterations in Japan's relations with the international arena generally, and with the Asian region more particularly.

Regime shift

For the past several years, Japan has been in the midst of a fundamental regime shift.[5] By 'regime', I mean the interrelated mixture of three things:

1 socio-economic cleavages and coalitions;
2 political and economic institutions; and
3 public policy profiles.

When regimes are stable they consist of a patterned set of ongoing, consistent, and mutually reinforcing relationships among all three. Such a combination provides the longstanding predictability and cohesion in a nation-state's political economy that allows one to talk meaningfully of a 'national pattern of politics', a *Weltanschauung*, a gestalt, an underlying 'mobilisation of bias', or prevailing paradigm.

In the case of Japan, comprehensive and linked changes have been taking place on numerous important fronts critical to the maintenance and stability of the regime that prevailed from roughly the early 1960s until the late 1980s. These have been more than simply the normal sequence of unrelated adjustments that are constantly taking place in any dynamic society. Rather, the very underpinnings of Japan's entire political economy have been undergoing sweeping overhaul. Among the most noteworthy changes were the following: a new electoral system, a reconfigured party system, and a massive dealignment of voters; the weakening of both the vertical and horizontal linkages connecting Japan's most powerful *keiretsu*; substantial reduction in the administrative tools available to economic bureaucrats; the pacification and emasculation of radical labour and leftist organisations; the economic and, to a lesser extent the political, marginalisation of organised agriculture; and a host of policy revisions that left the national budget deeply in the red, the official discount rate at its lowest in fifty years, the exchange rate of the yen swinging wildly, national debt at a higher per cent of GNP than in almost any other industrialised country, and the national treasury facing massive demands for gargantuan payouts for the debacle of bad loans throughout the financial sector, the enhanced threat to underfunded pension funds, growing interest payments, and the seemingly insatiable demands from electorally-fearful politicians for increased public sector spending for patronage projects. National economic performance had deteriorated substantially for almost the entire period 1990–99, following the collapse of the asset bubble created during the late 1980s, and little promise of a quick reversal.[6]

In all of these ways, the socio-economic, institutional and policy underpinnings of the old regime have shifted substantially. Virtually none of the changes noted above are likely to be reversed to their earlier forms. Japan's old regime has been jolted wildly out of its previous orbit of equilibrium. Within Japan, numerous political actors are currently battling over the extent and direction of desirable changes but no clear agenda yet commands a majority of popular support. Deep structural changes are taking place but how they will eventually be resolved is less clear. Ultimately, until some clarity emerges, predictions about specific policy directions for Japan – internationally, regionally, or otherwise – will perforce be predicated on highly dubious assumptions about specific evolutions in the nature of Japan's domestic political economy.

All the same certain recent changes can be mapped and the predominant directions that appear to be taking shape can be highlighted. From there it will be possible to examine the possible implications for Japan's foreign and regional policies. Three areas are critical – electoral and party system changes; bureaucratic and regulatory changes; and changes in the systems of financial and corporate governance.

Electoral reform and party system reorganisation

Japan has been going through a comprehensive set of changes in its electoral system and in the organisation of its various political parties. While some of these changes had earlier roots, they can be traced most tangibly to the split in the long-ruling Liberal Democratic Party in July, 1993.[7] Thirty-eight years of LDP hegemony over governmental posts gave way to a series of rolling and short-lived coalitions which over the next three years saw eleven different political parties sharing power and four individuals holding the office of Prime Minister. Less than two years after its split, the now smaller, post-split LDP returned to government in an alliance with its erstwhile enemies, the Socialists (and a smaller reform party). Subsequently, still further party reorganisations and recombinations took place with little predictable rationale. As of this writing in late 1999, the LDP dominated a different governing coalition that included the (ideologically conservative) Liberal Party and the (Buddhist-backed) New Komeito.

In the midst of this party reorganisation, and in part contributing to it, Japan scrapped its longstanding multi-member district system for elections to the Lower House of Parliament. In its place came one in which 300 parliamentarians were selected from single member districts, and an additional 200 were chosen from eleven regional districts on the basis of party-lists and proportional representation. The roughly four to one rural bias of the old system was dramatically reduced, and within the single member districts, at least, a premium on two candidate competition replaced the previous competition among five or more relatively viable candidates.

In the first election held under the new system, in 1996, six parties won ten or more seats. With the exception of the Japan Communist Party (JCP) and the LDP, all were substantially new or reformulated parties, not at all reflective of the party system that had prevailed from the 1960s until 1993. Four drew the bulk of their members from the old LDP. Although the LDP did the best of all the parties, and indeed increased its post-election seat total by 28 despite a shrinkage in the total number of Lower House seats by 11, it was by no means the cohesive electoral vehicle for conservatism that it had once been.

Four major trends now seem to be emerging: first, the demise of Japan's traditional left; second, the dominance of electoral politics by a host of competing conservative parties; third, an extensive voter demobilisation; fourth and finally, a consequent end to the longstanding electoral and party divisions over foreign policy that had long dominated post-war Japanese politics. The cumulative effect of these was the likelihood of at least a short-term continuation of a highly fluid linkage among political parties, party platforms and voters.

The Japan Socialist Party had been on a rather constant electoral downslope almost from its beginnings. Nonetheless, the party typically held 20–25 per cent of the seats in parliament through most of the 1970–80s, had spiked upwards in its support and seats with the 1990 elections, and was consistently the largest opposition party in the country. Along with the Japan Communist Party (JCP) and to a lesser extent the Democratic Socialist Party (DSP), and the Clean Government Party (CGP), the JSP had been an ideological standard bearer favouring dramatically curtailed ties to the United States, the elimination or constraint of Japan's own military forces, opposition to what it perceived as symbols of excessive nationalism and ties to pre-war authoritarianism, and a sweeping foreign policy of pacifism.

Ironically, it was under the temporary socialist-led coalition government of Murayama Tomiichi that the JSP scrapped most of the major policy positions the party had long advanced. Instead of being 'rewarded' for its 'realistic' policy shifts, however, in the 1996 elections the JSP found itself cut in half (from 30 seats to 15). Meanwhile, several minor, ideologically-leftist, parties that had previously taken 7–10 per cent of the vote merged into larger groupings. (The Japan Communist Party remained the only significant exception to this generalisation, nearly doubling its numbers from 15 to 26). More than anything else, the 1993 and 1996 elections italicised the historical decimation of Japan's parties of the left.

In the 1993 election three new conservative parties – the Japan New Party, the Japan Renewal Party and the New Party Sakigake – all competed with the LDP for conservative votes.[8] In the 1996 elections, three broadly conservative parties, the LDP (239 seats), the New Frontier Party (156 seats) and the Democratic Party (52) had become the principal parties and most importantly, nearly 90 per cent of the Lower House could be categorised as conservative.

Following the 20 October 1996 election and as of this writing, the LDP was the largest party in parliament and the major party in government. Yet, the party no longer enjoyed the same predominance that it had enjoyed prior to its split. Nor did it serve any longer as the single vehicle within which conservative politicians would contest national elections.

Although it had won 47.8 per cent of the seats in the 1996 election, other conservative parties drew 42.0 per cent. Beyond these simple numbers, the LDP had further clear-cut vulnerabilities, most notably linked to the difficulties of mobilising once loyal voters. Thus, while the LDP won 53 per cent of the seats contested in single member districts, it won only 35 per cent in the proportional representation districts. The other three conservative parties, including the Democratic Party that formed only weeks before the election, won a much more impressive 47.5 per cent.[9] The Democrats also did exceptionally well in the 1998 Upper House elections. Clearly, a battle for the institutional representation of Japanese conservatism was still underway, and by no means fully resolved in favour of the LDP.

Within Japan, there was a comprehensive voter demobilisation and increased partisan fluidity among once solidly pro-LDP interest groups. Voters who nominally 'supported' the LDP in principle had consistently correlated with actual party voters at levels of between .859 and .884 in the elections held between 1980 and 1990. In the 1993 election, this correlation fell to .756; LDP supporters were clearly deserting the party in a systematic demobilisation of voters.[10] The lack of clear LDP support was part of a broader trend toward voter dealignment. In the 1960s, fewer than 10 per cent of Japan's voters identified themselves as 'independents'. By the 1993 election that figure was up to 38 per cent; and in January, 1995, it was 50 per cent.[11]

Erstwhile conservative interest associations had also become more fragmented. Farm groups, small business associations, and even the big business federation, Keidanren, lost much of their earlier coherence and ability to speak for unified constituencies. The cumulative effect of these interest groups changes was to make the process of political co-ordination – for both conservative political parties and bureaucratic agencies – far more complicated than it had been when there were a smaller number of more comprehensive organisations. Linkages among interest groups, parties and bureaucratic agencies became far less automatic and predictably pro-LDP than was true at the height of conservative power. Still, while perhaps broadly 'conservative', larger and larger numbers of Japanese voters stayed home. Voter turnout in the 1996 election was the lowest it had ever been in the post-war years, falling to below 60 per cent.[12]

The major consequence of these changes in parties and elections was that the classic business versus labour, conservative versus socialist division that once shaped much of Japan's foreign policy debate, had been historically settled. Similarly resolved were many of the broad questions surrounding security relations with the United States as well as many longstanding nationalist-pacifist issues with predominantly domestic manifestations. Fifty years of economic transformation and the end of the Cold War had made many of them moot at earlier periods, but not until the comprehensive party realignment did it became clear that Japanese elections would no longer be contested over the same bipolar divisions as in the past.

By the middle of the 1990s, Japan's once vibrant political left had surrendered to conservatives on most of the issues that had once divided the two camps throughout the previous thirty-odd years; conservatism as a broad philosophy had undeniably triumphed over socialism in ways not likely to be reversed. Parties that espoused a left-of-centre agenda had simultaneously lost most of their electoral appeal.

The government-opposition divide at the end of the 1990s was no longer along traditional left–right, business versus labour, pro-Western versus pro-neutralist/communist lines, but instead was one between an ideologically undifferentiable conservative government and conservative opposition. For the most part, Japan's conservative parties outdid one another in repeating the same talismantic chants about 'reform', 'anti-corruption', 'foreign policy normalcy', and 'new vision'. But specific differences among their policy positions on key issues were few.

Such blurring of policy differences was a sharp setback to the hopes held out by many advocates of the new electoral system. Instead of presenting clear-cut policy alternatives, most of the conservative parties parroted one another's rhetorical positions on key issues in an apparent search for the mixture that would somehow mobilise the voting population. At the end of the 1990s, Japan's party realignment remained crystallised more around personalities and past party groupings than around fundamental issue differences; few generated much national voter appeal.

This is not to say that future political battles in Japan will not be fought over issues of economic distribution or over the constitution, military spending, US troops or the symbols of Japanese nationalism. Almost certainly these will emerge.

But the domestic articulation of any such issues in the next ten to fifteen years will almost certainly bear little resemblance to the forms and ideological banners under which they arose over the last 40–50 years. It is clear that any future domestic disputes about foreign and security policies are not likely to be heavily shaped by the once-strong positions of the JSP. Any electorally-important debates are likely to form around new polarities.

Moreover, with very few exceptions, the current political parties have been unwilling or unable to articulate policy positions capable of presenting very clear differentiations among themselves. Whether any such clarity will emerge in the near future remains an open question. Clearly, nearly 40 per cent of Japan's non-voters are available to be mobilised if and when a particular political party or candidate could provide them with sufficient motivation to turn out and vote. And such mobilisation could clearly take place on any of a host of issues faced by Japan – including many in foreign policy. But in the late 1990s, there were few such voices within the kaleidoscope of changing political parties, nor among Japanese citizens as a whole.

Administrative and bureaucratic reform

Just as conservative politicians were no longer united under a single electoral umbrella, and various conservative voters and interest associations had lost some of their earlier institutional unity, so too, Japan's national bureaucratic agencies no longer stood unified behind any hegemonic project in the way they had earlier been cohesive in their support of rapid economic growth. Nor did these agencies, for the most part, continue to enjoy their unchallenged positions at the commanding heights of policymaking. Instead, the Japanese bureaucracy had become more internally fragmented and its power was the subject of relentless political and popular attacks.

Japanese government agencies have long been noted for their reluctance to co-operate with one another.[13] Yet, rapid growth had generally induced at least the facade of considerable agency-to-agency co-operation; by the 1990s, such co-operation around an overriding agenda had been dramatically curtailed.[14] By that time, several agencies (particularly MPT, Agriculture, Transportation, Construction, and Home Affairs) had become heavily colonised by conservative politicians, in large measure through the LDP's Policy Affairs Bureau (seimu chōsakai), the actions of so-called *zoku* politicians (politicians with special connections to the interest associations and government agency concerned with some particular functional area of policy), and most especially by the Tanaka-Takeshita political machine. Generally, agencies with the largest influence over highly lucrative sectors of the economy and those ripe for pork-barrel politics and political contributions developed the tightest 'iron triangle' links among politicians, interest associations and government agencies.[15] Increasingly, their previously general economic missions gave way to the more particularistic mission of generating benefits for conservative politicians and their allies.

Other agencies (MITI, MOF, MPT, MOFA, and MOE to mention only the most prominent) while somewhat less prey to such political penetration and iron triangles, were at a minimum, caught up in the extensive competition over 'turf'. Numerous battles pitted agencies against one another over their respective responsibilities for emerging technologies such as biotechnology, development and regulation of HDTV, computer usage in schools, telecommunications, and the like.

During the mid 1990s, the national bureaucracy was also mired in a series of gaffes and unparalleled ineptitudes that dramatically undermined its credibility as the stalwart guarantor of national success. During the years of Japan's economic successes, the national bureaucracy was widely lauded at home and abroad for its extensive plans, regulations, and controls over wide segments of Japanese society that were presumed to have minimised many of the social problems that pervaded other countries. Despite numerous downsides, Japan had developed trains that ran on time, schools that provided a skilled and loyal workforce, businesses whose dynamism was not dependent on 'excessive competition' or massive layoffs during downturns, a health care system that resulted in low infant mortality rates and longevity for the elderly, crime rates that were low and declining, and so forth. With full justification or not, Japan's bureaucrats basked in the credit for most of these accomplishments. This all changed with a series of bureaucratic scandals, of which the most visible were the bureaucratic failure to deal adequately with the Kobe earthquake, the Aum poisonings, the HIV-tainted blood scandal, illegal licensing of old age homes by bribed MHW bureaucrats, several nuclear power plant meltdowns, and most importantly, the collapse of asset prices in stocks and property, the sweeping financial scandals in banks and brokerages, and the revelations that the financial sector had amassed a stunningly large collection of potentially unrecoverable loans.[16] Cover-up followed cover-up. By the end of 1997, the problems that once seemed concentrated in relatively minor outposts of the complex financial system, such as the *jūsen*, were shown to have infected all but the most solid banks, insurance companies and brokerages. A sequence of high officials, including several administrative vice-ministers, were implicated and/or forced into early resignations.

Bureaucratic sleaze affected local officialdom as well. Officials in 20 of Japan's 47 prefectures were revealed to have squandered millions of dollars by wining and dining one another along with officials from Tokyo. Fabricated and padded expense accounts, bogus trips, and non-existent staff were exposed as deeply entrenched 'norms'. At least three governors quit and some 13,000 officials were disciplined.[17]

A 1997 Mainichi poll showed that only 10 per cent of respondents thought government officials were seeking to fulfil the public good.[18] Politicians had long been viewed as corrupt; that the bureaucracy had come to be seen as little better was new and shocking.

Along with their revelations of incompetence and sleaze, high level bureaucrats began to show their political colours more clearly. Several former MOF officials, for example, resigned to run on the platform of Ozawa's Shinshintō in 1993, while the coalition government of 1993 attempted to purge certain senior bureaucrats deemed too close to the LDP. By the late 1990s, intra-conservative battles over deregulation and bureaucratic reorganisation saw particular agencies linking their fortunes to one or another party presumed most likely to champion its interests.

Not surprisingly, these shifts fed the overall demise of the bureaucracy's image as 'above politics' and operating in the 'national interest'. The scandals noted above revealed that large numbers of high ranking civil servants had been deeply enmeshed in extensive bribery schemes and closely tied to particular LDP leaders or groups. All of this contributed to a demise in bureaucratic prestige. A very simple measure of this decline can be found in the competition rate for positions in the senior civil service. At the height of conservative dominance and high growth, as many as 43 individuals competed for every one who was successful. By the early 1990s, that was down to fewer than 15 candidates for each opening.[19] More and more of Japan's best and brightest were opting for jobs in other arenas.

Within this broad context, pressures grew, from the media and the general public, for a new wave of 'administrative reforms'. The most widely touted proposals were those put forward by the Administrative Reform Council in 1997. These called for deregulation in six broad arenas, including bureaucratic restructuring, budgeting, economic structure, finance, education and social welfare. The most trumpeted proposals called among other things for the privatisation of the postal savings system, the division of functions once the sole responsibility of the Ministry of Finance, a reduction in the number of public corporations, massive cuts in Japan's 10,000 permits and licenses, and a substantial slimming of government agencies.[20] Meanwhile, a 'Big Bang', began in April, 1998, that involved substantial deregulation of the banking, securities and insurance sectors.[21]

As such measures were being carried out, they substantially eroded the policy-making autonomy of the national bureaucracy. Few government agencies advanced such reforms autonomously and most reforms enjoyed at best weak institutional support.[22] Political parties were divided on most of the 'reform' details, even as they united in their endorsement of the reform principle. Interest groups likewise favoured 'reform' of agencies to which they themselves were not linked, while opposing changes in the behaviour and power of 'their' agencies.

Thus, the truly important question for any future Japanese regime will be the extent to which such a deregulatory position gains institutionalised political expression and in turn becomes the catalyst for new policy directions. Will political organisations gravitate around the two opposite polls of 'protection' versus 'openness', and 'regulation' versus 'deregulation'? Or, as was successfully done by the LDP for the bulk of its time in power, will politicians, government agencies, and political parties blur, rather than sharpen these divisions? Absent any political or institutional vehicles by which these divisions can be articulated and resolved politically, the divisions themselves are likely to remain little more than latent for a long period. New policy initiatives based on the emerging socio-economic divisions remain unlikely. Moreover, in the current climate of hostility toward bureaucratic agencies, it will also remain difficult for those agencies to begin advancing major policy initiatives or to take any particular lead in shifting elements of Japan's foreign or regional policies. Instead, it is most likely that these agencies will remain in a collective effort to 'circle the wagons' and protect their existing powers and policy positions will be the outgrowth of such actions.

Financial liberalisation, corporate internationalisation, and the 'Big Bang'

Into at least the late 1970s, Japan's capital markets and its currency were insulated from world currency markets and were essentially 'national' in character. With accelerating speed during the 1980s both became ever more integrated into world markets. The Japanese yen, fixed at ¥360 to the US dollar from 1947 until 1971, more than quadrupled in value to about ¥80 at one point in 1995; then, just as suddenly it weakened to ¥125 by the middle of 1997. The ability of the Ministry of Finance and the Bank of Japan to set exchange rates had become vastly super-seded by that of international markets and currency speculators. This overall integration with world capital markets, coupled with important changes in privatisation of previously public enterprises and the increased multinationalisation of many of Japan's largest firms combined to erode many of the economic foundations that previously given rise to notions of 'Japan, Inc'.

The internationalisation of exchange rate values had begun with the breakdown of the Bretton Woods system in 1971. It accelerated when Japanese financial markets were substantially liberalised, particularly with the revision of the Foreign Exchange and Control Law (1980) and the deregulation of the corporate bond market. It reached an early apex as a result of the efforts by the G–5 finance ministers to co-ordinate monetary rates under the Plaza Accord of 1985 and the Louvre Accord of 1987.[23]

By the mid-1990s, individual Japanese companies and financial institutions had become free to issue overseas bonds in whatever was the most suitable currency and then swap the proceeds into yen. Japan had become the world market's major supplier of capital.[24] And indeed, individual Japanese corporations by the late-1990s were opting to finance even domestic business deals denominated in dollars as a further evidence of both their corporate autonomy and their independence from MOF oversight.

At home, privatisation and de-regulation were simultaneously underway. By the 1990s, once nationalised industries such the Japanese National Railways (JNR), Nippon Telephone and Telegraph (NTT), International Telegraph and Telephone (KDD) and the Tobacco and Salt Monopoly had all been substantially privatised. Other industries such as the airlines, energy, the finance sector, and various pension systems had undergone varying degrees of deregulation.[25] Numerous areas of the once highly protected Japanese economy had thus become more open to influence by stockholders on the one hand and to foreign corporations and investors on the other.

In addition, whereas during the 1960s government economic energies had been focused largely on assisting Japan's high value added, technologically sophisticated firms to gain greater international competitiveness, by the end of the 1990s, far more substantial governmental effort was being directed toward Japan's declining industries. MITI was particularly active in supporting cartels in such industries as aluminium, cement, and petrochemicals,[26] while, in other oligopolistic industries with high employment such as steel, shipping and textiles, MITI policies encouraged economic adjustment but within a still-protected domestic market.[27]

Japanese fiscal policy had also been transformed. During the mid-1960s, government revenues had come largely from corporate and personal income taxes while the Ministry of Finance pursued 'overbalanced budgets' that served to keep down government expenditures, and to allow conservative politicians to offer periodic and popular tax cuts. In 1964, for example, the budget was balanced and only 1.35 per cent of the general budget was devoted to debt service. By 1995, nearly one-quarter of the government's revenues were derived from consumption taxes; over one-quarter of the budget was financed by borrowing; and debt service had risen to 18.6 per cent.[28] This latter figure put Japan ahead of the United States (13.9 per cent), the U.K. (17.5 per cent), Germany (10.7 per cent) and France (17.9 per cent).[29] Even more remarkably, Japan's cumulative debt by 1997 topped nearly 100 per cent of GNP and it continued to rise as Japan approached the millennium. Among the OECD countries only a few such as Belgium, Canada, and Italy confronted bigger gross debts.[30]

Monetary policies were also quite different. Trying to cover the fallout from the bubble, in 1992 the government abandoned previous monetary restraint, driving down official rates to 0.5 per cent by the middle of the decade, the lowest levels in Japanese history. Moreover, the government launched a series of huge supplementary budgets between 1992–95 which in total exceeded ¥70 trillion while also dramatically expanding spending by the Fiscal Investment and Loan Programme. Both monetary and fiscal policies had become vastly more loose than ever before in post-war Japan.

Individual firm behaviour reflected this general loosening of monetary and capital controls. Foreign direct investment by Japanese firms in the mid-1960s had been minuscule; by 1993 cumulative Japanese investment abroad totalled some $260 billion, making Japan the world's second largest overseas investor (behind the US at $549 billion).[31] Once subject to heavy MITI and MOF directions designed to ensure conformity to government industrial plans, firms, by the end of the 1990s, were far freer to pursue their business strategies uncompromised by the earlier club of government capital controls. Technology transfer agreements leaped across national boundaries with nary a governmental signature. Profitable companies were free to finance activities through retained earnings. Others raised capital through domestic equity markets, overseas warrants, international currency swaps, domestic bond issues, and the like. They were thus far freer to pursue strategies determined primarily by internal, company-specific needs rather than by external government directives or national industrial policy proscriptions.

Deregulation of the corporate bond market was an important part of this process. As late as 1979 only two companies, Toyota Motors and Matsushita Electric were qualified to issue unsecured convertible or straight bonds. A decade later some 300 firms could legally issue straight or warrant-attached bonds while 500 firms could issue unsecured convertible bonds.[32] Deregulation also allowed many corporations to shift their sources of debt financing from the main banks to bonds. Bonds, including those issued abroad, gained an increased role. In 1965 ¥391 billion worth of bonds were issued by Japanese industrial companies; none were issued overseas. In 1989, the former figure was up to ¥9,284 billion while an even larger ¥11,129 billion was issued overseas.[33] Such changes reduced the internal cohesion among the *keiretsu* while allowing individual firms, whether *keiretsu* members or not, far greater autonomy in their capital generation and their overall business strategies.

Corporate and product entry into Japan had also become easier. Formal trade barriers and limits on foreign direct investment had been largely eliminated. Foreign brokerages not only held seats on the Tokyo Stock Exchange, but their total market share came to surpass that of Japan's big four (and after the failure of Yamaichi, Japan's big three). A number of foreign banks were involved in government-bond underwriting while others had entered trust banking. Japanese imports, including imports of manufactured goods, increased substantially from the 1960s. Many Western firms had become $1 billion companies within the Japanese market, including IBM, Coca-Cola, Schick, Motorola, Texas Instruments, Nestle, Olivetti, Warner-Lambert, Mercedes Benz, and Amway. Coca-Cola in the 1990s, for example, drew a higher share of its world profit from Japan than from the US, with 'profit margins per gallon' at four times the US rate. Also successful were direct merchandisers such as Wella, Eddie Bauer, Compaq, Dell Computer, Proctor and Gamble, McDonalds and Haagen Daas. Large department stores were more widespread, many stocking foreign products. The service sector continued to show surplus sales for foreign firms. Clearly, the Japanese market had shed much of its earlier mercantilist character.

In the midst of all of these changes in government finance and corporate control, the Hashimoto government began promising a massive financial deregulation, generally known as the 'Big Bang'. As of 1 April 1998, a host of existing controls over the convertibility of foreign currencies were lifted. In principle at least, corporations and individual citizens alike became free to convert yen into other currencies and/or to invest directly in foreign stocks, mutual funds, insurance programmes and the like. More importantly, the 'Big Bang' unleashed a wave of foreign direct investments in Japan, mostly through mergers, but some through hostile take-overs that substantially de-nationalised the heights of Japanese capitalism.

As larger numbers of Japanese firms, including many of their subcontractors, became more truly multinational, and as the 'Big Bang' took effect, numerous strategic alliances tied Japanese-owned companies to foreign-owned firms.[34] At the core of the once privileged banking sector, Japan's Long Term Credit Bank forged an alliance with the Swiss Credit Bank involving an investment of 1 billion Swiss francs ($671 million), while Barclays and Hokkaido Takushoku Bank developed joint asset management and investment banking services that would allow the Japanese bank to deliver the UK bank's products. Meanwhile in manufacturing Toyota was teamed up with GM and Kia among others and Nissan had been bought up by Renault; in electronics, Fujitsu, NEC, Hitachi and Toshiba all had alliances with American and European companies; NTT and KDD had done the same in telecommunications; Softbank and TV Asahi had various partners in software and commercial television; Mitsubishi Heavy Industries was in a venture with Daimler Benz while Kawasaki Heavy Industries and Ishikawajima Harima Industries also teamed up with foreign partners in a variety of military production technologies. These were merely the tips of an international alliance iceberg that accelerated madly by 1998–99, particularly in brokerages, insurance and finance. Indeed, Canon went so far as to adopt as its corporate slogan for the 1990s 'Symbiosis with Global Partners'.[35] The very 'nationality' of once unmistakably Japanese firms came into question, both as regards ownership but more importantly as regards the place and nationality of the workforce.[36] Although many Japanese-owned companies were often still international export powerhouses, their products were no longer manufactured exclusively – or in some cases predominantly – within Japan. From 1990 to the first quarter of 1996, Japanese exports grew by only 4 per cent, the lowest rate in one 12 country OECD survey. (During this period, eight countries had export growth of 25 per cent or more) Conversely, Japanese imports grew by 41 per cent, the third largest figure in the survey.[37] Even more symbolically, in 1995, Japan manufactured more overseas (¥41.2 trillion) than it exported from the home islands (¥39.6 trillion).[38]

Though these changes were taking place in many segments of Japanese business, they were by no means universal. Numerous firms in traditional industries such as cement and construction proved either unable or unwilling to invest abroad or to partner with foreign firms, enmeshed as many were in domestic public works projects advanced on their behalf by Japanese politicians. Similarly, while some of the subcontractors of Japan's larger manufacturers did follow them in setting up overseas operations, far more, particularly the smallest, remained in Japan only to watch their market shares dwindle. The number of manufacturing jobs in Japan fell by over one million in the four years 1992–95 alone, catalysing national fears about the possible 'hollowing out' of Japan.

Many of the most protected industries, including those within important service sectors such as insurance, brokerage houses, and even many commercial banks, remained unable or unmotivated to compete internationally. They remained locked into the domestic market, contributing heavily to the financial crisis of the 1990s.[39] The result of all of these shifts was to drive a series of wedges into a business community that had once been almost uniformly supportive of, and the automatic beneficiaries of, the politics of 'embedded mercantilism'.

Just as with political and party reforms, and the changes in bureaucratic structure and regulatory control, so too the changes in finance and corporate governance hold out the promise of dividing the once comfortably integrated and oligopolistic world of Japanese business. They also promise further fragmenting of the extensive intra-corporate ties that have underpinned Japan's vertical and horizontal *keiretsu*. At the same time, and equally importantly for foreign policy, these changes make it more and more difficult for the Japanese government to articulate clear-cut policies with any automatic expectation that official monetary and financial tools will allow them to count on semi-automatic corporate compliance with government policies. Instead, corporate interests are likely to be far more independent of governmental goals and far more reflective of the emerging power of capital markets and their own enhanced autonomy.

Regime prospects

The changes described above are all in progress; how they will be finally resolved remains unclear. It will almost certainly take considerable time before some newly equilibrated Japanese regime with predictability and stability emerges from the current frictions. At the same time, it is possible to suggest some of the major prospects for such a new regime. What are the most probable interlacings among current lines of socio-economic cleavage; the institutions through which these might gain expression; and Japan's probable public policy profile?

Turning first to socio-economic cleavages, the major division confronting Japan at the end of the century is that between its internationally competitive and its non-competitive sectors, firms, and socio-economic groups. At one extreme stands a Japan composed of the nation's truly multinational successes: world spanning, technologically sophisticated, high value added firms using skilled workforces that produce internationally competitive products, high profits, and expanding market shares. Around this same poll at the individual level are Japan's cosmopolitans – citizens with extensive quality education, highly marketable skills, good incomes, and an interest in sharing in a consumerist lifestyle. To such people, a Japan of greater internationalisation and economic openness are far more appealing than ominous.

At another extreme are Japan's more protected, less sophisticated firms with mixtures of low-skilled, undertrained or bloated workforces whose profitability is more a function of political protection and governmental subsidisation than internationally competitive products. Individuals at this poll tend to be less well-educated, with few cutting edge skills, lower incomes and a desperate anxiety about the downside risks of rapid economic change.

Such a division in itself suggests that Japan's future political economy will involve a relatively simple zero sum struggle between these two competing forces. Reduced to its journalistic expression, the future of Japan will come down to questions about whether Japan will deregulate its economy or not, whether trade and investment will become substantially more open or not, and ultimately whether Japan will recapture its role at the cutting edge of economic developments or instead will it remain mired in extensive regulations, protectionism, and anti-consumerist biases. From this one-dimensional perspective, the prospects for any new regime are twofold: 'forward or back', 'regulated or not', 'open or closed', 'market-driven or crony capitalist'.

Yet, socio-economics is not the only important division in Japan. Subsidiary splits fall along lines of whether or not to continue a predominantly pacifist role for Japan in foreign affairs or whether Japan should become 'a normal country'. There is also a strong contingent of citizens anxious to see an end to the corruption built into the prevailing political system. Such issues were of high salience in elections during the middle to later years of the 1990s for many Japanese voters. Issues of regulatory control and oversight also remain critical. Other issues have also catalysed voter interest at various times and promise to do so in the future. But as the previous section made clear, none of them have clear-cut institutional vehicles – political parties or bureaucratic agencies – by which to guarantee a permanent spot on the national agenda. Hence, whether party system reorganisation and/or bureaucratic deregulation will crystallise such sharp policy and programmatic alternatives remains highly questionable.

Party reorganisation in 1993 seemed to promise just such an institutionalised vehicle for the advocates of substantial internationalisation, bureaucratic deregulation, and a dismantling of the old system. Prime Minister Hosokawa had an admittedly inchoate coalition government, only a few members of which were outspoken advocates of sweeping reform. Yet, the coalition as a whole was committed to breaking with the past; it enjoyed widespread popular support for its agenda; and it began to put forward various reform proposals. But Hosokawa and his movement proved exceptionally short-lived.

The New Frontier Party (NFP) under Ozawa Ichirō also held out some promise of being a vehicle for change. In one survey of parliamentarians' attitudes, it was clear that the NFP members did differ in important ways from the LDP on the desirability of extensive reforms.[40] Still, neither was a clear-cut advocate of one or the other side. And more importantly, the NFP – the more pro-internationalist of the two – deteriorated rapidly in voter appeal and by early 1998 had fragmented drastically, thus eliminating any chance it may have had of serving as an electoral vehicle for reformists and internationalists.

In the Upper House elections of 1998, the Democratic Party won a substantial victory behind a platform geared to urban voters, a reduction in bureaucratic powers and the promise of sweeping economic reforms. It too proved to have a short span of influence. Thus, as of 1999, Japan's internationalist/urban contingent continued to lack any institutional vehicle through which to advance its particular socio-economic interests.

Such vehicles could well develop in the future. Party realignment has hardly ended. Moreover, given the vast number of businesses, citizens, and geographical constituencies likely to benefit from less bureaucratic regulation, more financial openness, and less protectionism, the ground remains ripe for cultivation by new political entrepreneurs anxious to tap into and to advance such interests. At the same time, most of Japan's politicians seem quite uncertain of where their best electoral advantages may lie, and hence few are quick to spell out proposed policy directions with great clarity.

The biases of the new electoral system tend toward such bifurcation. Combining as it does both single seat districts with regionally-constituted proportional representation seats, the new electoral system could modulate some of the preponderantly local bias in the preceding system which in turn has been critical to today's well-entrenched protection and regulation. Some anti-local pressures are almost certain to be generated by the party-style competition built into the proportional representation districts. Yet, the new single member districts are considerably smaller and more compact than those they replaced, and these are almost certain to provide an even greater spur to electoral parochialism. Moreover, if as happened in the 1996 election, parties use p.r. victories to seat parliamentary candidates who failed to win single-member seats, the likelihood of clear-cut party divisions along socio-economic, or any other lines, is thereby further limited.[41] Furthermore, in the run-up to the 2000 elections the LDP-led government to reduce by twenty the number of seats allocated by proportional representation.

Overall, the now smaller individual districts will almost certainly retain or expand their strongly 'local' caste and this will have a broader political influence. Two or more candidates competing in any single district are far more likely to attempt to outdo one another in 'local' variations of pork barrel promises than they are to articulate differences on major policy positions (although this could be complicated by the economic or security character of the district). But few individual candidates are likely to offer voters sharply competing alternatives between protectionist and anti-protectionist policies or between sweeping deregulation or continued regulatory controls; or on any other major issues calling for new directions on foreign or domestic policy. Any 'serious' candidates will almost certainly hew to whatever localistic focus seems most predominant. Thus, in some districts, electoral competition will involve two or more candidates advocating local protection, while in other districts, competitors will be attempting to outdo one another in their demands for deregulation and more open markets.

At the same time, while the old system had an anti-urban bias that was as high as 4:1, the new system is far more favourable to urban areas with the worst over-representation of rural areas being little more than 2:1. Thus, urban consumers who presumably will benefit disproportionately from a less regulated and more internationalised economy will undoubtedly gain an increased electoral voice. Even more importantly, internationally successful business firms will have the possibility of supporting parliamentary candidates (and parties) committed to policies likely to benefit them economically.

Consequently, one very probable basis for party realignment would see one (or more) parties taking positions favourable to Japan's international businesses, unions employed in export industries, those who would benefit from a more open Japanese market (such as urban consumers) and the like. Gravitating toward an opposing poll would be one (or more) party more narrowly nationalistic and representative of Japan's small shopkeepers, farmers, and less favourable to foreign direct investment and foreign imports. Some hint of this was reflected in the somewhat disproportionate 'internationalist' orientation of many NFP members, and the conversely more 'protectionist' biases and constituencies of those in the LDP, but this division is hardly clear-cut. Some such nationalist–internationalist realignment may occur in the future, but it is far more likely that any large party or parties will contain mixtures of both tendencies than that two parties will gravitate around different and antagonistic poles. Certainly, Japan's past political history suggests the importance most successful politicians and parties have placed on avoiding, rather than on exacerbating, class tensions and socio-economic divisions. Unless, or until, economic conditions in Japan become even more extreme than they are today, such a tendency is likely to remain strong.

Nor are Japan's elected officials alone in their protectionist biases. Most of Japan's bureaucratic ministries also focus inward. The exception of course is the Ministry of Foreign Affairs as well as the new Financial Supervisory Agency. But most other ministries such as Agriculture, Forestry and Fisheries; Education; Construction; Home Affairs; and Transportation are constituent-oriented. They are likely to remain so under any 'new' political arrangements, and even under new bureaucratic arrangements.[42] MITI is somewhat more mixed as is MOF. Yet both agencies, and MOF in particular, have been biased in favour of protecting longstanding constituents and the protection of their own regulatory frameworks. Vogel has identified what he sees as the most distinctive feature of recent Japanese regulatory reforms: 'the ministries' effort to turn liberalisation into a protracted process in which their ability to determine the timing and conditions of new market entry generates a powerful new source of leverage over industry'.[43] Hence no Japanese ministry has been a consistent advocate of massive deregulation or vastly more open markets, particularly when these have seemed, as they do at the end of the century, to involve a reduction in the very regulatory powers from which the power of those agencies flows.

In short, a relatively clear-cut socio-economic bifurcation is emerging between a deregulatory and internationalist poll on the one hand and a regulatory and nationalist poll on the other. However, the former has at best a very limited institutional representation and only a minimal voice within the upper echelons of government. Internationalism and deregulation may have stronger voices in the top ranks of business, but thus far, even business has been slow to press for any clear-cut political expression of its more internationalist/deregulatory views. This may well change, but the chances for a rapid institutional reflection of Japan's underlying socio-economic divisions seem slight.

Yet, it is similarly difficult to imagine the development of any policy profile that would somehow satisfy both major constituencies in the ways that high growth was so successfully capable of doing from the 1960s through the 1980s. At this point, the policy choices confronting Japan seem far more zero-sum as between regulation and deregulation and financial openness or not. Making such choices however is politically exceptionally difficult. Making them under the current conditions of slow-to-no growth will be even more painful. Nor are any new directions likely without exacerbating demands for payouts to alleviate the pain of any losers under new policies unless Japan were willing to abandon its longstanding political commitment toward inclusionary politics and shared social burdens.

For the moment, Japan is finding some stability around continued protection of the politically well-entrenched, if economically uncompetitive, sectors of society, along with grudging acceptance of deregulation and more open markets. Such stability, however, is unlikely to remain for a long period. It is almost impossible to see Japan's economy recovering even moderate rates of growth under such policies. Moreover, there are simply too many voters and too many important Japanese businesses that would be seriously disadvantaged if it were to continue for long.

Thus, a third scenario for a stable regime seems more plausible, one that involves neither sharp bipolar electoral politics between internationalists and nationalists, nor the victory of one over the other. The third scenario might well be called the 'Italianisation of Japan'. Under such a situation, Japanese electoral politics would involve a more muddied mix of politicians and parties redolent of Italy in the 1970s or 1980s. Elected politicians would increase their constituent popularity through shared pilferage of the treasury allocated to increased patronage and public works. They would continue to protect the country's farmers, small businesses, marginalised regions, protected sectors, and troubled industries. Voters who thus benefited would provide such politicians with electoral backing while those voters unhappy with the limited choices they were offered would simply stay home in greater numbers, as happened in Japan's 1996 elections. Meanwhile, internationally-successful and/or multinationally-based firms would go about their business without excessively frustrating interference from, or inordinate dependence on, the world of politics. In effect, Japan's socio-economic divisions would play out in ways that saw the economically-non-competitive sectors in control of electoral politics, while the more competitive sectors would find their successes within domestic and world markets.

So long as international pressures for an opening of Japanese markets remains diffuse and product specific, and so long as the economic pinch of protectionism is not too sharply felt by the truly successful firms or by large numbers of consumer/voters, such a system could well continue for a long period of time. It would not generate the exceptional economic transformations and high growth of two decades earlier, but it could muddle along without serious challenge for a considerable period.

Within this context of a changing regime in Japanese domestic politics, what can plausibly be expected for Japan's involvement with Asia? I believe that few major changes are likely in Japan's policies, but it seems helpful to examine the possibilities for the future less in terms of clear-cut predictions and more in terms of three central tensions that have long existed in the past and are likely to continue to shape Japanese foreign policies in the future.

Three central tensions

Japan's foreign policies and regional policies toward Asia are likely to be the outcome of three central tensions. The first tension is that between domestic and international forces. What works well for domestic Japanese politics and economics is frequently at odds with what is conducive to an improved position for Japan internationally. This tension was one of the major issues dividing Japanese conservative and progressive forces throughout the post-war period. It was also alive within the ranks of the Liberal Democratic Party (LDP) before the party split; it was acute within the Murayama coalition, as it debated across a wide ideological gap such issues as participation in PKO, the constitutionality and mission of Japan's Self-Defense Forces, how to deal with Japanese military activities in Asia during the Pacific War, and other issues. It remains alive in different forms in intra-conservative debates over US troops and bases on Okinawa, as well as over the extent to which Japanese policies should tilt toward the US or toward Asia.[44] This tension is critical to understanding the extent to which domestic politics will lead to any new Japanese policies internationally or whether domestic politics will constrain any such moves.

The second tension is between regionalism and internationalism. Despite China's size and population, Japan's remains the most powerful economy in Asia. Yet, Japan's leadership is far from unquestioned within the region. Simultaneously, however, as a member of the G-7 and an economic power with extensive international interests beyond Asia, Japan has concerns that extend far beyond the region. Quite frequently, Japan's broader international orientations conflict with those inherent in any emerging regional role. The central questions here concern the extent to which Japan will emerge as the leader of Asia as well as whether any such regional role will be compatible with, or competitive with, the country's being a much more internationally-oriented player throughout the world.

The third and final tension concerns the different dimensions through which Japan will act. Three central dimensions are relevant: economic, diplomatic, and military. The lines separating these are somewhat blurry; yet, the extremes of the three poles remain quite distinct. Since 1945, Japan has relied principally on economic rather than on diplomatic or military means to achieve its foreign policy goals. Whether that pattern will continue in the future remains unclear.

The widespread shifts discussed in the preceding sections suggest that future governments in Japan will confront greater pressures to become more internationally proactive than were earlier governments. Nevertheless, within electoral circles and within the national bureaucracy, the pressures for continuity remain overwhelming. Numerous powerful groups and organisations clearly prefer to keep things more or less the same and to retain a focus on domestic problems, rather than to deal pre-emptively with what is going on elsewhere in the world. The evidence from the developments in Japanese politics discussed above suggests that Japanese politics is likely to remain primarily 'local politics'.

Dramatic changes in external conditions might well alter this domestic bias. So might various party reorganisations or independent bureaucratic initiatives. But it is hard to envision actions that might catalyse the nation toward a dramatically more activist international role. Absent some dramatic shift, Japanese politicians and government officials seem concentrated on the country's domestic problems and the principal bias of Japan's domestic politics and economy remains toward a retention of the status quo, perhaps modulated by a reluctant, tentative, and gradual movement toward greater foreign policy activism. But these moves are unlikely to result in any substantially increased role for, or activism by, Japan in the Asian region or the world at large.

What of the balance between and internationalist and a regionalist Japan? Japan has the most powerful economy in Pacific Asia and stands as an economic Gulliver in a region of Lilliputs.[45] Its gross national product (GNP) is about six times greater than the combined GNP's of Taiwan, South Korea, Singapore, and Hong Kong. Although China has been growing fast and is projected to have the region's largest GNP by 2015, Japan easily surpasses the Middle Kingdom in per capita income, finance, trade, advanced industrial production, and research, and will do so for many decades to come.

Many would even suggest that Japan is also the most powerful military presence in the region, even though many countries have more troops under arms. China has three million troops; India and North Korea each have over one million, Japan has only 245,000; it also has relatively few combat aircraft and limited force projection capability. But, except for the US, Japan's is by far the most technologically sophisticated military force in the Asia Pacific.

As Europe has moved to create a unified economic zone, and as NAFTA has gained momentum as a North American trade unit many pundits have suggested that Asia, with Japan at its centre, would emerge logically as a third regional bloc, quite possibly the most economically dynamic of the three. In this way the world's three most powerful national economies (the US, Germany and Japan) would each be at the core of a regionally-based trade and investment bloc – all three highly competitive with one another, a scenario vaguely reminiscent of George Orwell's nightmarish dystopia, 1984.

Considerable evidence can be mustered in support of such a scenario. Approximately 70 per cent of Japanese foreign aid is directed toward Asia, and virtually all major recipients of Japanese aid are Asian. As labour costs have risen in Japan, labour-intensive Japanese firms have taken advantage of their enhanced autonomy and financial incentives to invest vast sums in search of cheaper labour. Initially this involved South Korea, Hong Kong, and Taiwan; subsequently the money moved to Thailand, Malaysia, Indonesia and Singapore. Numerous Japanese firms have begun integrated world wide production with Asian factories as key components.[46] Japan is the largest foreign investor in Indonesia, Malaysia, and Thailand and the second largest investor in Singapore and the Philippines. The amounts of Japanese money – most of it private – that has moved into all of these economies has been ratcheting upwards annually. Intra–Asian trade has also been on the rise.

Nonetheless, any growing role for Japan in Asia is unlikely to be unilateral or uncomplicated. Japan's predominance in Asia will confront at least three competing trends over and above the basic bias now within the country to focus on domestic problems: first, the US military's continued presence in Asia; second, the growing role of Asian powers not so dependent on Japanese capital or technology; and third, the strong non-regional, broadly internationalist pressures and aspirations felt by Japan. Such pressures work, less against Japan's being a pre-eminence in Asia, and more against Japan's definition of itself primarily as 'the' regional power, or even as 'a' regional power. To the extent that Japan becomes a regional power, it will do so primarily with an eye toward ensuring an open, rather than a closed, Asian regionalism. Certainly, Japan proved unable to create an independent regional leadership role for itself during the economic crisis that began in 1997, hemmed in as it was by US and IMF reluctance as well as its own domestic economic problems.

Japan's activities in a host of international economic and political organisations also work against its limiting its perspective to that of 'first among Asian equals'. Any extensive focus on its potential political and economic role in Asia runs the risk of causing Japan to lose sight of its far broader linkages with the rest of the industrialised world. Indeed many other countries in Asia are becoming increasingly trans-regional as well. All are solidly linked to Japan, but all are fundamentally dependent on US markets as well. And in the case of Japan, the linkages extend even more widely, to Europe, Latin America, and even the Middle East.

The US market remains for Japan four and a half times larger than Japan's number two export market. In addition, Japan is vitally dependent on US companies for critical products such as food supplies and oil. Thus, even with its long-running recession, Japan remains a 'world economic superstar' in terms of its GNP, capital holdings and per capita income. At the same time, Japan is far less a world economic power in terms of diversified market capabilities, and continues to rely heavily on the US market for its exports.

When the question turns to security, Japan's continued dependence on the United States and Western Europe is even more stark. The US–Japan Security Treaty can in no way be replaced by any intra–Asian security agreement. Indeed, the 1996 revisions in that treaty reaffirmed for both Japan and the United States the continued importance of security linkages between the two countries, and guaranteed a continuation of the security relationship and US bases in Japan. Not surprisingly, many of Japan's Asian neighbours were delighted at this indication of continuity in the US–Japan security relationship.

Any new policy directions for Japan, in the Asian region or elsewhere in its foreign policy profile, is likely to continue to reflect glaring imbalances among its economic, diplomatic, and security dimensions. Generally speaking, Japan has been at its most international and regional economically, while it has been least international and regional in security matters. Its political and diplomatic activities fall in between, but have been much closer to the relatively passive position it has taken in security affairs.

None the less, despite problems in many sectors, many Japanese firms and many Japanese technologies remain highly competitive in world markets. Economic prowess remains Japan's strong suit. Overall strength in manufacturing seems likely to keep many Japanese-owned firms playing a major role in Asia and the world over the next decade. To the extent that Japan moves to exert greater regional or international leadership, the sphere of economics is most likely to provide Japan with the greatest comparative advantage.

Politically, Japan has been far less visibly present in either the Asian region or in the world at large. At least since Prime Minister Ikeda (1960–64), Japan has endeavoured to 'separate economics from politics' in its foreign policy. Indeed, into the early 1980s, Japanese foreign policy involved largely lockstep imitation of US actions. Independent consideration of Japan's foreign interests and political or diplomatic means to achieve those ends were comparatively rare.

By the 1990s, Japan was showing a greater willingness to pursue more autonomy in certain limited areas of its foreign policy. The country was not willing to follow the US in imposing economic sanctions against either Viet–Nam or China. Rather, it pursued independent policies in both countries. Similarly, Japanese diplomats have been far less willing than either their US or German counterparts to worry about internal Russian political or economic stability (at least until the four Northern Islands are returned or at least promises of their return are ensured). Unlike virtually all of the other industrialised democracies, in deference to Japan's Arab oil ties, Japan did not send a high level political delegation to the funeral of Menachem Begin. In such areas, Japan during the 1990s showed an increased ability and willingness to separate various of its foreign policy interests from those of the US and to use diplomatic, and not just economic, means to achieve these ends. If Inoguchi is right in suggesting that an emerging 'bigemony', will replace US hegemony, Japan will clearly be a less docile and quiescent partner than it once was.[47] Nevertheless, given its domestic economic problems, and its inward looking politics, the entire notion of 'bigemony' now seems farfetched.

Outside of the economic sphere, Japan's independent policy actions remain largely at the margins of international significance. They hardly pose major challenges to the overarching political directions pursued by the US, for example. Nor is it easy to identify Japanese ends that were purely strategic or political (with the possible exception of the Northern Islands issue). Far more frequently, manifestations of Japanese policy autonomy have been largely reflections of the pursuit of longstanding economic interests, most typically the interests of Japan's least internationally competitive corporations.

The first tool of diplomacy for Japanese officials is likely to remain that of economics. This is unlikely to change quickly even though Japan's domestic economy has been stagnant for nearly a decade. Furthermore, most Japanese actions in diplomacy and strategy have continued to be closely co-ordinated with the United States and/or various international bodies. Japan has given little indication that it is anxious to move independently or aggressively in most international problem areas. Indeed, given Japan's recently parlous financial straits, the country will find it difficult even to exercise economic leadership.

Conclusions

This paper has outlined what I believe are the major changes taking place in Japan's domestic political economy, as well as the three major tensions that are most likely to shape Japan's future role in the world's evolving political economy. In working their way into the twenty-first century, Japan's leaders are likely to find themselves forced to confront simultaneously both domestic tensions and competing international demands and opportunities. Constructing cohesive national policies will by no means be easy. Given the competing pulls of domestic pressures, plus the competitiveness among international tensions, cohesiveness is far less likely than a series of inconsistent zigs and zags. Certainly, developments inside the electoral, party system and bureaucratic arenas within Japan militate against the easy emergence of any stark and clear-cut policy directions, domestically or in foreign policy.

The strongest pulls for Japan to play a more international role, to internationalise its domestic economy, and to shape behaviour in Asia, are likely to come from economic, rather than from diplomatic or military forces. Japan's economy has reached a stage of development where it is increasingly difficult for the country's political and bureaucratic leaders to resist the tremendous international impact of currency flows, overseas investment, the needs of Japanese and other multinational corporations, and the technological and labour market imperatives of an increasingly integrated world economy.

Similarly, Japan is likely to play an increased role, economically and (perhaps) politically and militarily, in Asia. But the country can do so successfully only if it does not ignore the far more compelling pull for it to be a major world player – reflecting its clear interests beyond the Asian region. In this way, although Japan will remain extremely critical to the countries of Asia, they are likely to diminish in inherent value to Japan. And to the extent that Japan's political focus remains introspectively driven, any matters of foreign policy, short of major crises, are less likely to receive serious political attention.

Japan might, for a variety of reasons, move to enhance its overall national influence over international and regional events. But there is little evidence to suggest that these moves will involve becoming a 'contender' for significantly greater international influence, if being such a 'contender' means seeking to rewrite the major rules and directions of international relations.

Rather, in groping toward any new role over the next decade or so, Japan is unlikely to move precipitously, unless confronted by major external threats. Moreover, it is most likely that Japan will continue to resist acting autonomously. Instead it will act primarily through collective frameworks, rather than through unconstrained and single-handed actions. In the past, Japan has been most comfortable operating within the collective framework of the United Nations, and other international organisations such as APEC, OECD, the World Bank, the IMF and WTO. Japan has historically sought to avoid international isolation, particularly after the disaster of World War II. Working through the collective security apparatus of the UN, as well as other international organisations, would be congruent with Japan's reluctance to stand alone as well as with Asian reluctance to see the resurgence of a strong, independent-minded, and potentially bullying, Japan. This pattern too is likely to continue.

Notes

1 Peter J. Katzenstein and Nobuo Okawara, *Japan's National Security: Structures, Norms and Policy Responses in a Changing World*, Cornell East Asia Series, Ithaca, 1993; Sato Hideo, *Taigai Seisaku* (Foreign Policy), Tokyo Daigaku Shuppan, Tokyo, 1989.

2 See my 'Regime Shift: Japanese Politics in a Changing World Economy', *Journal of Japanese Studies*, Summer, 1997, pp. 333–61. See also *Regime Shift: Comparative Dynamics of the Japanese Political Economy*, Cornell University Press, Ithaca, 1998.

3 Walter Hatch and Kozo Yamamura, *Asia in Japan's Embrace: Building a Regional Production Alliance*, Cambridge University Press, Cambridge, 1996.

4 Kozo Yamamura, 'The Cost of Rapid Growth and Capitalist Democracy in Japan', in Leon N. Lindberg and Charles S. Maier (eds), *The Politics of Inflation and Economic Stagnation*, The Brookings Institution, Washington, DC, 1985, p. 468.

5 My views on this regime shift can be found in 'Regime Shift', *Journal of Japanese Studies*, Summer, 1997, and in my book *Regime Shift: The Comparative Dynamics of the Japanese Political Economy*, Cornell University Press, Ithaca, 1998.

6 Noguchi Yukio, *Baburu no Keizaigaku* (The Economics of the Bubble Economy), Toyo Keizai Shimbunsha, Tokyo, 1992, p. 25.

7 On the process of the LDP split, see Ōtake Hideo, 'Jimintō Wakate Kaikakuha to Ozawa Guruupu "Seiji Kaikaku" o Mezashita Futatsu no Seiji Seiryoku', (The LDP's Young Reformers and the Ozawa Group – Two Strands of Political Power focusing on Reform) *Leviathan*, vol. 17, 1995, pp. 7–29.

8 On this election see, *Leviathan*, vol. 15, 1994.

9 Akarui Senkyō Saishinkyōkai, *Dai41kai Shūgiin Sōsenkyō no Jittai* (Realities of the 41st General Election for the Lower House), ASSK, Tokyo, 1996, p. 38.

10 Kabashima Ikuo, 'Shintō no Tōjō to Jimintō Ittō Yūitaisei no Hokai' (The Rise of New Parties and the End to the Liberal Democratic Party's Single-Party Dominance), *Leviathan*, vol. 15, 1994, p. 19; Tanaka and Weisberg, 'Political Independence in Japan in the 1990s: Multi-dimensional Party Identification During a Dealignment'. Paper presented at the Annual Meeting of the American Political Science Association, San Francisco, 29 August–1 September, 1996. See also Tanaka and Nishizawa, 'Critical Elections of Japan in the 1990s: Does the LDP's Comeback in 1996 Mean Voter Realignment or Dealignment?'. Paper delivered at the World Congress of the International Political Science Association, 17–21 August 1997.

11 Tanaka and Weisberg, 'Political Independence in Japan in the 1990s: Multidimensional Party Identification During a Dealignment', p. 1. See also Tanaka and Nishizawa, 'Critical Elections of Japan in the 1990s', 1997, p. 5, Figure 2.

12 It should be noted however that the LDP allowed many of its contestants in single member districts to take spots on the proportional representation lists, in effect guaranteeing those who lost in the first arena that they would still retain their seats. As might be imagined, this was one of the features of the new system that came in for explicit voter criticism as its results became clear.

13 One of the classic statements on this is Tsuji Kiyoaki, *Nihon no Kanryōsei*. See also Muramatsu Michio, *Sengo Nihon no Kanryōsei*.

14 An excellent example of this kind of co-operation was that between the Ministry of Finance and the Ministry of International Trade and Industry on many projects where the expertise of each was needed by the other in order to carry out their respective missions. See Masaru Mabuchi, 'Financing Japanese Industry: The Interplay between the Financial and Industrial Bureaucracies', in Kim, et al. *The Japanese Civil Service and Economic Development*, Oxford University Press, Oxford, 1995, pp. 288–310.

15 Inoguchi Takashi and Iwai Tomoaki, *'Zoku-Giin' no Kenkyū* (A Study of the 'Diet-Tribesmen'), Nihon Keizai Shimbunsha, Tokyo, 1987; Iwai Tomoaki, *'Seijishikin' no Kenkyū* (A Study of 'Political Contributions'), Nihon Keizai Shimbunsha, Tokyo, 1990).

16 David Asher, 'What Became of the Japanese Miracle?', *Orbis*, Spring, 1996, p. 10.

17 Yomiuri Shimbun as cited in *Washington Post National Weekly Edition*, 13 January 1997, p. 17.

18 *Washington Post National Weekly Edition*, 13 January 1997, p. 17.

19 Japan, National Personnel Authority, annual reports; the data is also compiled on an annual basis in T.J. Pempel and Michio Muramatsu, 'Structuring a Proactive Civil Service', p. 46.

20 'Reform Proposals Get Mixed Start', *Nikkei Weekly*, 25 August 1997.

21 '"Big Bang" Programme Taking Clearer Shape', *Nikkei Weekly*, 16 June 1997.

22 Steven K. Vogel, 'Japan as a Liberal Market Economy? All in Favor, and All Opposed', *Social Science Japan Journal*, July 1997; also 'When Interests Are Not Preferences: The Cautionary Tale of Japanese Consumers', *Comparative Politics* (forthcoming)

23 For my analysis of the consequences of these accords on Japan, see T.J. Pempel, 'Structural "Gaiatsu": International Finance and Political Change in Japan', *Comparative Political Studies*, 32, 8 December 1999.

24 Japan was the world's largest creditor nation in 1996 with 16.7 per cent of its GDP or $742 billion in net foreign assets. 'Financial Indicators', *The Economist*, 9 November 1996, p. 123.

25 Otake Hideo, *Jiyūshugiteki Kaikaku no Jidai* (The Era of Liberal Reforms), Chūō Kôronsha, Tokyo, 1994, Part II, Chaps. 2, 3, 4, 5, 6, pp. 78–161. At the same time, as Steven Vogel argues, in many instances the processes involved 'more rules'. *Freer Markets; More Rules*, Cornell University Press, Ithaca, 1996.

26 Mark Tilton, *Restrained Trade: Cartels in Japan's Basic Materials Industries*, Cornell University Press, Ithaca, 1996.
27 Robert M. Uriu, *Troubled Industries: Confronting Economic Change in Japan*, Cornell University Press, Ithaca, 1996.
28 My calculations from Nihon Kokusei Zue, *Suji de Miru Nihon no Hyakunen*, p. 392 (for data on 1964); *Nihon Kokusei Zue 96/97*, p. 414 (for data on 1995).
29 Keizai Kôhô Center, *Japan*, 1996, p. 91.
30 'The Japanese Numbers Game', *The Economist*, 2 March 1996, p. 71; 'The New Twist in Japan', *The Economist*, 26 October 1996, p. 18. It should be noted that Japanese government authorities argue that this figure leaves out the assets of Japan's postal savings system and public-sector pension funds. Yet even this net figure has grown dramatically.
31 Jetro, *White Paper on Foreign Direct Investment*, Tokyo, Jetro, 1995.
32 John Y. Campbell and Yasushi Hamao, 'Changing Patterns of Corporate Financing and the Main Bank System in Japan', in Aoki, M. and Hugh Patrick (eds) *The Japanese Main Bank System: Its Relevance for Developing and Transforming Economies*, Oxford University Press, Oxford, 1995, p. 330.
33 J. Mark Ramseyer, 'Explicit Reasons for Implicit Contracts: The Legal Logic to the Japanese Main Bank System', in Aoki and Patrick (eds) *The Japanese Main Bank System*, 1995, p. 240.
34 On the general subject see Michael E. Porter, 'Towards a Dynamic Theory of Strategy', *Strategic Management Journal*, vol. 12, Winter 1991, pp. 95–117. On such alliances by Japanese electronic companies, see Fred Burton and Freddy Saelens, 'International Alliances as a Strategic Took of Japanese Electronic Companies', Nigel Campbell and Fred Burton (eds) *Japanese Multinationals: Strategies and Management in the Global Kaisha*, Routledge, London, 1994, pp. 58–70.
35 As cited in Yoshiya Teramoto et al. 'Global Strategy in the Japanese Semiconductor Industry', in Campbell and Burton, *Japanese Multinationals*, 1994, p. 82.
36 At the same time, there were important differences between Japanese multinationals and those of the US and Germany as Louis W. Pauley and Simon Reich point out, 'Enduring MNC Differences Despite Globalization', *International Organization*, vol. 51, no. 1, Winter 1997, pp. 1–30.
37 *The Economist*, 23 November 1996, p. 11.
38 *Far Eastern Economic Review*, 4 July 1996, p. 45.
39 Noguchi, *Baburu no Keizaigaku*; David Asher, 'What Became of the Japanese Miracle?', 1996, pp. 1–21.
40 Uchida Kenzō, Kunemasa Takeshige, and Sone Yasunori, 'Nihon no Kiro o Tō (Japan at the Crossroads) *Bungei Shunjū*, August 1996, p. 96–99. LDP 'conservatism' was also evidence in its 1996 budget which was heavily laden with public spending programmes.
41 Parties were able to do this by co-ranking multiple candidates, and then choosing after the election, on the basis of single seat competition results, which of the co-ranked candidates to actually seat. See Margaret McKean and Ethan Scheiner, 'Can Japanese Voters Ever Throw the Rascals Out? Electoral Reform Enhances Permanent Employment for Politicians' Paper presented at the Conference on Democratic Institutions in East Asia, Duke University, 8–9 November 1996.
42 Muramatsu Michio, Ito Mitsutoshi, and Tsujinaka Yutaka, *Sengo Nihon no Atsuryoku Dantai*, Tōyō Keizai Shimposha, Tokyo, 1986, esp. Chaps. 4, 5. Proposed bureaucratic reorganisation would merge several of the more protectionist oriented agencies, such as MAFF, Construction and Transport into a single Ministry of Land Development, making for an even larger bastion of regulatory control.
43 Steven Vogel, *Freer Markets, More Rules*, p. 257.
44 'Cracks Form in Newly Forged Opposition Party', *The Nikkei Weekly*, 5 December 1994, p. 1.
45 T.J. Pempel, 'Trans–Pacific Torii: Japan in the Asian Region', in Peter J. Katzenstein and Takashi Shiraishi (eds) *Network Power: Japan and Asia*, Cornell University Press, Ithaca, 1997.
46 Hatch and Yamamura, *Asia in Japan's Embrace*
47 Takashi Inoguchi, 'Japan's Images and Options: Not a Challenger, But a Supporter', *Journal of Japanese Studies*, vol. 12, no. 1, 1986, pp. 95–119.

4 The rise of an environmental superpower?

Evaluating Japanese environmental aid to Southeast Asia

Peter Dauvergne

Environmental aid is the cornerstone of Japan's initiative in the 1990s to become a regional and international environmental power. Formidable internal and external factors, however, impede effective environmental aid. Powerful Japanese economic ministries, such as the Ministry of International Trade and Industry and the Ministry of Finance, overwhelm environmentally oriented state bodies, such as the Environment Agency. This contributes to environmental aid that stresses technological solutions, environmental exports, and corporate interests. Bureaucratic disputes and power struggles undermine policies and contribute to inefficient management. Vague environmental guidelines and weak enforcement mechanisms compound problems. Japan also relies primarily on data and information from recipients to assess environmental impacts. In addition, environmental reviews often have unclear procedures and are poorly co-ordinated. Even the definition of environmental aid is vague, which has allowed Japan to increase the amount of environmental aid by simply reclassifying traditional projects, such as sewage and water systems. This has also contributed to concessional loans accounting for the bulk of environmental aid. Within Southeast Asia, corrupt officials, a stress on economic growth, and inefficient and ineffective managers further aggravate the problems with Japanese environmental aid. As a result, despite large amounts of environmental aid, this aid has only contributed to marginal improvements to the environments of Southeast Asia. Meanwhile, the ability of Japanese environmental aid to foster goodwill or improve Japan's environmental image in Southeast Asia is constrained by negative perceptions of Japan within Southeast Asia, Japan's environmental, economic, and aid legacy, and inconsistent effects of actual environmental aid projects. These problems and constraints suggest that Japan's environmental aid is unlikely to provide an effective foundation for environmental leadership.

Introduction

Japan is now a global power in environmental aid.[1] Since 1991 Japan has been the world's largest aid donor. In FY1997 (1 April 1997 – 31 March 1998), Japan's Official Development Assistance (ODA) was nearly US$9.4 billion. During that period around 20 per cent of Japan's ODA was classified as environmental aid. This paper evaluates Japanese environmental ODA, as a tool to improve environmental management, as a tool to improve Japan's image in Southeast Asia, and as a foundation for environmental leadership. The amount of environmental aid has expanded considerably in the 1990s, contributing to additional funds for environmental research and technical assistance. Yet the effectiveness of this aid has been mixed, in part because of domestic constraints and in part because of resistance within recipient countries. Within Japan, new environmental guidelines at the loan and aid agencies are vague, poorly integrated into decision-making, and rely heavily on the honesty and data of potential recipients. Environmental aid itself is in part simply a reclassification of traditional aid, such as water and sewage projects, which in the past were considered infrastructure projects. Poor co-ordination and rivalries within the bureaucracy further undermine environmental aid. The Ministry of International Trade and Industry (MITI) has hijacked part of this aid to support corporate technology exports. Meanwhile, the Environment Agency has little input while key units, such as the Forestry Agency, have shown little interest. Mismanagement, corruption, and indifference within Southeast Asia compound these internal constraints on effective environmental aid. As a result, Japan's environmental aid has been plagued by problems and has only contributed to incremental improvements in environmental conditions in Southeast Asia. This aid has also done little to foster goodwill and trust or alter Japan's image as an economic and environmental exploiter. This is partially because of the limited impact of much of Japan's environmental aid; and partially because of Japan's military, economic, ODA, and environmental legacy within Southeast Asia, which has left many Southeast Asian elites suspicious of the motives behind environmental aid.

The chapter begins by sketching Japan's foreign aid from the 1950s to the late 1990s. The next section explains the organisation of Japanese aid. The third section analyses the factors that have impeded effective aid, especially the ability of aid and loan agencies to internalise environmental concerns. Building on this overview, the paper then examines Japan's environmental aid programme and the environmental guidelines at the ODA and loan agencies. The paper then proceeds to analyse the effects of this aid on Japan's regional image. The conclusion reflects on the broader implications of the problems with environmental aid for Japan's drive to become a regional, and perhaps even a global, environmental superpower (defined as a world environmental leader, in terms of financing, human resources, technology, and ideas). It also considers the possible impacts of administrative reforms on Japan's environmental aid.

Evolution of Japanese ODA

Japanese aid began in the 1950s as bilateral reparation payments to countries occupied in World War II. Japan became a member of the Development Assistance Committee (DAC) of the Organisation for Economic Cooperation and Development (OECD) in 1960. As Japan's economy continued to surge in the 1960s, the United States began pressuring Japan to increase aid to the Southeast Asian region.[2]

By the end of the 1960s, Japanese aid had begun to Thailand, Cambodia, Laos, and South Vietnam. At this time, Japan was also a major donor to Indonesia, providing one-fourth of aid from 1967–70. Throughout the 1960s and 1970s, Japanese aid financed large infrastructure and energy projects, often directly or indirectly supporting Japanese exporters and investors and helping to maintain steady and substantial natural resource imports, especially from Southeast Asia. This aid also helped gain the confidence and respect of North America and Europe and reintegrate Japan into the Asia–Pacific region after World War II. Over this period, the amount of ODA increased steadily, from US$116 million in 1964 to US$1.1 billion in 1976. In 1976, Japanese reparation payments ended. After this, the quantity of aid continued to grow quickly. It also began to focus more on strategic and political concerns, as part of a comprehensive security approach.[3] By 1989, Japan had become the largest donor, distributing around US$9 billion.

Japanese aid was guided by fairly pragmatic and often ad hoc concerns from the 1950s until the late 1980s. It had a reputation into the 1980s of being linked, even more so than other donors, to self-interest. This view was particularly strong among Asian political, business, and academic elites. Among donors, the reputation of Japanese aid over this time was also tarnished by long-term support for repressive regimes with poor human rights records – especially important trading partners like Indonesia, China, and the Philippines under President Ferdinand Marcos.[4]

Compared to other donors, Japanese tied aid, which requires recipients to buy goods and services from the donor, is now low. The Japanese government claimed, for example, that 95.8 per cent of new loans were totally untied in 1992.[5] Even the OECD estimates that only 11 per cent of bilateral aid was tied in 1993, far lower than France (40 per cent), Germany (36 per cent), the United Kingdom (35 per cent), and the United States (29 per cent).[6] Yet, even though little Japanese aid is now officially tied, Japanese companies apparently still press recipients to request aid projects that support Japanese business interests. Moreover, as David Arase argues, tied aid 'alone is not a reliable indicator of whether policy is strongly determined by commercial and economic interests'. Far more important in the case of Japan is the 'structural inclusion of private sector actors in policy making and implementing structures'. As a result, even though Japanese ODA has shifted since the mid-1980s away from supporting export promotion and resource development and more toward Japanese investment in manufacturing, it still 'continues to be closely co-ordinated with the commercial agendas of private sector actors and with the strategic economic agendas of the economic ministries'.[7] In this context, a high proportion of Japanese aid has supported economic infrastructure and services, especially transportation and energy projects. In the 1980s, economic infrastructure and services accounted for about 40 per cent of ODA, well over the DAC average.[8] In 1995, around 45 per cent of aid supported economic infrastructure projects.[9]

Japan has allowed recipients more control over ODA projects than most other donors. This partly arises because potential recipients must request assistance. It is also partly a result of a high loan-to-grant ratio. In 1988, for example, Japanese concessional loans to Indonesia reached US$842 million, while total grants were only US$143 million. In the Philippines, loans were US$404 million; grants US$131 million.[10] In 1995, 46.6 per cent of Japanese ODA was distributed as grants. In that year, the average for the members of the DAC was over 75 per cent.[11]

The bulk of Japanese aid has been distributed in Asia, a logical extension of the commercial and strategic importance of this area for Japan. Southeast Asia has been especially important. In the 1980s, for example, Southeast Asia received 43.9 per cent of Japanese ODA. In recent years, Japan's aid has started to take a more global approach. Yet even in 1995, 54 per cent of total Japanese aid still went to Asia; and one-quarter of total bilateral aid went to Southeast Asia. In that year, China was the largest recipient of Japanese aid (US$1,380 million), followed by Indonesia (US$892 million), Thailand (US$667 million), India (US$506 million), and the Philippines (US$416 million).[12]

Starting in the mid-1980s, Japan began to develop a more assertive, confident, and coherent aid philosophy. Officials and government documents began to stress the need to foster self-reliance among recipients and provide long-term incentives to move beyond aid. This provides a justification for the emphasis on concessional loans (although in recent years Japan has nevertheless increased the total amount of grants and humanitarian aid). Sone Kenko, a Japanese government Economic Officer, argues: 'We believe aid quality has more than one meaning. In our view, lending money enforces some discipline on the recipients and encourages them to use the resources more productively than if we just gave them away'.[13] These new 'philosophical' principles also provide a justification for a request-based aid system as well as support for large-scale infrastructural projects – such as transportation, communication, and energy projects – which are seen as essential to promote and accelerate industrialisation. The emphasis on infrastructure and energy projects in turn bolsters the argument that Japanese corporations, which have extensive experience in these areas, are logical partners in aid projects.

Japan further clarified its aid philosophy in 1991. The government announced that future aid decisions would consider military spending, nuclear weapons development, the strength of democratic practices, the extent of market reforms, and human rights. This primarily affected authoritarian regimes with poor human rights records. For example, Japan suspended aid to Haiti after the October 1991 coup. Although sometimes for only a short time, Japan also suspended aid to Sudan, Kenya, Malawi, Guatemala, and Sierra Leone following human rights abuses. In addition, Japanese aid representatives have raised human rights abuses in East Timor during discussions with Indonesian officials.[14] In 1992, an ODA Charter refined these principles further, adding in particular environmental concerns. The first Principle of Japan's ODA Charter states that 'environmental conservation and development should be pursued in tandem'.[15]

Since the early 1990s, Japan has also promoted South–South cooperation, supplying financial and technical assistance to facilitate ties between more advanced developing countries in East Asia and less developed countries in places like Africa. Owada Hisashi, the Japanese Ambassador to the United Nations, argues that: 'We have had great achievements in drafting and spreading the concept of South–South cooperation since 1993. Now we will get into the second stage of promoting the implementation of such co-operation'.[16] Japanese officials have also argued in recent years that, as a late developer and an Asian country, Japan has a particularly important role in the regional aid network, providing a bridge between Asia's developing states and richer Western ones. Japan has advocated that aid is a global duty of developed countries, partly for humanitarian reasons and partly to enhance peace and security. As part of the moves to develop a more coherent and assertive aid programme in the 1990s, Japan has also tried to respond to international and domestic critics. Japan is now, for example, more receptive to co-ordinating aid projects with other bilateral and multilateral donors. More support is also provided for nongovernmental organisations. In FY1995, Japan allocated ¥4.5 billion in grants for grass-roots organisations, up 50 per cent from the previous year, although this still represents a relatively small amount of total ODA, and is far less than other donors.[17] While the ODA Charter and more coherent aid principles have strengthened the intellectual base of Japanese aid, serious problems remain with the administration of aid.

Organisation of aid

By FY1995, total Japanese ODA had reached US$14.5 billion, making Japan by far the largest donor. In the next fiscal year this fell to US$9.44 billion, largely due to the depreciation of the yen, cuts to the aid budget, and the suspension of aid to China. It was still higher, however, than any other bilateral donor, although it was only 0.20 per cent of Gross National Product, a fall from 0.28 per cent in 1995 and the lowest ratio in two decades. In FY1997 the amount of ODA again fell slightly in US dollar terms, to US$9.36 billion, although in terms of a per cent of GNP it increased to 0.22. The quantity of Japanese aid remains impressive, however, and Japan will likely continue as the world's largest donor for some time.

     Over a dozen government bodies are responsible for administering ODA. The most important ministries and agencies are the Ministry of International Trade and Industry, the Ministry of Foreign Affairs, the Ministry of Finance, and the Economic Planning Agency. The two implementing organisations are the Overseas Economic Cooperation Fund (OECF) and the Japan International Cooperation Agency (JICA). The OECF provides concessional loans. It is officially under the Economic Planning Agency, although the Ministry of Finance has considerable influence. In FY1995, the OECF made loan commitments of about ¥1.1 trillion. Over 80 per cent went to Asia (15.6 per cent to Indonesia; 13.6 to the Philippines; and 11.7 per cent to Vietnam). As in the past, most of these loans financed infrastructure and energy projects. Only 3.2 per cent financed, for example, agriculture, forestry, and fisheries projects. JICA administers grants and technical assistance.[18] JICA is mainly under the control of the Ministry of Foreign Affairs, although any ministry or agency steering funds through JICA can have considerable influence. The OECF and JICA also lend funds to Japanese companies to promote direct investment in the South, generally at low interest rates. JICA provides these loans to companies that do not qualify for OECF or EXIM Bank loans. Both OECF and JICA loans are usually part of packages of overseas economic assistance and private capital.[19]

The Export–Import (EXIM) Bank of Japan is not officially part of Japan's ODA. The distinction between OECF and EXIM Bank loans, however, is in some respects simply definitional. A small change in the DAC definition could shift OECF 'aid' to EXIM Bank 'loans'. It is therefore reasonable to consider the EXIM Bank in a discussion of Japanese aid. The EXIM Bank lends money to Japanese companies that do not qualify for ODA loans. The Bank also provides export, import, and investment credits to foreign governments and corporations. A key priority of the Bank is the 'development and import into Japan of natural resources'.[20] The Ministry of Finance has official control, although MITI also plays a prominent role. As of March 1996, cumulative commitments of the EXIM Bank had reached ¥33 trillion.[21]

Constraints on effective aid

A fragmented aid administration impedes efforts to develop an effective aid programme.[22] Administrative struggles create unnecessary delays, and foster ad hoc and inconsistent decisions. MITI often supports business interests, while Finance stresses fiscal management, and Foreign Affairs advocates particular foreign policy goals. Even JICA and the OECF do not co-operate well. One OECF official complained that: 'We get better co-operation with USAID (United States Agency for International Development) than we do with JICA'.[23]

The huge volume of Japanese aid presents further difficulties. Measured in US dollars, the amount of Japanese ODA increased markedly with the appreciation of the yen after the 1985 Plaza Accord. In the 1980s and first half of the 1990s, Japan also steadily increased the aid budget. Staff hiring did not reflect these increases and there are now insufficient staff to handle aid volumes. Around 1,100 people work at JICA and just over 300 at the OECF. Including staff from other ministries and agencies the total ODA administration is about 1,900, far lower than, for example, the United States and Germany which both have nearly 4,000 foreign aid staff.[24] Japan's ODA staff are now overworked and are responsible for huge aid budgets. Their ability to handle complex problems, such as environmental assessments, is further hindered by frequent rotations, language barriers, and few specialists. Many staff also have minimal field experience. Only about five per cent of JICA staff live overseas, compared to around fifty per cent of USAID staff.[25] Package deals that involve aid and private capital also undercut effective environmental management by obscuring ties between Japanese companies and aid projects, thereby undermining monitoring and accountability. According to Richard Forrest, 'even if the ODA portion is covered by environmental or other restrictions, the auxiliary funding and secondary projects that often follow are outside the scope of environmental assessments, and have no policies to guide or regulate them'.[26]

Japan's support for infrastructure and energy projects also increases the difficulties of effective environmental management. By their very nature, dams, roads, and large-scale development schemes create significant environmental change. The high loan-to-grant ratio also thwarts effective environmental management.

Compared to grant recipients, it is far harder to require borrowers to follow environmental guidelines. Moreover, considering that recipients frequently turn to unsustainable resource extraction to service foreign debts, and considering that the poorest countries often suffer from the greatest environmental degradation, it is questionable whether any loan should be considered as 'environmental aid'. Other internal factors also impede effective environmental management of aid projects. Project evaluations are often inadequate. Japanese ODA guidelines assert that aid decisions will consider the environmental record of potential recipients. But Japanese aid agencies rely largely on reports from these recipients, rather than on Japanese or independent studies. Technology transfers are also often inappropriate – a problem that is aggravated as recipients request, and at times insist, on the most advanced technology.[27] Compared to other donors, Japan also has few links with nongovernmental groups, reducing the scope for alternative approaches and community involvement in projects.

Obstacles to effective aid do not of course only arise from within Japan. Corruption, incompetence, and indifference within developing countries are often crucial. Southeast Asian elites are often far more interested in promoting economic growth than in improving environmental conditions. Recipient actions are particularly important for Japanese aid because of the request-based system and the large percentage of concessional loans, which allow less direct Japanese participation. As part of a campaign to promote 'Good Governance' in developing countries, Japan recently introduced a new aid contract clause to try and reduce the amount of grant aid lost to corruption. If a recipient country violates the 'corruption' clause, they must repay the funds or Japan will cancel the contract.[28] It is too early, however, to assess the impact of this new clause.

In sum, formidable forces undermine effective Japanese aid projects, especially ones concerned with environmental issues. Of course, to some extent all donors face similar problems, although the fragmented administration of Japanese aid, the volume of aid, the emphasis on concessional loans and infrastructure projects, and the small and relatively inexperienced staff leave Japan with particularly acute problems. These problems are magnified by specific limitations with environmental aid and environmental management at the OECF, the EXIM Bank, and to a lesser extent, JICA.

Environmental aid

Background

Multilateral and bilateral donors have not agreed on a definition of environmental assistance. Even within Japan definitions vary. The Japanese Foreign Ministry defines it as 'assistance conducive to the resolution of environmental problems' including 'the improvement of the living environment, forestry conservation and afforestation, disaster reduction, pollution control, the conservation of the natural environment (including the conservation of biological diversity) and the protection of the ozone layer'.[29] JICA simply lists environmental aid projects as: 'pollution control, improving living environment (water supplies, sewage and waste management), forest conservation/afforestation, conservation of the natural environment and biodiversity, disaster prevention, capacity development and improvement for solving environmental problems, energy conservation, protection of natural resources (agriculture, fishery and soil), and countermeasures against desertification'.[30]

In 1989, Japan announced a significant increase in environmental aid funds, promising ¥300 billion over the next three years. This sum was surpassed by over ¥100 billion. At the London Summit in 1991 and the Earth Summit in 1992, Japan announced that environmental aid priorities would include forest conservation and reforestation, energy conservation and technology, pollution control, wildlife and soil conservation, water and atmosphere preservation, and strengthening environmental capacity in developing countries. In 1992, Japanese environmental assistance reached US$2.8 billion, about 17 per cent of total aid.[31] At the Earth Summit in 1992 Japan announced a ¥900 million to ¥1 trillion target for environmental aid over the next five years. Japan reached this target a year early, having distributed ¥980 billion in environmental aid by FY1995. By FY1996 this had reached ¥1.5 trillion. These figures, however, are somewhat misleading. Environmental aid partially reflects a reclassification of traditional projects to environmental ones.[32] Much of this aid supports environmental management rather than environmental protection. Even dams are considered environmental projects, as part of flood and disaster prevention. From FY1989–FY1992, much of this aid funded urban water and sewage projects; and concessional loans comprised over 70 per cent.[33] The amount of concessional loans as a percentage of environmental ODA increased even more in the mid-1990s, to almost 90 per cent from FY1994 to FY1997.[34]

Japanese environmental aid has contributed to some important programmes and initiatives. Japanese grant aid has funded conservation centres in Indonesia, Thailand, and China. JICA has transferred important environmental technologies, including ones to monitor and control pollution and conserve energy. Environmental experts from JICA have gone abroad; and numerous people from developing countries have visited Japan for environmental training. JICA has also conducted studies to identify environmental problems in countries that may not have the experience, expertise, or political will to request environmental aid (such as in China, Macedonia, and Zimbabwe in 1995). In addition, JICA has assisted recipients with environmental plans and impact assessments. Through a bilateral co-operation framework with the United States, Japan has also supported natural resource conservation, including biodiversity projects in Indonesia.[35] Yet despite these contributions, bureaucratic struggles, and vague, nonbinding environmental guidelines at the OECF, EXIM Bank, and JICA have undermined the overall effectiveness of Japanese environmental aid.

Bureaucratic politics of environmental aid

As the amount of environmental aid grew in the 1990s, various ministries and agencies jockeyed for control. Foreign Affairs has supported some of the environmental initiatives of international organisations. Most of their input, however, has been through JICA. MITI now has a major role in international environmental affairs. Through the Environmental Policy Division, MITI has stressed technological solutions and corporate technology exports to improve global environmental management, especially energy conservation.[36] Under MITI's guidance, the International Centre For Environmental Technology Transfer (ICETT) was created in 1991 to transfer Japanese pollution abatement technology to developing countries. MITI also announced a Green Aid Plan in the same year (about 20 per cent is considered ODA). In FY1992, this Plan supplied approximately ¥2.7 billion to developing countries, mostly for technological support for water and air pollution, waste treatment and recycling, and energy conservation. MITI also supports the Research Institute of Innovative Technology for the Earth (RITE). This institute, established in 1993, brings together industry, academia, and government researchers. It focuses on developing environmental technologies, especially to conserve energy and address global warming.[37] MITI, along with the Agency of Industrial Science and Technology, also folded together three existing projects to create the New Sunshine Programme 'to develop innovative technology to create sustainable growth while solving energy and environmental issues'.[38]

The Environment Agency plays a minor role in environmental aid. It is also a relatively weak bureaucratic actor, especially compared to MITI, Foreign Affairs, and Finance. In 1990, it did, however, establish a Global Environment division. This division participates in some JICA projects.[39] It also attempts to *encourage* Japanese companies to consider overseas environmental effects.[40] Some signs suggest that the influence of the Environment Agency may be increasing, although this is inconsistent and constrained by a small budget and staff. Some Environment Agency officials do claim, however, that informal input has increased since the early 1990s.[41]

Aid Agencies and environmental guidelines

In the late 1980s and early 1990s, the OECF, JICA, and the EXIM Bank developed environmental departments and guidelines. In 1989, the OECF announced guidelines to encourage potential recipients to request environmentally sound loans. These were also designed to enable the OECF to evaluate applications.[42] In addition, the OECF appointed an environmental adviser and senior environmental manager, and created an Environment Committee.[43] In 1993, the OECF created the Environment and Social Development Division. As part of tougher environmental standards, the OECF also sent teams to evaluate possible requests. Because these teams encouraged potential borrowers to integrate environmental concerns, according to one official, in the first half of the 1990s, the OECF rarely rejected loan applications on environmental grounds.[44] OECF commitments for environmental projects have increased steadily since the early 1990s. In FY1991, the OECF committed ¥96.2 billion for 13 environmental projects (8.4 per cent of total commitments). By FY1995, this had increased to ¥218.6 billion for 25 environmental projects (20 per cent of total commitments).[45] In FY1998, the OECF agreed to lend ¥322 billion for 32 environmental projects, accounting for 29.0 per cent of total OECF commitments. This was well above the FY1994 commitment of ¥108.4 billion (12.3 per cent of total ODA loans), but only marginally more than the commitment in FY1996 of ¥318.9 (25.1 per cent of total ODA loans).[46]

In 1995 the OECF revised their environmental guidelines. In that year the OECF also established a programme to provide favourable conditions and terms for environmental projects, including interest rates that are 0.2 per cent lower than normal OECF loan rates. The new guidelines require potential borrowers to submit an environmental impact assessment for large-scale development projects. They also provide support for these assessments. They include stronger terms for resettlement and conservation projects. And they provide an environmental checklist for potential borrowers. To provide time to meet these new requirements, these guidelines only apply to loans requested after 1 August 1997. The OECF is using them to evaluate loan requests, although they still rely on materials supplied by potential recipients to assess these requests. Furthermore, as the guidelines note: 'Responsibility with regard to environmental consideration of a project rests ultimately with the recipient country'.[47]

The EXIM Bank developed environmental guidelines in 1989, revising these in 1991. These guidelines are confidential. The Environmental Affairs Section is responsible for reviewing loans with potential environmental implications. In theory, the EXIM Bank can reject loan applications for environmental reasons. However, this seems to rarely, if ever, occur.[48] For example, from April 1993 to April 1994, the Environmental Affairs Section did not reject any applications, although apparently some conditions were set. In 1994, a Bank official also claimed that more loans were being made to promote better environmental management.[49] Without access to confidential Bank records, however, it is impossible to verify these claims or definitively evaluate the effectiveness of environmental guidelines.

OECF and EXIM Bank environmental guidelines and sections appear designed primarily to appease critics. More concrete changes have occurred at JICA. JICA established an Environment Section of the Planning Department in 1989. The next year JICA announced environmental guidelines for development projects. In 1993 the Environment Section was elevated to a division and expanded to include environment, women in development, and global affairs. Since the late 1980s JICA has worked to integrate environmental factors into grants and technical assistance. This has contributed, for example, to a greater stress on conserving old-growth tropical forests and rehabilitating secondary forests.[50] In 1993, JICA established an environmental database. By the mid-1990s JICA had 20 environmental experts, although only five were officially registered as 'environmental specialists'. In addition, JICA provides intensive environmental training courses. JICA has also added more environmental experts to development study teams (even when the project is not directly connected to an environmental issue). The number of development study teams with an environmental specialist increased from 65 in 1993 to 92 just two years later.[51] Like the OECF, JICA has also increased the amount of funds for environmental protection. In 1985, JICA allocated ¥4.4 billion to the environmental sector. In 1989, this had increased to ¥10.0 billion, about 10 per cent of JICA's budget. By 1993, it had reached ¥21 billion, or 16.3 per cent of the budget. JICA's total environmental aid jumped to over ¥30 billion in 1997, 19.2 per cent of the budget.[52]

Despite these admirable changes, however, JICA's environmental record in the 1990s is far from exemplary. Environmental Impact Assessments are still frequently inadequate. Generally, the environment division, together with a regional division of the Planning Department, assess whether an Environmental Impact Assessment is needed. When necessary, one of JICA's sectoral departments then outlines the parameters of the assessment. Private consultants and JICA officials (often with little environmental training) generally conduct the assessment. Environmental guidelines are also often optional and nonbinding, while project details usually remain confidential. As well, there is generally no post-project environmental evaluation. Poor co-ordination and co-operation among aid agencies and relevant ministries and agencies further undermine JICA's environmental projects. Environmental guidelines and reviews are often poorly co-ordinated or inconsistent; as a result, environmental standards can shift as a project develops.[53]

In short, Japan's environmental aid programme and environmental guidelines within the aid agencies have significant problems. Environmental aid is in part just a reclassification of traditional projects. Bureaucratic overlaps and struggles have distorted policies and implementation. Vague and nonbinding guidelines often allow aid agencies to treat environmental concerns in a superficial way, especially at the OECF and the EXIM Bank. At JICA some important changes have occurred, although even here environmental concerns are still frequently mishandled. Combined with the general problems with Japanese aid outlined earlier, as a result, significant setbacks and frequent failures have plagued Japanese environmental aid, and overall this aid has only contributed to minor improvements in environmental conditions in Southeast Asia. In some cases it has even exacerbated problems. It has supported inappropriate technology transfers and Japanese corporate interests. And in the case of environmental loans (which comprise the bulk of environmental aid), despite the OECF programme to provide more favourable terms, these will eventually increase foreign debt and provide further incentives for unsustainable resource extraction.[54] In part because of these limited results, in part because of general problems with Japanese aid, and in part because of Japan's legacy in Southeast Asia, Japanese environmental aid is also doing little to build trust, goodwill, appreciation, and confidence with the governments of Southeast Asia.

Environmental aid and Japan's image in Southeast Asia

An image is a very broad concept; an image that transcends a region is even broader. It reflects a mixture of facts, misunderstandings, confusion, prejudice, and stereotypes. There are, moreover, always multiple images that vary depending on the context, time, and area. Collapsing complex and diverse views into the simple category of 'Japan's regional image in Southeast Asia' undeniably masks diverse experiences, attitudes, and fluid perceptions. It also inevitably reifies a complex set of often contradictory images and meanings. But the concept of an image also allows for an understanding of a broad set of attitudes and perceptions that consciously or unconsciously shape negotiations, reactions, and state relations.[55]

Southeast Asians have generally perceived Japan as an adept economic manager, although this has changed somewhat with Japan's economic setbacks in the 1990s. Several countries have tried to imitate Japan's economic model, including Singapore which began a campaign in 1978 to 'Learn From Japan' and Malaysia which announced a 'Look East' campaign in 1982.[56] Southeast Asian leaders, officials, and corporate executives have also all sought Japanese investment, technology transfers, and aid. Yet at the same time many elites strongly resist perceiving Japan in a positive light. Positive images of economic competence and ingenuity are mixed with suspicion and distrust of Japan's political and strategic motives and goals. Japan's campaign to establish a Greater East Asia Co-Prosperity Sphere left deep scars on Japan–Southeast Asian relations after World War II. Even officials born after the war still grew up hearing stories of Japanese atrocities.[57] Japan's rapid economic recovery after the war also contributed to resentment among the post-war generation as Japan apparently prospered in part by exploiting Southeast Asia's natural resources. Although Japan has tried to cultivate more positive attitudes among Southeast Asian elites through cultural, technical, and educational exchanges, these efforts have had only minor effects.[58] These efforts have also left little sense that Japan is generous or supportive. As Anny Wong notes, 'historical memories of Japanese hostility, notorious trade practices, and traditional aloofness from regional interests have sustained Japan's negative image as a self-centred economic animal'.[59] Sato Masaru argues that:

> Asian neighbours need Tokyo as a source of low-interest loans and high-technology as well as being a potentially big market for their products. But memories of Japan's war-time rule and environmentally unfriendly behaviour of Corporate Japan have deterred governments from hailing Japan as a benign big brother.[60]

These perceptions have contributed to an overall image among Southeast Asians of Japan as an environmental predator – that is, an image of Japan as systematically exploiting Southeast Asian resources to fuel economic growth at home, often leaving behind severe environmental degradation.

Japan's image as an eco-predator partly reflects Japan's actual impact on Southeast Asia. With a population over 125 million, few natural resources, and large industries, Japan has relied heavily on natural resource imports to fuel rapid economic growth. Japan imports over 90 per cent of its mineral and primary energy needs (such as oil, natural gas, and coal). At the height of the log export booms in the Philippines (1964–73), Sabah Malaysia (1972–87), and Indonesia (1970–80), Japan imported over half of the total combined log production of these places. Japan now accounts for around 50 per cent of log exports from Sarawak Malaysia, the Solomon Islands, and Papua New Guinea. Japan is also the world's largest tropical plywood importer, most of which comes from Indonesia and Malaysia. Much of this wood has been used as panels to mould concrete (*konpane*), which has been commonly discarded after two or three uses. Japan is also the world's largest consumer of marine products, accounting for about 15 per cent of the global fish catch. Again, much of this comes from Southeast Asia. About 90 per cent of Japan's shrimps and prawns are, for example, from this region. After the United States, Japan is the second largest consumer of wildlife products, and a major importer of endangered species (again particularly from Southeast Asia). Japan has a poor record for supporting measures to conserve biodiversity. Environmentalists have strongly criticised Japan for whaling and dumping hazardous waste. And Japan has exported pollution as companies relocated factories, especially to Southeast Asia, in part to take advantage of lower environmental standards.[61]

So far Japanese environmental aid appears to have had little influence on Japan's environmental image in the region. In part this is occurring because Japanese aid projects are simply not visible to the people in recipient countries.[62] More important, however, is Japan's legacy and image as an economic and environmental exploiter, limiting the extent that Japanese environmental aid is seen as altruistic and supportive. This is compounded by the mercantilist past of Japanese aid, the perceived links between US interests and Japan's aid distribution, the perception that Japanese aid is a tool for economic expansion within Asia, and the limited concrete benefits of this aid for improving environmental conditions in Southeast Asia.

Conclusion: a global environmental superpower?

In the early 1990s, Japanese policymakers began to discuss the possibility of Japan becoming a major international and regional environmental power.[63] A 1995 editorial in the *Nikkei Weekly* called for Japan 'to take up the sword of leadership … to preserve and protect the global environment'.[64] Some scholars are optimistic about Japan's leadership in this area. Rowland Maddock predicts 'that by 2010 Japan will indeed have assumed the mantle of environmental leader'.[65] Environmental aid is a cornerstone of this initiative. The findings in this paper, however, suggest that Japan's ambitious moves to become a global, or even a regional, environmental leader will face formidable obstacles. Various factors impede effective environmental aid. The strength of economic interests, such as MITI and Finance, compared to environmentally oriented groups, such as the Environment Agency, contributes to an emphasis on technological solutions, environmental exports, and corporate interests. Bureaucratic factionalism also distorts policies and fosters inefficient management. Current administrative reform proposals in Japan could help. On 1 October 1999, the EXIM Bank of Japan merged with the OECF to create the Japan Bank for International Cooperation (JBIC). There have also been proposals to make the Environment Agency a Ministry, or perhaps merge the Environment Agency with the Ministry of Education or the Science and Technology Agency.

These reforms may reduce some administrative overlap and inefficiencies; but they are unlikely to change aid fundamentally. The EXIM Bank–OECF merger has no clear vision or administrative rationale, and appears to be primarily a political compromise.[66] It also does not appear to involve a change in the functions of the OECF and the EXIM Bank, although it may give Japanese aid an even greater commercial focus.[67] The ultimate outcome for the Environment Agency is still unclear, although all of the proposals have involved merging historically weak bureaucratic agencies.[68] A Ministry of the Environment is therefore unlikely to have significantly greater powers, especially compared to MITI, the Ministry of Foreign Affairs, and the Ministry of Finance. Moreover, other factors will continue to impede effective environmental aid. Concessional loans form the core of environmental aid. Yet considering the links between unsustainable resource exports and debt servicing, and considering that the poorest countries tend to have the most severe environmental problems, labelling any loan as 'environmental aid' is highly questionable. Environmental guidelines are vague and contain no effective enforcement mechanisms. Environmental evaluations rely largely on data and information from recipients. Environmental reviews are badly co-ordinated and lack transparent procedures. The definition of environmental aid is also unclear, and much of this aid is merely a reclassification of traditional projects, such as sewage and water systems. Factors within Southeast Asia compound the difficulties of effective environmental aid. Many environmental aid projects are managed inefficiently and ineffectively. Corrupt Southeast Asian officials often aggravate these problems. And finally, Southeast Asian perceptions and stereotypes, Japan's environmental and economic legacy, the history of Japanese ODA, and the peripheral and inconsistent effects of environmental aid projects limit the power of environmental aid to generate trust, respect, confidence, and gratitude. All of these problems and constraints suggest that despite the substantial sums involved, Japan's environmental aid is unlikely to provide a solid foundation for either regional or global environmental leadership and is even less likely to recast Japan's image as eco-friendly.

Notes

1   I am grateful for the constructive comments of Mike Danaher and Jeff Graham, the discussants for my paper at the workshop, 'Regionalism and Japan: The Bases of Trust and Leadership', 8 January 1998, Griffith University, Brisbane. I also appreciate the input of Javed Maswood and Kathy Morton as well as the research assistance of Tanaka Yuki. An earlier version of this paper titled 'Japan's Environmental Aid to Southeast Asia', appears in Department of Japanese Studies, eds, *Proceedings of The Sixth International Conference on Japanese Studies 1999: Japan Southeast–Asia Relations* (Singapore: National University of Singapore, 2000), pp. 56–66.

2   Apparently, the United States even linked the return of Okinawa with an increase in ODA to Southeast Asia. Takashi Shiraishi, 'Japan and Southeast Asia', in Peter J. Katzenstein and Takashi Shiraishi, eds, *Network Power: Japan and Asia* (Ithaca: Cornell University Press, 1997), footnote 21, p. 180.

3   Robert M. Orr, Jr and Bruce M. Koppel, 'A Donor of Consequence: Japan as a Foreign Aid Power', in Bruce Koppel and Robert M. Orr, Jr, eds, *Japan's Foreign Aid: Power and Policy in a New Era* (Boulder, CO: Westview Press, 1993), pp. 2–3.

4   Steven W. Hook, *National Interest and Foreign Aid* (London: Lynne Rienner, 1995), p. 79.

5   Susan J. Pharr, 'Japanese Aid in the New World Order', in Craig Garby and Mary Brown Bullock, eds, *Japan: A New Kind of Superpower?* (Washington, DC: Woodrow Wilson Center Press; Baltimore, MD: Johns Hopkins University Press, 1994), p. 171.

6 Summarised in Tomoko Fujisaki, Forrest Briscoe, James Maxwell, Misa Kishi, and Tatsujiro Suzuki, 'Japan as Top Donor: The Challenge of Implementing Software Aid Policy', *Pacific Affairs* 69, no. 4 (Winter 1996/97), p. 522.

7 David Arase, 'Public–Private Sector Interest Coordination in Japan's ODA', *Pacific Affairs* 67 (Summer 1994), pp. 171–3. Also see, David Arase, *Buying Power: The Political Economy of Japan's Foreign Aid* (Boulder: Lynne Rienner, 1995).

8 Summarised in Fujisaki et al., 'Japan as Top Donor', p. 522.

9 Christopher B. Johnstone, 'How Much Bang for the Buck? Japan's Commercial Diplomacy in Asia', *Japan Economic Institute Report*, no. 13A, 4 April 1997, p. 9.

10 Hook, *National Interest and Foreign Aid*, p. 86.

11 Economic Cooperation Bureau, Ministry of Foreign Affairs, Japan, *Official Development Assistance: Annual Report 1996* (Tokyo: Association for Promotion of International Cooperation, 1997), p. 24.

12 *Ibid.*, pp. 25–6.

13 Quoted in Hook, *National Interest and Foreign Aid*, p. 80.

14 Pharr, 'Japanese Aid in the New World Order', pp. 168–9.

15 OECF, *OECF Annual Report 1993* (Tokyo: OECF, 1993), p.18.

16 Quoted in Wada Tsutomu, 'Japan aid heads to Africa via Asia', *The Nikkei Weekly* 4 August 1997.

17 Dennis T. Yasutomo, *The New Multilateralism in Japan's Foreign Policy* (London: Macmillan, 1995) outlines Japan's recent aid philosophy, pp. 27–30.

18 For current information on JICA and the OECF, see http://www.jica.go.jp and http://www.oecf.go.jp

19 JICA, *Support for Japanese Enterprises in Developing Countries: Long-Term, Low-Interest Financing System* (Tokyo, JICA, undated); and JICA, *Development Loan and Investment Programme* (Tokyo, JICA, 1991).

20 EXIM Bank of Japan, *Guide To The Export-Import Bank of Japan* (Tokyo: EXIM Bank of Japan, February 1994), p. 1.

21 Johnstone, 'How Much Bang for the Buck?', p. 3.

22 During interviews in 1994, numerous officials at the OECF and JICA mentioned their frustration with administrative procedures. For a critique of Japan's aid administration, see Alan Rix, *Japan's Foreign Aid Challenge: Policy Reform and Aid Leadership* (London: Routledge, 1993), chapter three.

23 Quoted in Robert M. Orr, Jr, *The Emergence of Japan's Foreign Aid Power* (New York: Columbia University Press, 1990), p. 50.

24 Fujisaki et al., 'Japan as Top Donor', pp. 532–3.

25 Richard Forrest, 'Japanese Aid and the Environment', *Ecologist* 21 (Jan/Feb 1991), p. 29.

26 ibid., p. 27. Also see Richard Forrest, *Japanese Economic Assistance and The Environment: The Need for Reform* (Washington: National Wildlife Federation, 1989).

27 Numerous officials and analysts pointed to this problem during interviews in the Philippines, Malaysia, and Indonesia in 1994.

28 'ODA Ni Oshoku Boshi-ho', (New ODA Clause to Prevent Corruption) *Nikkei Shimbun* 20 September 1997. For a study of the impact of recipients on Japanese aid, see David M. Potter, *Japan's Foreign Aid to Thailand and the Philippines* (New York: St. Martin's Press, 1996).

29 Japanese Ministry of Foreign Affairs, *Japan's ODA 1993* (Tokyo: Association for Promotion of International Cooperation, 1994), p. 175.

30 JICA, *The Environment and JICA: International Cooperation to Deal With Global Environmental Problems* (Tokyo: JICA, March 1996), p. 2.

31 Peter Evans, 'Japan's Green Aid', *The China Business Review* 21, no. 4 (July–August 1994), p. 40.

32 David Potter, 'Assessing Japan's Environmental Aid Policy', *Pacific Affairs* 67, no. 2 (Summer 1994), p. 206; and Interview, Friends of the Earth, Tokyo, 25 May 1994.

33 Louise do Rosario, 'Green at the Edges', *Far Eastern Economic Review* (12 March 1992), p. 39; Japanese Ministry of Foreign Affairs, *Japan's ODA 1993*, p. 178; and Pat Murdo, 'Japan's Environmental Foreign Aid: What Kind of Edge?', *Japan Economic Institute Report* 12 August 1994, p. 2 (available at http://www.gwjapan.com/ftp/pub/policy/jei/1994/a-series/0812-94a.txt).

34 Calculated from the data at http://www.oecf.go.jp and http://www.jica.go.jp

35 Economic Cooperation Bureau (of Japan), *Official Development Assistance*, p. 58; and JICA (Environment, Women in Development, and Other Global Issues Division), 'Environmental Assistance of Japan International Cooperation Agency', Tokyo, January 1997, p. 4.
36 Interview, MITI official, Environmental Policy Division, Tokyo, 27 April 1994.
37 Based on International Center For Environmental Technology Transfer, *ICETT* (Yokkaichi, Japan: International Center For Environmental Technology Transfer, June 1993); MITI, 'Green Aid Plan', internal document, supplied by a MITI official, April 1994; and Research Institute of Innovative Technology for the Earth, *RITE* (Tokyo: Research Institute of Innovative Technology for the Earth, March 1992).
38 MITI, and the Agency of Industrial Science and Technology, *New Sunshine Programme* (Tokyo: New Sunshine Programme Promotion Headquarters, 1993), p. 4.
39 In mid-1995, the Environment Agency was involved in 7 technical co-operation aid projects. Fujisaki et al., 'Japan as Top Donor', p. 527.
40 Interview, Office of Overseas Environmental Cooperation, Environment Agency, Tokyo, 5 April 1994.
41 Various interviews, Global Environment Department, Environment Agency, Tokyo, 9 June 1994.
42 Interview, OECF Environment and Social Development Division, Tokyo, 11 April 1994. Also see OECF, *OECF Environmental Guidelines* (Tokyo: OECF, 1989); and OECF, *OECF and The Environment* (Tokyo: OECF, 1993).
43 Rix, *Japan's Foreign Aid Challenge*, p. 125.
44 Interview, OECF official, Tokyo, 11 April 1994. For a list of typical OECF environmental loans, see Environment and Social Development Division, Project Development Department, OECF, 'Typical OECF Environmental Projects', Tokyo, OECF, 20 February 1997.
45 *OECF News Letter*, 'Environment Special: Development and Environment', July 1996, p. 2.
46 See http://www.oecf.go.jp
47 The Overseas Economic Cooperation Fund, *OECF Environmental Guidelines (2nd Version)* (Tokyo: The Overseas Economic Cooperation Fund, August 1995), p. 1.
48 One EXIM Bank official claimed that loans are sometimes informally rejected to allow the applicant to withdraw and save face. Interview, senior official, Environment Section, EXIM Bank, Tokyo, 11 April 1994.
49 Interview, senior official, Environment Section, EXIM Bank, Tokyo, 11 April 1994.
50 Interview, senior JICA official, Tokyo, 12 April 1994.
51 JICA, 'Environmental Assistance of Japan International Cooperation Agency', pp. 5–7.
52 See http://www.jica.go.jp for current data.
53 Potter, 'Assessing Japan's Environmental Aid Policy', p. 208.
54 The overall impact of Japan's environmental aid is difficult to assess precisely, in part because it is exceedingly difficult to obtain information about these highly sensitive projects. Moreover, the effects and implementation of ODA vary to some extent across projects, sectors, and areas. See Marie Söderberg, ed., *The Business of Japanese Foreign Aid: Five case studies from Asia* (London: Routledge, 1996). In such a short paper, it is not possible to analyse these variations across Southeast Asia. The few detailed studies that exist, however, indicate consistent and significant problems. For Thailand, see Potter, 'Assessing Japan's Environmental Aid Policy', pp. 211–15. For the impact on the forest sectors of the Philippines, East Malaysia, and Indonesia, see Peter Dauvergne, *Shadows in the Forest: Japan and the Politics of Timber in Southeast Asia* (Cambridge, MA: The MIT Press, 1997).
55 See Benjamin Odartei Botchway, *The Impact of Image and Perception on Foreign Policy: An Inquiry into American Soviet Policy During Presidents Carter and Reagan Administrations, 1977–1988* (Munchen: Tuduv Verlag, 1989); Bruce Stronach, *Beyond the Rising Sun: Nationalism in Contemporary Japan* (Westport, Conn: Praeger, 1995); and Greg Fry, 'Framing the Islands: Knowledge and Power in Changing Australian Images of 'the South Pacific'', *The Contemporary Pacific 9*, no. 2 (Fall 1997), pp. 305–44.
56 For a discussion of Japan's impact on Malaysian development, see K.S. Jomo, ed., *Japan and Malaysian Development: In the shadow of the rising sun* (London: Routledge, 1994).
57 Of course, perceptions of Japan are not uniform across Asia. As T. J. Pempel notes, 'Memories of wartime Japanese atrocities remain relatively strong in China, Korea, Singapore, and the

Philippines, for example. Such memories are far less vivid or relevant in Thailand, Burma, Indonesia, or even Malaysia, and are hardly a factor in India and the rest of South Asia'. T. J. Pempel, 'Transpacific Torii: Japan and the Emerging Asian Regionalism', in Peter J. Katzenstein and Takashi Shiraishi, eds, *Network Power: Japan and Asia* (Ithaca: Cornell University Press, 1997), p. 75.

58 Anny Wong, 'Japan's National Security and Cultivation of ASEAN Élites', *Contemporary Southeast Asia* 12 (no. 4, March 1991), p. 306. To some extent Japan's image has improved. According to Lee Poh-ping, since the end of World War II Japan has 'taken efforts to improve its image, so that the perception of Japanese as '*samurai* in business suits' is weaker'. Lee Poh-ping, 'Japan and the Asia–Pacific Region: A Southeast Asian Perspective', in Craig Garby and Mary Brown Bullock, eds, *Japan: A New Kind of Superpower?* (Washington, DC: Woodrow Wilson Center Press; Baltimore, MD: Johns Hopkins University Press, 1994), p. 131.

59 Wong, 'Japan's National Security and Cultivation of ASEAN Élites', p. 313.

60 Sato Masaru, 'Japan Seeks Asian Leadership Role At G7 Summit', 5 July 1993, Reuters Limited, Reuters News Service.

61 Owen Cameron, 'Japan and South–East Asia's Environment', in Michael J.G. Parnell and Raymond L. Bryant, eds *Environmental Change in South–East Asia: People, Politics and Sustainable Development* (Routledge: London and New York, 1996), pp. 70–1, p. 78, p. 84.

62 Kyodo News Service, 'Japan Should Overcome Foreign Aid 'Scepticism' Says White Paper', 3 October 1995, BBC Monitoring Service, in Reuters News Service.

63 On Japan's changing global role, see Edward J. Lincoln, *Japan's New Global Role* (Washington, D.C.: The Brookings Institute, 1993); Danny Unger and Paul Blackburn, eds, *Japan's Emerging Global Role* (Boulder: Lynne Rienner, 1993); Rob Steven, *Japan and the New World Order: Global Investments, Trade and Finance* (London: MacMillan, 1996; New York: St. Martin's, 1996); and Reinhard Drifte, *Japan's Foreign Policy in the 1990s: From Economic Superpower to What Power?* (New York: St. Martin's Press, 1996).

64 'Nation's Diplomatic Policies Should Center on Environmental Protection', *Nikkei Weekly* 16 January 1995, p. 6.

65 Rowland T. Maddox, 'Japan and Global Environmental Leadership', *Journal of Northeast Asian Studies* XIII, no. 4 (Winter 1994), p. 46. For an overview of recent environmental initiatives in Japan, see Miranda A. Schreurs, 'Japan's Changing Approach to Environmental Issues', *Environmental Politics* 6 (no. 2, Summer 1997), pp. 150–6.

66 'Kazuawase Yusen, Koritsu Atomawashi', (Merger as a Result of Compromise) *Asahi Shimbun* 15 March 1995, p. 3.

67 'Enjyo To Shobai O Togo', (How to Integrate Aid and Business) *Asahi Shimbun* 1 March 1995.

68 Shioya Yoshio (Chief Editor), 'Kagaku Bunka Ni Oikaze', (Boost for Science and Technology Related Government Agencies) *Nikkei Shimbun* 16 August 1997, p. 10.

5 Japan's position on human rights in Asia

Watanabe Akio

Introduction

Japan is frequently criticised as having a foreign policy that is devoid of moral principles. This criticism may appear to be particularly applicable to the issue of human rights because moral considerations are important in the handling of this issue. In recent years, the United States and some members of the European Union (EU) have given considerable emphasis to the promotion of human rights in other countries. This has provoked an angry response from many Asian governments. As a member of advanced western economies and a shared geography and history with Asian neighbours, Japan now finds itself in an awkward dilemma. In this chapter, I will look at Japanese governments' handling of human rights issues and the extent to which such matters are a source of potential conflict between Japan and its Asian neighbours, or between Japan and the Western nations, and what Japanese responses tell us about Japan's preferred position in the East–West debate. These are questions often raised about Japan's foreign policy in general and its human rights diplomacy in particular.

Let me begin by first describing recent developments in Japan's human rights diplomacy in the context of international interest in the issue. I will then identify some characteristics of Japanese thinking on this and illustrate it with reference to Myanmar and China. In doing so I will clarify the relationship between humanitarianism and human rights issues; distinguish between substance and style or between rhetoric and reality; and assess and explore the effectiveness or limitations of human rights diplomacy. I will argue that human rights diplomacy should be understood in the context of domestic politics and national interests. Human rights diplomacy is defined here as an assembly of words and deeds of a government with regards to human rights issues in diplomatic relations with foreign governments. Non-governmental organisations (NGO) and other societal actors are taken into consideration as far as their behaviour has a bearing on governmental policies.

Organisation of human rights diplomacy

Japan has a well-developed system of legal institutions for promoting and protecting individual human rights. These rights are guaranteed in Chapter III of the Japanese

Constitution of 1947. Today, Japan is, if not perfect from the viewpoint of human rights, as democratic as many Western societies as far as the domestic aspect is concerned.

Internationally, Japan ratified, in 1979, both the International Covenant on Social, Economic and Cultural Rights (which came into force as of 3 January 1976; hereunder ICSECR) and the International Covenant on Civil and Political Rights (which came into force as of 23 March 1976; hereunder ICCPR). Japan became a member of the Commission on Human Rights for the first time in 1982. Japan's participation in the international human rights regime[1] was not necessarily tardy because as one expert on the United Nations writes, 'it is only the present (third) phase (i.e. 1979 onwards) that the member states of the United Nations have made any serious efforts to respond to violations (of human rights) in a manner that all purports to be objective and even-handed'.[2]

Nevertheless, it can not be denied that Japan has not been active in giving shape to the regime in its present form. The criticism of Japan also is that it has been rather slow and cautious in the field of human rights diplomacy. It was only in July 1984, for instance, that the Japanese Ministry of Foreign Affairs (MFA) created a new division specifically in charge of human rights and refugees (jinken/ nanmin ka). This new division was established as part of organisational changes to MFA's Bureau of United Nations. The immediate reason for the creation of the new division was the fact that Japan, as mentioned above, became a member of the Commission on Human Rights in 1982. (Until that time, human rights issues were handled by the Political Division of the United Nations Bureau).

Another reorganisation in August 1993 transferred the Human Rights/Refugees Division to the newly created Bureau of Foreign Policy (sogo gaiko seisaku kyoku). This organisational reform was a part of the MFA's attempt to adapt to the changing agenda in the post-Cold War international society especially in view of the experiences of the Gulf Crisis/War of 1990–91.[3]

Formulation of human rights issues

The trend of changing governmental attention to human rights issues is indicated in Table 5.1. For purposes of comparison, the table shows the number of references (in terms of lines) to human rights, refugee and environmental issues, typically three categories of 'global issues'.

The first reference to human rights issues in 1967 followed the adoption, in the UN General Assembly (UNGA) on 7 November 1967, of a declaration on non-discrimination of women. References to human rights in the early years, i.e. 'the first phase' that covers roughly the period ending the late 1970s, merely described discussions in the Third Committee of the UNGA. In these discussions, Japan was a noncommittal observer and concentrated on issues relating to the environment. An interesting new phrase of 'frontier diplomacy' appeared in volumes 16 and 17 of the *Diplomatic Bluebook* that covered Japan's diplomatic activities in 1971 and 1972. This was intended to signify a 'new type of diplomatic agenda as distinguished from military, political and economic issues that had hitherto formed the traditional

Table 5.1 References to human rights and other global issues in Japanese diplomatic bluebook (number of lines allocated to each category)

Year	(Vol.)	Human Rights	Refugees	Environments
1967	(12)	17	–	–
1968	(13)	7	–	–
1969	(14)	20	–	19
1970	(15)	19	–	48
1971	(16)	25	–	113
1972	(17)	47	–	181
1973	(18)	28	–	91
1974	(19)	17	–	59
1975	(20)	25	–	42
1976	(21)	36	5	62
1977	(22)	30	–	38
1978	(23)	36	38	53
1979	(24)	32	63	63
1980	(25)	67	13	36
1981	(26)	60	38	42
1982	(27)	74	30	45
1983	(28)	58	27	48
1984	(29)	53	26	49
1985	(30)	63	27	45
1986	(31)	51	20	19
1987	(32)	41	15	–
1988	(33)	42	36	134
1989	(34)	71	45	99
1990/91	(35)	–	146	135
1991/92	(36)	–	173	238
1993	(37)	62	59	111
1994	(38)	54	59	89
1995	(39)	38	25	54
1996	(40)	51	40	63

Note:
The number in the brackets following the year indicates the volume number of the Diplomatic Bluebook. For instance, Volume 40 (published in 1997) describes Japan's diplomatic activities for the year 1996.

agenda of diplomacy', with concrete examples being nuclear energy, use of space and ocean for peaceful purposes and 'environmental diplomacy'. These issues were characterised as those that require international co-operation and 'multilateral diplomacy'.[4] In other words this concept closely resembled the current expression of 'global agenda'. The impact of this new thinking is clear in the drastic increase in spaces allocated to environmental issues in the early 1970s (see Table 5.1). Not only UN but also OECD (Organization for Economic Cooperation and Development) and bilateral talks between the United States and Japan were regarded as important international fora for this purpose.[5] It is interesting that environmental issues were defined in this period as part of 'international economy' and therefore regarded principally as an agenda for cooperation among the advanced economies (i.e. members of the OECD).

The second phase of Japan's human rights diplomacy began in the late 1970s but was not accompanied by any significant increase in the space allocated to this issue area in the *Diplomatic Bluebook*. As pointed out earlier, Japan ratified both ICSECR and ICCPR Conventions in 1979 and joined the Geneva-based Commission for Human Rights three years later. These actions coincided with the greater attention given to human rights protection within the UN. Since then Japan progressively enlarged its participation in the international human rights regime. In 1986 the Bluebook proudly reported that Japan was a member of all the major fora concerning human rights issues (i.e. UNGA, UNECOSOC, Commission for Human Rights and Subcommittee on Prevention of Discrimination and Protection of Minorities).[6]

In this period, references to the human rights issues in the Bluebook were of a more concrete nature, indicating an increased familiarity with and maturity of thinking about the issues. For example, discussions at the 32nd session of UNGA on human rights issues were summarised as consisting of the following three points:

1 that civil and political rights cannot be fully realised unless accompanied by a fulfilment of economic, social and cultural rights;
2 that human rights issues should be treated in a comprehensive way taking into considerations such things as specific social conditions, respect for individual dignity and necessity for social development and for promotion of welfare; and
3 that the establishment of a new international economic order was an essential element for the effective enhancement of human rights and fundamental freedom.[7]

Although these were reported as 'facts', the manner of the reporting seemed to indicate Japan's preference for narrowing the gap between the advanced nations (which tended to favour civil and political rights) and the developing nations (which tended to favour of economic, social and cultural rights). As will be discussed later, this attitude closely resembled the position taken by the Japanese representative at the 1993 Vienna conference on human rights.

Japan's global diplomacy entered a new era in the late 1980s and the early 1990s, when two items, the environment and refugees, gained prominence. After the first wave of enthusiasm in the early 1970s, Japan's environmental diplomacy had moved to the back burner until 1988–89 when it was reactivated, in response to the heightened international environmental awareness in the post-Cold War era. The issues were placed on the agenda of many international conferences to which Japan was a party. The US–Japan Joint Programme Coordinating Committee (which was set up in accordance with US–Japan Agreement for Cooperation in the fields of environment protection) met in May 1989 to specifically discuss matters related to global environmental issues. The Ministerial Committee of the IEA (International Energy Agency) also met in May of the same year and took up the issues of energy and environment including the question of global warming. The annual ministerial council meeting of the OECD held in June 1989 took cognisance of the necessity of more systematic and effective co-ordination of economic and environmental policies and the G–7 Summit Conference in July 1989 also paid great attention to environment issues to the extent that about one third of its economic declaration was allotted to this subject. Clearly, Japan regarded environmental diplomacy as part of international co-operation especially among the advanced economies in view of the fact that such institutions as the OECD, IEA and G–7 played the important role of agenda setting for Japan's environmental diplomacy.[8]

Another group of issues in the broad category of 'global diplomacy' was that of refugees. In the early years Japan's concern with refugee problems was limited to that of refugees from Vietnam. Since the 1980s Japan began to pay more attention than before to Africa with regard to refugee issues. Foreign Minister Kiichi Aichi made a speech on that subject at the meeting of international conference for assisting African refugees held in April 1981 at Geneva, pledging financial assistance needed for emergency relief and emphasising the necessity for international assistance from a longer term perspective.[9] As the refugee problem became more aggravated in the aftermath of the Gulf War, relief activities for refugees in Africa, the Middle East and other places gained a larger place in Japan's global diplomacy. The appointment of Ogata Sadako as the UN High Commissioner for Refugees in 1991 also contributed to Japan's heightened interest in the refugee issues.

Table 5.1 gives an impression that there was no dramatic change in Japan's level of interest in human rights issues throughout the whole period under investigation. Unlike the other two issue areas (refugees and environment), no particular international events, including the Tiananmen massacre in 1989, helped to invigorate visibly Japan's human rights diplomacy. This does not necessarily point to Japan's lack of interest in issues of human rights.

Human rights diplomacy: Japanese style

Japan's human rights diplomacy is based on the following four pillars:

1 Use all available opportunities to express Japanese concern over human rights violations to respective governments;
2 Urge foreign governments to improve domestic human rights conditions through government-to-government policy dialogue;
3 Offer technical assistance to governments which are willing to establish or improve legal institutions necessary to promote and protect human rights; and
4 Review Japan's ODA (Official Development Assistance) to those governments whenever there are clear problems in light of Principle IV of the ODA Charter.[10]

The ODA Charter is the most important, if not the only, policy instrument, which the Japanese government can and does apply for the purpose of human rights. The 1992 ODA Charter established the following four principles:

1 that environmental conservation and development should be pursued in tandem;

2 that any use of ODA for military purposes or for aggravation of international
   conflicts should be avoided;
3 that full attention should be paid to trends in recipient countries' military
   expenditures and their exports and imports of arms etc.; and
4 that full attention should be paid to efforts for promoting democratisation
   and introduction of a market-oriented economy, and the situation regarding
   the security of basic human rights and freedoms in the recipient country.[11]

Of these, Principle 4 is directly relevant to the present subject. Since ODA is the
single most effective measure that Japan can hopefully use as leverage in the field
of human rights, it is worthwhile to undertake a further analysis of Japanese government's thinking behind this new ODA policy. The following extract from the ODA
annual report is suggestive.

> The third and fourth principles (of the ODA Charter) … are designed to
> encourage positive efforts of recipient countries in light of these principles.
> When there are clear problems in light of these principles from the perspective
> of Japan and the international community, Japan reviews its aid policy to
> such countries. In such case, however, it is not proper to apply the third and
> fourth principles mechanically because it could hinder flexible implementation
> of official development assistance. Therefore, Japan tries to apply these
> principles from a broader perspective through closely watching the trends on
> those matters.[12]

The purpose of the new ODA policy is not so much to 'punish' errant countries as
to 'encourage' them to improve human rights situations by themselves. What follow
are some concrete examples of how Principle IV of Japan's ODA Charter has
been applied to some problem countries.

Nigeria: Japan suspended its aid, except emergency and humanitarian relief, to
Nigeria in March 1994 when the military junta took over the government and
dissolved the national assembly and political parties, and banned political rallies.
(Japan was the top donor to that country in 1992, with its aid amounting to $42.55
million).

Kenya: In light of human rights situation, corruption, and slow economic reforms,
Japan, together with other DAC countries, suspended aid in support of Kenya's
balance-of-payments in November 1991. In July 1993, Japan resumed Yen loans
in conjunction with the World Bank to support Kenya's balance of payments
position as the country began to show signs of improvement in the areas mentioned
above(e.g. the holding of elections at the end of 1992). Other donor countries
agreed at the November 1993 meeting of DAC to lift suspension of aid. Japan
played an intermediary role in co-ordinating differences between Kenya and donors
in the process of resuming aid. (Japan was the top donor to that country in 1992,
with aid amounting to $128.67 million).

Malawi: Japan held back additional aid to support Malawi's balance of payments
in May 1992 because of a worsening human rights situation. As Malawi adopted
pluralistic democracy and held a national referendum in a peaceful manner in

June 1993, Japan reviewed the possibility of resuming aid and eventually in January 1994 exchanged notes with Malawi's government with a view to providing yen loans for entrepreneurial development and drought recovery programmes. (Japan was the fourth largest donor to that country in 1992, following Germany, UK and USA, with its aid amounting to $23.68 million).

Sierra Leone: Japan decided to restrict its aid to emergency and humanitarian relief because of violation of democratic processes and human rights after the coup d'etat of December 1992. However, once the junta officially announced its plan to transfer power to a civilian government and after the human rights situation had improved in the following months, Japan decided in October 1993 to resume aid except for balance-of-payments support. (Japan was the fifth largest donor to that country in 1992, following Italy, USA, Germany and France, with total Japanese aid amounting to $3.84 million).

Haiti: Japanese aid was suspended after the democratically elected President Jean Bertrand Aristide was expelled in September 1991 by a military junta. Japan considered the possibility of resuming aid when an agreement was reached between Aristide and the leader of the junta through the intermediation of the OAS (Organization of American States), providing for the restoration of democratic process and return of the expelled President. The junta went back on this promise and as a result Japan's aid to this country remained suspended. It was eventually lifted in October 1994 following the return of President Aristide and restoration of legitimate government.[13]

The emphasis on 'flexible implementation' of the ODA Charter and the above examples of actual application of Principle IV clearly indicate Japan's inclination for positive rather than negative sanction as a strategy to promote democracy and human rights. Japan, as a leading donor country, does apply negative sanction to a problematic recipient but that action is more often than not meant as warning rather than punishment. Japan is quick to resume its aid at the earliest signs of improvement of the situations in question (e.g. Malawi, Sierra Leone, Haiti and most notably Kenya). Although such an attitude sometimes invites cynical comments about its slipperiness and elements of hypocrisy, the good intentions of the government's strategy can not be denied.

Based on these observations one can identify several characteristics of Japanese human rights diplomacy. The first is its non-confrontational approach. This is intrinsically related to its dislike of 'politicising' an issue. Many official documents indicate a preference for avoiding unnecessary politicisation of human rights issues. For example, the 1988 version of the *Diplomatic Bluebook* made the following comment:

> The strong tendency of politicisation of talks on human rights continued unabated throughout 1987. Given the past history of controversy, deliberations on the Resolution of 'human rights situation in Cuba', introduced by the United States was in the spotlight at the 44th session of the Commission on Human Rights. Fierce manoeuvring was inspired between the United States, which strongly pushed its adoption, and Cuba, which tenaciously opposed

such a move. The verbal fighting was brought to an end when a resolution calling for the dispatch of a fact-finding team to Cuba introduced by Central American countries was adopted without a vote. From the standpoint that substantive improvements in the human rights situation in Cuba should be realised, Japan, by conferring consistently with the United States of America, Cuba and other countries concerned, contributed to co-ordinating their position to adopt the proposed resolution.[14]

The phrase 'substantive improvements in the human rights situation' in the above quotation is indicative of Japan's *pragmatic approach* to the issues of human rights, which can also be identified as the second characteristics of the Japanese diplomatic style. Japan's foreign policy officials are apparently of an opinion that verbal fighting is not conducive to 'substantive improvements in the human rights situation' in Cuba or for that matter in any other countries. What seems best to them is to help these countries create legal institutions, which are necessary for the protection of human rights. Institution building is a time-consuming endeavour, but such an indirect approach can, in the long run, prove more productive than exerting direct pressure upon the targeted countries. This was the philosophy behind the Japanese initiative for 'Partnership for Democratic Development' (PDD) advocated by Prime Minister Hashimoto Ryutaro at the Lyon Summit in June 1996. It was from these considerations that Japan offered technical assistance in the field of human rights to several countries such as China, Cambodia and others in recent years.

The third characteristic is Japan's preference for a *multilateral approach* to human rights diplomacy. Human rights are, in the eyes of Japanese diplomatic officials, an agenda for international co-operation and as such should be dissociated as much as possible from the arena of power political games between states. In this sense, a regional approach is seen as a preferable alternative. Unfortunately, however, for obvious reasons, this alternative is not readily available in the Asia Pacific region.[15] Before turning to Asia and the Pacific, a couple of more general comments about Japan's human rights diplomacy are necessary.

The first point concerns the distinction and interrelation between humanitarian (i.e. refugees for example) and human rights issues. Although both types of issues are dealt with by the same Division in the MFA and are often difficult to separate, there seem to be subtle and important distinctions between the two both in theory and in practice.

The distinction is fundamentally related to the difference between humanitarian and human rights law. The purpose of the former is to protect victims of war, either those between states or within a single state, by regulating unfortunate consequences stemming from such armed conflicts, while the latter is intended to secure individuals' rights to their fullest extent during peace. Both are concerned with protection of individuals' rights and are often inseparable in concrete circumstances. Nevertheless, historically speaking, the two categories of legal instruments have developed separately and mechanisms of protection provided by each are also different. More importantly, matters related to human rights are often highly political, while exercise of political rights has nothing to do with humanitarian law. Thus, the International Red Cross, whose function is to rescue war victims, often has to enter the territory of individual states and is cautious not to offend the sovereign rights of that state. Politicisation of issues is therefore anathema to those who are engaged in humanitarian activities. However, human rights activists (say Amnesty International) sometimes regard it as useful to make open accusations against problematic governments with the intention of arousing public attention.[16]

In practice, humanitarian activities are more often than not necessitated in emergency situations (like international war or breakdown of domestic political order) and therefore require quick measures: but the problem of human rights needs a longer-term approach since it presupposes the existence of a minimum level of political order in a given state and requires the progressive development of legal institutions to comply with international instruments concerning human rights. It is one thing to extend emergency relief to restore the normal state of affairs; it is another to assist a country to build institutions that can function effectively.

This leads to the next issue of the inseparability of various aspects of human rights issues in concrete situations, which require a comprehensive approach in practice. The discussion thus far has assumed that we can separate the different aspects of human rights issues and highlighted those problems primarily related to political and civil rights. Such a method may be appropriate because political and civil rights are a focal point in the contemporary international debate relating to East Asian countries like China and Myanmar. But in the real world various aspects of human rights cannot be easily separated from each other. Refugee problems, for example, are regarded as that of humanitarian emergency relief but the realities of broken states, which produce refugees, is such that emergency relief alone is not sufficient. Moreover, they can even be harmful unless such humanitarian assistance programmes are conducted in tandem with long term efforts of state building. The need for a greater consistency between short-term humanitarian activities and long-term development assistance projects is becoming widely recognised among those who are concerned with improvement of UN system in the fields of economic and social development.[17]

Similarly, it is sometimes argued that civil and political rights cannot be fully realised unless accompanied by fulfilment of economic, social and cultural rights. As pointed out earlier, Japanese foreign policy statements, as early as the 1970s, had indicated their inclination for a comprehensive approach to human rights issues. As for the manifold meanings of human rights, one well-known method is to classify them into three categories, or 'generations'. The first category is that of civil and political rights (based on the idea of 'liberty'); the second category includes economic and social rights (based on the idea of 'equality'); and the third category is that of human rights (based on the idea of 'fraternity'). The third category of rights, according to proponents, covers the rights to peace, to a healthy environment, to share in the exploitation of the common heritage of mankind, to communicate, and to humanitarian assistance. Many of these still remain very controversial but a right to development (one component of the third category) was codified in a 1986 UNGA Declaration (GA Resolution 41/128). Commenting on this declaration, the *Diplomatic Bluebook* of the year wrote that 'it is worthwhile to note that a right to development, a long standing issue, has been finally codified, reflecting the opinion among the developing nations that North–South problem should be treated as a matter of human rights'.[18] This is a cardinal issue about which there is a sharp difference between the North and the South (or shall we say 'clash of civilisations' between the West and the Rest?) in the recent debate on human rights.[19]

Although the Japanese government has not openly defended the developing countries on the issue of human rights, it is more sympathetic to their concerns than are the other developed nations. The 1993 Vienna Conference on Human Rights admitted that human rights were a universal value and that all states had the responsibility to respect and promote them, the Vienna Declaration and Programme of Action (25 June 1993) took note also of (a) interdependence and indivisibility of economic, social, cultural, civil, and political rights and (b) recognition of rights to development as inseparable part of fundamental human rights.[20] This was a clear compromise, which while ideologically grotesque to some Western intellectuals, was a welcome sign of constructive trends in the eyes of Japanese diplomats.[21] Commenting on these points (a & b), the Japanese representative at the Vienna conference, Ambassador Matsunaga Nobuo, stated as follows:

> This Conference gives us an opportunity to address the question of the relationship between development, democracy and human rights.
>
> While social and economic development may facilitate enhanced respect for human rights, I believe that fundamental freedoms and rights should be respected by each and every country, whatever its culture, political or economic systems, or stage of development.
>
> Human rights should never be sacrificed to development. Rather, development should serve to promote and protect rights – economic, social, cultural and political. Respect for human rights will facilitate development by bringing about a society in which individuals can freely develop their own abilities.
>
> Convinced of this, Japan believes that development assistance should also contribute to promotion of the human rights of individuals.[22]

Significantly, Ambassador Matsunaga asserted that 'development may facilitate enhanced respect for human rights' in one place and that 'respect for human rights will facilitate development' in another. This seemingly circuitous logic is what is actually meant by 'interdependence and indivisibility of economic, social, cultural, civil, and political rights'. As a matter of fact, however, we are often forced to decide upon which end of the continuum to start, an extremely difficult decision. Japanese diplomacy has to walk a tightrope between 'civil and political rights' (emphasised by the West) and 'economic and social rights' (emphasised by the Rest). At any rate, preference for *comprehensive approach* can be depicted as a fourth characteristic of Japanese style of human rights diplomacy in addition to the three already mentioned ones.

Human rights issues in Asia and the Pacific

All the characteristics of Japan's human rights diplomacy – non-confrontational, pragmatic/indirect, multilateral and comprehensive – are clearly discernible in Japanese policies towards Asian countries, where human rights situations have been in the spotlight in recent years. Earlier, countries in Africa (South Africa), Latin America (Chile, Bolivia, El Salvador, Guatemala), the Middle East (Israel, Iran, Afghanistan) and the Socialist camp (Poland, Cuba) used to attract most international attention in the UN and other international fora on human rights. In the post-Cold War era, world attention has shifted first to transition economies of the former Soviet Union and the Eastern Europe and then to developing economies in Asia. When apartheid used to be a burning issue in the international society, Japan, a leading trade partner of South Africa, found itself in an awkward position, facing bitter criticism from many Black African nations. When Japan stood for a non-permanent seat of the UN Security Council in 1986, it won only with a very narrow margin due to, among other things, great dissatisfaction among African nations with regard to economic sanctions against South Africa.[23] Japan is now having similar, or even harder, experiences in human rights diplomacy in relation to Asia. The most controversial cases among them are Myanmar and China.

Myanmar

Myanmar has severely tested Japan's human rights diplomacy in Asia. Since the establishment of the State Law and Order Restoration Council (SLORC) in September 1988, Myanmar has been a constant target of criticism from those who are concerned with human rights issues. The chronology of major events and Japan's responses to them are as follows.

- In July 1988 the dictatorship of General Ne Win, who had ruled the country since 1962, collapsed in the face of uprisings involving discontented citizens, students and Buddhists. The uprising began in March in Yangon but spread throughout the country. In the middle of political upheavals, General Saw Maung took over the government and established SLORC in September. Paralleling the US Government's decision to cut economic assistance to Myanmar, Japan also suspended ODA except for the aid projects that had started prior to the coup d'etat. Portions of the emergency/humanitarian aid were also exempted from suspension. As a result, Japan's ODA disbursements to Myanmar declined from $ 259.55 million in 1988 to $71.41 million in 1989. (See Table 5.2). (Japan had been the top donor to Myanmar, providing 60–70 per cent of the total amount received by that country).
- In February 1989 Japan gave recognition to the government of General Saw Maung in light of some signs of recovery of political order. At the same time Japan resumed its ODA to Myanmar, although no new projects were approved. In May 1990, general elections were held and the SLORC suffered a humiliating loss to the National League for Democracy (NLD) led by Ms. Aung San Suu Kyi. The SLORC cancelled the results of the election and suppressed the

NLD, placing Suu Kyi under house arrest. In the midst of harsh criticisms of the military regime all over the world, Japan suspended its ODA except the previously agreed projects.

• After General Saw Maung stepped down in April 1991 there were some positive developments in political situation in Myanmar, such as the successful conclusion of peaceful negotiations with minority groups (except for the Karens), preliminary steps towards constitutional government, and discussions between the SLORC leaders and Suu Kyi, even though the opposition political parties, including NLD, remained under strict government control. While the Japanese Government continued its policy of aid suspension, it decided, in February 1994, to extend aid to non-government organisations such as the Red Cross of Myanmar which were engaged in activities to strengthen medical aid services. Similarly, approximately ¥1.6 billion in grant was offered for the planned extension of a nursing college in October 1995. In the meantime Japan kept open channels of communication both with SLORC leaders and, informally, with Ms Suu Kyi with a view to bringing about political reconciliation between the government and opposition. For instance, Japanese Foreign Minister Kakizawa Koji met his counter part (Mr Ong Jo) in June 1994 to urge SLORC to expedite democratisation. Again in November 1995 Kakizawa's successor, Kohno Yohei, met Mr Ong Jo and reiterated the same point.

• In December 1994 Chinese Premier Li Peng visited Yangon. ASEAN Foreign Ministers' Meeting invited Myanmar as a guest for the first time in July 1994 (Bangkok) and a similar invitation was repeated the next year (Brunei). The ASEAN members gave an observer status to Myanmar in July 1996 and finally in July 1997 Myanmar was accepted as a full member of that organisation. The United States and some European members of the ASEM (Asia–Europe Meeting) strongly opposed that decision, applying visa suspension and economic sanctions against the SLORC but ASEAN leaders justified their position by using the concept of 'positive engagement'. Although Japanese government has never publicly endorsed the ASEAN's position, its policy has been closer to that of ASEAN than to that of the US and West European governments.[24]

Table 5.2 Japan's ODA disbursements to Myanmar (in $ million)

Year	Grant aid	Technical co-operation	Loan aid	Total
1987	55.43	11.34	104.73	172.00
1988	81.69	9.56	168.29	259.55
1989	40.36	3.52	27.53	71.41
1990	30.18	3.16	27.98	61.32
1991	37.17	4.54	42.81	84.52
1992	31.58	4.98	35.51	72.06
1993	35.98	5.77	26.86	68.61
1994	99.95	7.37	26.49	133.82
1995	139.27	12.16	−37.19	114.23
1996	101.98	9.87	−76.65	35.19

It was in this context that the Japanese government announced its decision to partly resume its yen loan to Myanmar on March 11, 1998. Japanese aid to Myanmar was an issue about which Japan and the US had disagreements at the Denver Summit of June 1997 (between Foreign Minister Ikeda Yukihiko and Secretary of State Madeleine Albright) as well as at the Vancouver meeting in November 1997 (between Foreign Minister Obuchi Keizo and Secretary of State Albright). On both occasions the Japanese Foreign Minister expressed his government's inclination to soften its Myanmar policy by emphasising the stability factor whereas the US Secretary of State opposed a soft approach as an implicit recognition of the military regime. In spite of US objection, the Japanese government officially announced its decision on March 11, 1998, to resume its yen loan (originally pledged in 1986 and suspended since 1988) for the construction of an international airport at Yangon (to the maximum of ¥27.17 billion of which some ¥2.5 billion were to be provided within this financial year). The Ministry of Foreign Affairs justified its decision by pointing to the practical necessity of physical safety while emphasising that this action should not be interpreted as an approval of the SLORC (renamed as SPDC, State Peace and Development Council, as of 15 November 1997) with regard to human rights and democratisation issues.

Although difficult to substantiate, geopolitical considerations (i.e. fears of increasing Chinese influence in Myanmar) were possibly a factor in this new policy toward Myanmar.[25] It is also reported that Secretary of State Albright had received a report from a high-powered mission (composed of three former high-ranking officials – Abramovitz, Armitage and Armacost) sent to Myanmar in October 1997 to look into the political situations of that country. The mission, on its return to Washington, apparently advised that the US Government should use the influence of ASEAN to induce Myanmar towards democratisation, a position not far from that of Tokyo. Given these circumstantial evidences, it may well be that the real difference between Tokyo and Washington was not as large as it appeared on the surface.[26]

One should bear in mind also the fact that there are differences in opinion among Japanese political leaders. There exist three groups of Diet members which are concerned with Myanmar: one led by Kosugi Takashi (member of the Lower House, LDP, Tokyo District 3) which is sympathetic towards Suu Kyi with the other two groups being in favour of the SLORC/SPDC.[27] Some objection was voiced from Democratic Socialists and Sakigake members of the coalition groups as well as from within the LDP itself about the recent government decision to resume ODA to Myanmar. Their objection was based on concern for the human rights situations. The Secretary General of the LDP, Kato Koichi, was among those who pushed for the government decision. Kato is said to be interested in a project to convert Myanmar's poppy-growing fields into Japanese soba cultivation (poppy is a source material of drug production). The dividing line is between those 'pragmatists' (such as Kato) who see the problem mainly from economic and strategic points of view and those who are more idealistic about democratisation. The picture of politics in Tokyo is not very different from that in many other capitals although the pragmatists appear to be stronger.[28]

China

Given the unique importance of China both in terms of its economic potentials and politico-strategic status in the post-Cold War era, human rights issues regarding China presents an even more serious challenge to Japan's diplomacy than the case with Myanmar. The problem is complicated by United States policy towards China, which has oscillated between the hard-liners (a strange combination of human rights oriented idealists and security-minded realists) and the soft-liners (a similarly strange alliance between commercial interests and Kissinger-type grand-strategists).

The first test was a diplomatic crisis which came with the advent of the Tiananmen incident in June 1989. Prior to the incident, Japan had enjoyed a very close relationship with China both in the field of economic and political affairs, despite relatively minor (and somewhat inevitable) frictions mostly related to 'historical legacy', like history text books for Japanese school children, an issue about a dormitory in Tokyo for Chinese students subject to a battle between Taipei and Beijing over legal title. China was also enjoying a relatively favourable international climate since its leaders had decided in 1978 to do away with its economic autarchy and to get on good terms with the advanced economies.

The Tiananmen incident had a profound impact on the international status of China. Its image deteriorated overnight, one of the earliest examples of the enormous impact of the news media, like the CNN, on international relations. The image of China as an anti-democratic (and by definition anti-human rights) regime became an instant reality and offered a sharp contrast with that of former Soviet Union and East European countries which seemed to be on the 'way towards democratisation'. Results of opinion polls in Japan before and after the event showed a dramatic change in Japanese perception about China. Those who named China as an attractive country declined from 17.3 per cent to 4.6 per cent whereas those who named China as a disagreeable country rose from 5.4 per cent to as much as 27.1 per cent.[29]

The Japanese government, however, responded somewhat differently from other democratic nations. Japan was the largest ODA donor for China but suspended its Third Term Yen Loan Programme on which an agreement had been reached the previous year.[30] The Japanese government also took additional measures to reduce the level of diplomatic contacts with China along the lines of most other OECD countries. Characteristically, however, Japan did not express its political position on the problem of China's democratisation itself, a clearly different style from the other OECD countries. When the Japanese government suspended ODA to China, it deliberately chose a low key style, avoiding straightforward reference to human rights and democracy. It instead simply pointed to the practical difficulties of implementing ODA-related negotiations under the confused conditions following the Tiananmen incident. In other words Japan carefully avoided depicting its decision as a 'sanction' against China. Japan's diplomacy towards China on this occasion did not differ very much from the other OECD countries in substance; it differed sharply in style.[31]

In international fora, Japan made efforts not to isolate China internationally while avoiding dissociating itself from other democratic countries. For instance, when the leaders of the G–7 nations met in the middle of July 1989, the Japanese Prime Minister, together with leaders of other nations, declared that 'human rights are a matter of legitimate international concern'. At the same time Japan successfully put its own idea into another declaration on China which read in part that 'we look to the Chinese authorities to create conditions which will avoid their isolation and provide for a return to co-operation based upon the resumption of movement towards political and economic reform, and openness'.[32]

The UN Subcommittee on Prevention of Discrimination and Protection of Minorities which met in late August of the same year also discussed China. Professor Hatano Riboh from Japan participated in the discussion. Anticipating a strongly-worded draft resolution that would force him to abstain, Hatano joined with nine other members to draft a resolution that would secure the widest possible support because a failure of the motion would have given Beijing an excuse for claiming that the subcommission had decided that Chinese government's behaviour on 4 June did not warrant censure. Finally, the Subcommission passed a resolution which, while avoiding any direct reference to the Tiananmen incident, simply expressed concern about 'the events which took place recently in China' and 'their consequences in the field of human rights', and made an appeal for 'clemency in favour of persons deprived of their liberty as a result of the above-mentioned events'. Hatano was among the fifteen members who supported the resolution while nine (including a Chinese representative) were against it, with one absentee and one non-vote (chairman).

Despite what may seem an excessively polite wording of the resolution, it was significantly the first case in which a human rights resolution on a permanent member of the UN Security Council was passed by the Subcommittee.[33]

This episode says something about the extent to which China could exert influence on multilateral diplomacy, or rather the limits of multilateral diplomacy. Even if some hard-liners (like the United States) had wished to censure China more openly, they had to take into considerations possible 'defectors' (smaller nations of the third world) which were vulnerable to intimidation by China. The United States, too, was not free of conflicting pressures domestically, as illustrated by heated debates over the Scowcroft/Eagleberger mission to Beijing and over the renewal of MFN (Most Favoured Nation) treatment to China.[34] These constraints more often than not resulted in an equivocal position. As for Japan, which had complicated relations with China, it would find itself in an awkward position if it was forced to choose between the United States and China.

Encouraged by the Bush Administration's decision to renew MFN to China in late May, 1990, the Japanese government quickly moved a step further in favour of a more lenient policy towards China. In preparation for the Houston Summit in July 1990, Tokyo worked hard to explain its intended policy of partially lifting its ban on ODA to China. As a result there was no open criticism of Japan's position on China. The summit ended with the Chairman's Statement which included only one paragraph devoted to China. It said,

We acknowledge some recent actions taken by the Chinese government, but for now the measures put in place at last year's Summit remain. We will explore, however, whether there are World Bank loans that would contribute to reform of the Chinese economy, especially to meet environmental concerns.[35]

The Chairman's statement issued at the end of London Summit in 1991 also included one paragraph related to China which read:

We welcome China's co-operation with the international coalition in opposing Iraqi aggression and over other regional issues. We hope to see further economic and political reform in that country, though we still have serious concerns about human rights there. Contacts with the Chinese have been re-built over the past year, and this process should continue. Unconditional extension of Most Favoured Nation status to China by the US would contribute to these goals.[36]

Likewise, the Chairman's statement issued at the end of Munich Summit in 1992 also include one paragraph related to China which read:

The recent developments towards economic reform in the People's Republic of China are encouraging. We also want to see China making greater efforts towards political reform. The situation with regard to human rights calls for considerable further improvement. We welcome China's accession to the Non-Proliferation Treaty and her application of the guidelines and parameters of the Missile Technology Control Regime. We hope that China will play a more constructive role in the international sphere.[37]

There was no mention of China in the political documents issued after the following two G–7 summit meetings in Tokyo in 1993 and in Naples in 1994. The G–7 leaders had apparently decided to tone down their criticisms of China's human rights. Japanese diplomacy probably was a catalyst for this change in international climate. Reciprocally, Japan's China policy carefully followed the gradual change in international climate of opinion especially that among the G–7 nations. Immediately before the Houston Summit, Prime Minister Kaifu Toshiki met President Bush to explain Japan's policy to China. Following that Summit conference, the Japanese government sent former Prime Minister Takeshita Noboru to Beijing to inform the Chinese of its intention to limit its loans to China in fiscal year 1990 to humanitarian items only and lift suspension of the Third Term Yen Loan Programme in a piecemeal manner. The first half of the following year (1991) witnessed frequent mutual visits at a ministerial level between Tokyo and Beijing (such as Finance Minister Hashimoto's visit to Beijing in January and Foreign Minister Qian Qichen's visit to Tokyo in June). Then in August 1991, just after the London Summit, Prime Minister Kaifu went to Beijing to announce his government's decision to resume Third-Term ODA programme to China.

Japan's adoption of the ODA Charter in June 1992 can be regarded as part of Japanese efforts to justify its ODA policy (to China in particular and to many other more or less 'problematic' recipients) at the G–7 or some other meeting of OECD countries such as the DAC. As mentioned earlier also, 'western' opinion was neither uniform nor uncompromising. It had been the case that since 1992 China had been a topic of discussion every year at the UN Human Rights Commission at Geneva.[38] Even though no decision was ever reached on the issue, a kind of success for Chinese diplomacy (which was active particularly among African countries), Beijing was displeased to see the issue taken up for discussion at that international forum. When the Commission met in 1997, China finally succeeded in killing a move sponsored by Denmark to take up the issue of China's human rights record. The failure of the Danish initiative was partly due to differences among the Western group. Germany, France and Canada, together with Japan, split from Denmark (supported by the US) and jointly moved a more compromising proposal based on a 'dialogue' approach. In the end, China's own 'non-action' won a majority (27 vs. 17, with 9 abstentions). One of the reasons for the softening of some of the western governments attitudes towards China was the fact that China subscribed to ICSECR in October 1997.[39]

All in all, the distance between Japanese 'realism' and Western 'idealism' about human rights issues is not very large in reality even when the matter is discussed in a closed circle of the advanced nations like G–7 and OECD. The distance, if any, that existed originally, had almost disappeared over time. It is more difficult for these nations to form a unified front at international meetings of a wider group of nations where 'third-world' countries outnumber the advanced nations. A compromise is a most likely result of multilateral discussions on this issue.

Bangkok (March 1993) and Vienna (June 1993) provided the opportunity to see how compromise was worked out. The Japanese representative who participated in the preparatory regional meeting for Asia in Bangkok sided with Western nations on fundamental principles on the one hand, and supported consensus in the form of the Bangkok Declaration, which articulated the 'Asian position', out of 'spirit of co-operation and compromise' on the other. Ambassador Matsunaga who attended the World Conference on Human Rights in Vienna reiterated the Japanese arguments in Bangkok.[40] Their actions may be described as diplomatic acrobatics played out on the precarious 'edge of chaos'. Their actions were made easier, however, because the 'edge' had become somewhat broader in a manner described in the above.

Conclusion

One of the assumptions of our discussion was that, given the sharp and wide difference between Asia and the West with regard to human rights issues, Japan, being a member of the group of advanced economies on the one hand and a country which shares much with its Asian neighbours both historically and geographically on the other, will find itself often in an awkward dilemma. An implied question was 'to what extent is this gap a source of potential conflict between Japan and its Asian neighbours, or between Japan and the Western nations?

One important conclusion to be derived from the above analysis is that, the distance between Japan and other Western nations is more in rhetoric than in reality. Diplomacy is governed by a variety of considerations including commercial and politico/strategic interests. Human rights, however important they may be, have to be balanced with considerations of national interests. It is to some extent inevitable, therefore, that Country A's human rights diplomacy towards Country B is a function of the degree of importance of Country B for Country A's national interests. Even the United States government, under strong domestic pressure for a tougher stance towards China, could not afford to ignore the fact that China is a very important commercial partner and will be more so in the future. It also needs, as it did at the time of the recent crises in Kuwait and North Korea, China's co-operation in dealing with difficult problems of international security. It is natural, therefore, that as long as some good excuse can be found, the US government tends to soften its stance on China's human rights issues. Thus the track record of US human rights diplomacy towards China is more like that of Japan in contrast to the human rights diplomacy towards, for example, Myanmar.

Likewise, countries such as Japan and Australia, which belong to the group of 'western' nations, but are more vulnerable than the US to diplomatic/commercial pressure from China, tend to be more conciliatory in their human rights diplomacy towards China. As Australia's white paper says,

> The Government recognises that, on occasion, support for human rights will create difficulties in Australia's bilateral relationships, including in our commercial relations. The best means of managing such difficulties is to focus on practical measure and to address human rights concerns in the context of a sound overall bilateral relationship. Linking human rights to trade serves neither Australia's trade nor its human rights interests.[41]

The 1995 edition of Japan's *Diplomatic Bluebook* says:

> Japan does not believe in a confrontational approach in raising an issue of human rights in a foreign country. It instead prefers a pragmatic approach in which the chief concern should be effectiveness with a view to bringing about meaningful improvements in human rights situation in the country concerned. It was from this belief that we played a role in formulating a UN Resolution in 1994 concerning Myanmar which, taking cognisance of some improvements so far made by the government of Myanmar, urged Myanmar's government to make further efforts. The resolution was passed unanimously at the 49th General Assembly.[42]

Recent behaviour of some EU nations (e.g. France and Germany) on this subject is not very different from those of Australia and Japan. This is not to say that human rights diplomacy is, by nature, an act of hypocrisy or of double standards. Principled behaviour is, indeed, one of the necessary requirements of good diplomacy. There is logical consistency in Japan's human rights diplomacy, which is well captured in the following excerpts from Ambassador Matsunaga's speech entitled 'Human Rights and Diplomacy' delivered before a symposium held at the United Nations University on 26 June 1995. Having said that 'diplomacy can play certain roles in the promotion and protection of human rights', the Ambassador cautioned that

> there is an inherent difficulty in diplomacy's roles in human rights issues. As human rights concerns the whole business of governing fundamentally, a governments' commitment to the promotion and protection of human rights must be accompanied by the governed people's internalisation of human rights as an essential part of their political values. This process of internalisation is the most critical determinant. By nature, it goes beyond what diplomacy can do. We need to have sober recognition of this inherent limitation of diplomacy's roles in human rights protection. Otherwise, human rights diplomacy may work counterproductively, as it frequently does.[43]

He sees a difficult dilemma because 'we wish to address human rights issues through foreign policies. Every nation of the world agrees that it is legitimate, but, no matter how legitimate it may be, its effectiveness is bound to be limited. The strategy we should take is, then, to find out areas where the effectiveness is not severely limited, and to focus our foreign policy to those areas to gain maximum possible effect.'

What should the strategy be like? According to Matsunaga, there are three factors which determine whether a government promotes and protects human rights:

1 the government's will to do so;
2 the government's ability or its availability of means to do so like an ample number of jurists and an ample number of law schools to train them; and
3 external conditions.

What is meant by the last mentioned item is whether the government concerned considers the promotion and protection of human rights as compatible with its other aims, such as security (the preservation of the regime included) and economic prosperity. Compatibility between human rights and other aims can be realised in many cases but cannot be taken for granted. As a result and notwithstanding the universality of abstract human rights, it is not easy for us to induce, through diplomatic means, a foreign government to carry out its duty of promoting/protecting human rights as is prescribed in the Vienna Declaration. This is the crux of the whole question of human rights diplomacy. It requires 'caution to address this factor of the prospect of the compatibility through diplomacy for many reasons'.

I agree with Ambassador Matsunaga in thinking that in addition to the importance of 'explicit demonstration of political will' by those who firmly believe in human rights with a view to influencing governments all over the world to confirm their *will*, an equally important area of human rights diplomacy is to help governments concerned to improve their *means* to promote and protect human rights.

The characteristics of Japan's human rights diplomacy – non-confrontational, pragmatic/indirect, multilateral and comprehensive approach – are an expression of the logic elaborated above. In this sense Japan's human rights diplomacy can be regarded as consisting of principled behaviour.

Notes

1   The international human rights regime is defined as consisting 'of those international norms, processes, and institutional arrangements, as well as the activities of domestic and international pressure groups, that are directly related to promoting respect for human rights'. See Alston, P. (ed.), *The United Nations and Human Rights: A Critical Appraisal*, Clarendon Press, Oxford, 1992, pp. 1–2

2   Alston, P., *ibid.*, 1992, p. 139. Alston divides the evolution of the Commission on Human Rights into three phases: the first phase (1946–66: Abdication of Responsibility); second (1967–78: A Gradual Assumption of Responsibility); and the third (1979 to the present: Evolution of Effective Response).

3   At this time a new Division for Global Issues was created. Those Divisions that fall under the Foreign Policy Bureau include International Security, Arms Control/Reduction, Atomic Science, UN Policy and UN Administration. See Gaimusho, *Gaiko Seisho* (Diplomatic Bluebook), 1993, vol. 1, Appendix.

4   *Diplomatic Bluebook*, vol. 16, 1972, pp. 74–9; vol. 17, 1973, pp. 79–86.

5   Since September 1970 when the US–Japan ministerial council for dealing with public hazard was created, the council met from time to time on an ad hoc basis until it emerged as a standing forum based on the treaty, US–Japan Agreement for Cooperation in the Fields of Environmental Protection, signed in August 1975. *Diplomatic Bluebook*, vol. 20, 1976, p. 199. The OECD established the Committee on Environment in July 1970.

6   *Diplomatic Bluebook*, vol. 29, 1986, p. 333.

7   *Diplomatic Bluebook*, vol. 22, 1978, p. 241.

8   *Diplomatic Bluebook*, vol. 33, 1989, pp. 43–4.

9   See the text of Aichi's speech in *Diplomatic Bluebook*, vol. 26, 1982, pp. 394–6.

10 Interview with Mr. Kaitani, Chief of Division on Human Rights and Refugees on 12 March 1998. See also *Diplomatic Bluebook*, vol. 41, 1997, pp. 1–17.

11 Ministry of Foreign Affairs, *Japan's ODA 1992*, Association for Promotion of International Cooperation, Tokyo, 1993, pp. 846–51.

12 *Japan's ODA 1994*, 1995, p. 112.

13 *Japan's ODA 1994*, 1995, p. 112.

14 *Diplomatic Bluebook*, vol. 32, 1988, p. 112.

15 As for various efforts to create regional human rights regimes at a non-governmental level, see Abe Koki, 'Ajia no jinken: chiiki jinken kiko eno michi', *Kokusai Mondai*, no. 449, August 1997, pp 2–16.

16 Maurice Torrelli, *Le Droit Internationale Humanitaire, Collection: Que Sais-Je?*, Presses Universitaires de France, Paris, 1985, pp. 12–15.

17 A call for US–Japan Joint Action: Strengthening the United Nations' Capability Development Cooperation, Japan Institute for International Affairs and Columbia University, 1998.

18 *Diplomatic Bluebook*, vol. 31, 1987, p. 256.

19   For an example of critical comments by a leading western scholar see Jack Donnelly, *Universal Human Rights in Theory and Practice*, Cornell University Press, Ithaca and London, 1989, p. 144.

20   For a brief comparison of the Vienna Declaration and the Bangkok Declaration, see Yamakage Susumu, *Japan Review of International Affairs*, vol. 11, no. 2, Summer 1999, pp. 118–37.

21   For an example of western response to the Vienna (and the Bangkok) conferences, see Olwen Hufton (ed.), *Historical Change and Human Rights: The Oxford Amnesty Lectures 1994*, Basic Books, 1995, pp. 132–3. There are intellectuals within Japan who share this opinion with western liberals, being very critical of the 'conservative' attitudes of the Japanese officials. See Ebashi Takashi (ed.), *NGO ga tsukuru sekai no jinken* (NGO builds human rights of the world), Akashi Shoten, 1996.

22   Statement by H.E. Matsunaga Nobuo, Envoy of the Government of Japan at the World Conference on Human Rights, Vienna, 18 June 1993.

23   Kawabe Ichiro, *Kokuren to Nihon*, Iwanami Shoten, Tokyo, 1994, p. 218. For the decision making of the Japanese government about economic sanctions against South Africa in 1986, see Noguchi Kunihiro, 'Japan's Economic Sanctions against the Republic of South Africa: 1986 – An Analysis of Policy Making Process' (in Japanese), MA Dissertation submitted to the Graduate School, the School of International Politics, Economics and Business, Aoyama Gakuin University, March 1997.

24   Although western government are taking severe policies against Myanmar, their private business interests are more actively engaged in Myanmar than Japanese counterparts. UK is the leading investor (six times larger than Japan) and the US is the fifth largest investor (three times larger than Japan) while Japan ranks ninth (about $200 million) as of early 1998. The US government announced in April 1997 to prohibit new investment by US firms. Measures of sanctions vary from country to country, but they include suspension of aid, visa for high ranking officials and arms sales. General attitudes toward Myanmar again vary from country to country. The US, UK, Denmark and Sweden belong to the group of hard liners whereas attitudes in Germany and France are relatively soft and closer to that of Japan. Australia, traditionally a hard liners, recently switched to a softer line especially after Myanmar's admission to ASEAN in July 1997. These observations are based on an interview with a Japanese diplomatic official on 12 March 1998.

25   See Sasajima Masahiko, 'Myanmar eno enshakkan saikai', in *Yomiuri Shinbun*, 6 March 1998.

26   *Asahi Shinbun*, 23 June and 28 July 1997. The Asahi tends to emphasise the distance between Washington and Tokyo on human rights in Asia.

27   The pro-Suu Kyi group includes Mr. Hatoyama Yukio of the Democratic Party and Ms. Takemura Yasuko of the Democratic Socialist. Those pro-SLORC (SPDC) groups are led by respectively Mr. Ozawa Tatsuo of the Liberal Party and Mr. Koga Makoto and Mr. Muto Kabun of the LDP.

28   Japan's export to Myanmar stood at $254 million and its import at $103 million in 1996. The direct air route from Osaka to Yangon opened in July 1996 while an office of JETRO was established in Yangon in January 1998. Despite these, Japanese direct investment (accumulated value as of January 1998 was about $200 million) is far behind Britain ($1.3 billion), Singapore, Thailand, Malaysia and the US. For Japan's ODA policy toward Myanmar see Juichi Inada, 'Democracy and Stability: Political Considerations in Japan's ODA to Myanmar and China', in Tatsuro Matsumae and Lincoln C. Chen (eds), *In Pursuit of Common Values in Asia: Japan's ODA Charter Re-evalued*, Tokai University Press, Tokyo, 1997, pp. 101–21.

29   See Takagi Seiichiro, 'Human Rights in Japanese Foreign Policy: Japan's Policy Toward China after Tiananmen', in James T.H. Tang (ed.), *Human Rights and International relations in the Asia Pacific Region*, Pinter Publishers, London, 1995, p. 100.

30   Since 1979, the Japanese government had already provided two major packages of Yen loan to China, the First Term Yen Loan Programme of ¥350 billion for the 1979–84 period and the Second Term Yen Loan Programme of ¥470 billion for the 1985–90 period. A pledge about the Third Term Loan Programme of ¥810 billion for the 1990–96 period was made by Prime Minister Takeshita during his visit to Beijing in August 1988. The Tiananmen Incident occurred just in the process of implementing the first portion of the Third Term Yen Loan.

31 For a more detailed analysis of Japan's response to the Tiananmen incident, see Takagi, Op. Cit., and Watanabe Akio, 'Japan's Foreign Policy Making in Crises: China (1989–90) and Kuwait (1990–91)', Department of Social and International Relations, Working Paper no. 34, Tokyo, April 1993, pp. 10–20.

32 The 1989 summit adopted four declarations on political issues: human rights, East–West relations, China and terrorism. Gaimusho Keizaikyoku (comp.), *Samitto kanren shiryoshu* (Materials related to G–7 Summit conferences), Sakaino ugoki sha, Tokyo, 1995, pp. 556–8 and 570–1.

33 Hatano Riboh, 'Jinken shoiinkai no kino: sono 'dokuritsusei' to 'seijisei' (The function of the Human Rights Subcommittee: Its 'independence' and 'political nature'), *Kokusai Jinken*, no. 1, 1990, pp. 44–47. Human rights Subcommittee is the shorter name for the Subcommittee on the Prevention of Discrimination and Protection of Minorities, the only subcommittee of the UN Commission on Human Rights, consisting of 26 persons who, although nominated by their governments, are supposed to serve as experts in their individual capacity rather than as governmental representatives. The subcommittee meets for four weeks every August in Geneva. The nine members who volunteered to become joint movers were, in addition to Hatano (from Japan), those from Norway, France, United States, Philippines, United Kingdom, Costa Rica, Netherlands, and Mexico.

34 President George Bush sent his Special Advisor for National Security Brent Scowcroft and Under-Secretary of State Lawrence Eagleberger to Beijing in early December 1989 in an attempt to mend fences with China. This action started a hot debate in Washington.

35 *Samitto kanren shiryoshu*, 1995, p. 586.

36 *Samitto kanren shiryoshu*, 1995, p. 620.

37 *Samitto kanren shiryoshu*, 1995, p. 648.

38 The UN Commission on Human Rights, a functional commission of the UN Economic and Social Council, is represented by 53 nations and meets for six weeks from late January to mid-March each year at Geneva. The geographic composition of the 53 nations is as follows: Africa (15), Asia (12), Latin America and Caribbean (11), Western Europe and other western Countries (10) and Eastern Europe (5). Japan falls into 'Asia' (not in other western countries).

39 The EU and US stepped back in 1998. Foreign Ministers of the EU met on 13 February and decided not to support a resolution censuring China at the UN Commission on Human Rights. One of the reasons given for this decision was the acceptance by the Chinese government of a proposed visit by UN High Commissioner for Human Rights, Ms Mary Robinson to China. Sir Leon Brittan of the EU is reported to have said that the best way to promote human rights in a reformist China was to strengthen the process of economic reform and maintain a constructive political dialogue, an argument that sounded much like the official Japanese position. The US government also decided, in defiance of Congressional protest, not to move a resolution on China at Geneva, quoting China's avowed intention to subscribe to ICCPR (President Jiang Zemin of China expressed his intention to that effect in his letter to UN Secretary General Kofi Annan dated 12 January 1998). *Asahi Shinbun*, 20 January 1998 (evening edition); 24 February 1998; 17 March 1998 (evening edition). For Brittan's comments see James Moorhouse, 'For Chinese, Economic and Political Progress Go Together', *International Herald Tribune*, 3 April 1998. Moorhouse, a British conservative in the European Parliament, is critical of the compromising stance of Britain and the European Commission.

40 'Statement by Otsuka Seiichiro, Minister, Embassy of Japan in Thailand and representative of Japan to the Regional Meeting for Asia of the World Conference on Human Rights' *Jiyu to Seigi* (Liberty and Justice), vol. 44, no. 112, 1993, pp. 105–6. For Matsunaga's statement see note 22 above.

41 Commonwealth of Australia, *In the National Interest: Australia's Foreign and Trade Policy*, Department of Foreign Affairs and Trade, 1997, pp. 13–14.

42 *Diplomatic Bluebook 1995*, p. 92.

43 Keynote statement by H.E. Matsunaga Nobuo, President of Japan Institute of International Affairs, 'Human Rights and Diplomat', delivered before a Symposium at the United Nations University, Tokyo, on 26 June 1995.

6 Reaction and action

Analysing Japan's relations with the Socialist Republic of Vietnam

Hirata Keiko

As Japan has become a world economic power, its foreign policy has come under increased scrutiny. A common view of Japan's international behaviour is that it is essentially reactivist. Japan is portrayed as passive, risk-avoiding, and ineffective in conducting foreign policy.[1] Though all states of course react to events and pressure from outside, Japan is seen as being purely reactive, lacking any substantial proactive policies of its own.

In this chapter, I examine Japan's policy toward the Socialist Republic of Vietnam (SRV), a nation at the heart of international political and military conflicts in recent decades. Through this analysis, I will show the limitations of the reactivist view of Japan and instead propose a hybrid model of foreign policy behaviour. I argue that Japan's diplomacy toward Hanoi has fluctuated greatly between reactivism and proactivism for the last decades and that this fluctuation has resulted from two competing foreign policy goals:

1 to become a regional leader in Asian political and economic affairs; and
2 to maintain close strategic relations with the United States.

While these goals are often compatible, at other times they conflict. The tension between these two goals requires Tokyo to carefully calibrate the external environment in order to promote policies, which maintain the proper balance.

I begin by first discussing the notion and applicability of the reactivist model to contemporary Japanese policy toward Vietnam. Next, I will outline the main features of proactivism in Japanese policy toward Vietnam and modify the reactivist model by proposing a hybrid analytic model combining reactivism and proactivism. Following that, I will briefly discuss the historical relationship between Japan and Vietnam prior to the establishment of the SRV. Finally, I illustrate Japan's reactive–proactive diplomacy by analysing recent Tokyo–Hanoi relations in three periods:

1 the early 1970s–1978 (initial proactivism following US withdrawal from Vietnam);
2 1979–the late 1980s (reactivism during the years of Vietnam's occupation of Cambodia); and
3 the late 1980s–present (renewed proactivism after the end of the Cold War).

Through this discussion, I will try to remedy the paucity of analysis on Japanese proactive foreign policy by proposing the hybrid analytic model of reactivism and proactivism. Although, I do not attempt to apply this hybrid model to Japanese foreign policy in general, it may be useful in understanding Japan's relations with countries such as Myanmar and China, where Japan has had strong political and economic incentives for active engagement. Further research is necessary to identify situations and issue areas where this reactive/proactive model holds true.

Reactivism

The main focus of the reactivist perspective is on the role of *gaiatsu* in Japanese policymaking. The reactivist school argues that *gaiatsu* provides a powerful stimulus to the Japanese domestic policymaking process – frequently characterised as immobile – and that *gaiatsu* is the foremost factor determining the direction of Japan's diplomacy. According to this school of thought, changes in Japanese foreign policy occur as responses to the international community rather than to domestic needs.[2]

Another main theme of the reactivist view is the centrality of the United States in affecting Japan's foreign policy. The reactivist school assumes that the external pressure on Japan usually comes from Washington.[3] Lincoln explains why Tokyo has so often yielded to US *gaiatsu*:

> The US government has been the principal source of the outside pressure, a role that has come about as a result of historical legacy (the war and occupation), a vague sense of international hierarchy (the Japanese still view the United States as more prestigious and powerful than their own country), and overwhelming focus on maintaining access to American markets for goods and investment (given the large shares of exports and investment destined to the United States), and a concern for maintaining the US–Japan mutual security treaty as the cornerstone of Japanese foreign policy.[4]

Many reactivists distinguish Japan's behaviour in economics from that in the political/strategic arena and argue that Japan is an aggressor in low politics but a dwarf in high politics. Some attribute Japan's reactiveness to the 'Yoshida Doctrine' of the 1950s, which emphasised post-World War II economic reconstruction and development, minimum defence, and reliance on the US–Japan Security Alliance that guaranteed American military protection of Japan. According to Hellmann, the Yoshida Doctrine has been kept intact by an international 'greenhouse' created by the United States in the early Cold War era. In his view, the Yoshida Doctrine under the protection of the international greenhouse has made Japan an economic superpower while allowing it to remain a dwarf in world politics. Hellmann asserts that because of Japan's special 'incubator' conditions under the greenhouse provided by the United States, Tokyo has never faced an urgent need to develop long-term strategic security planning.[5] According to him, 'Japan was and still remains essentially a passive actor on the world political state, more a trading company than a nation-state, a nation without a foreign policy in the usual sense of the word'.[6] Similarly, Funabashi argues that Japan has eschewed political involvement in international affairs while focusing on economic gains since the end of World War II. He claims that for the last four decades 'all the nation's (Japan's) energy and resources were mobilised exclusively for economic reconstruction and expansion' and that security issues were placed on the back burner.[7]

By contrast, other reactivists do not draw a line between politics and economics and maintain that Japan is reactive even in the economic sphere. According to Calder, Japan is a typical 'reactive state' in economic policymaking, possessing the following 'essential characteristics' of the reactivist state:

> (1) the state fails to undertake major independent foreign economic policy initiatives when it has the power and national incentives to do so; and (2) it responds to outside pressures for change, albeit erratically, unsystematically, and often incompletely.[8]

From Calder's point of view, Japan avoids taking independent economic policy initiatives despite the country's 'manifest economic and geostrategic resources and its demonstrated ability to operate strategically within its national boundaries'.[9] Calder wonders why, despite its enhanced national capacity, Japan has been reactive to international events and has been more deferential to US *gaiatsu* than have most middle-range powers such as major European states.[10]

While divergent opinions exist as to whether Japan is reactive only in high politics or whether it is reactive even in low politics, there is consensus among reactivists over the manner in which Tokyo conducts foreign policy. The unanimous view is that Tokyo's reactive policymaking involves minimalist, passive, and risk-averse diplomacy. Blaker describes the essence of Japan's foreign policy as 'coping'. In his view, Japan merely copes with situations created by others and that Japan's foreign policymaking involves

> carefully assessing the international situation, methodically weighing each alternative, sorting out various options to see what is really serious, waiting for the dust to settle on some contentious issue, piecing together a consensus view about the situation faced, and then performing the existing situation with the fewest risk.[11]

Another view on Japan's foreign policy shared by the reactivists is that Japan's foreign policy approach is ineffective. As Calder claims in the above statement that Japan responds to foreign pressure 'erratically, unsystematically, and often incompletely',[12] many scholars argue that Tokyo unsuccessfully implements a new policy after an impetus of *gaiatsu*. According to Blaker, Japan's 'minimalist, coping approach has become jarringly inappropriate to Japan's vastly expanded, international presence today'.[13]

A well-cited example of Tokyo's ineffective reactivist policy is the country's role in the Gulf War in 1990–91. Lincoln claims that Japan failed to take a clear stand or to quickly join the war effort, but instead reacted defensively to US pressure. He points out that Japan's tardy response to the war invited severe criticism from the United States and other countries despite Tokyo's eventual contribution of $13 billion, roughly 20 per cent of the total cost of Desert Storm.[14]

The reactivist perspective is useful in explaining the importance of *gaiatsu*, particularly US pressure, in influencing Japanese foreign policymaking. The proponents of the reactivist perspective are correct in their assessment that US–Japan relations should be a focal point of analysis of Japan's foreign policy. Their view that Japanese foreign policymaking is slow and risk-averse is also accurate and useful to understanding Japan's behaviour.

This reactivist model, however, is by itself insufficient to explain Japan's foreign policy in many regions in the world, such as Southeast Asia, a region where Japan has taken important diplomatic and economic policy initiatives. The main problem with the reactivist model is its premise that changes in Japanese foreign policy occur only as a result of *gaiatsu*. This model neglects proactive policy initiatives by Japan and instead postulates that a reactive, passive, minimalist approach prevails at all times any places. Closer examination of Japan's foreign policy reveals that Japan does indeed take indigenous initiative to pursue its interests. One well-cited example of Japan's activism is its recent Official Development Assistance (ODA) policy, demonstrated by such initiatives as aid doubling plans and four debt relief plans for debt-plagued developing countries in the 1980s.[15] Japan's Vietnam policies in the post-Vietnam War era have similarly been proactive. Japan has consistently sought to pursue its political and economic interests in Indochina since the 1970s, succeeding at some times and failing at others.

Another significant problem with the reactivist model is its failure to clearly delineate Japanese foreign policy at times when Japan does not face *gaiatsu*, particularly from the United States. The reactivist model implies that Japan always faces a constant flood of *gaiatsu* from the United States and that Tokyo incessantly adjusts itself to American demands. But the United States does not necessarily make demands on Japan when there are no high stakes for Washington. For example, Washington did not exert much pressure on Tokyo over Japanese policy toward Vietnam in either the 1970s or the 1990s. An oversimplified image of US–Japan relations – that the United States constantly pressures Japan and Japan grudgingly accommodates US demands – obscures the more complex reality of US–Japan relations. While United States sometimes exerts strong pressure on Japan regarding issues of critical importance to Washington, at other times the United States remains sanguine or at least tolerant of Japan's foreign policy role, as seen for example in Vietnam.

Balancing act: dual relationship with the United States and Asia

Japan's reactivism/activism takes place within the framework of Japan's dual relationships with the United States and Asia. As reactivists correctly point out, US–Japan relations have been a crucial point of reference for Japanese international behaviour. The bilateral relationship has provided a critical link for Japan to the global system by keeping Tokyo closely aligned with Washington's policies in world affairs. At the same time, Japan has cherished its relations with other Asian countries. Asia has been the central stage for Japan's economic and political activism. Asia has provided a significant market for Japanese products and has been the largest recipient of Japanese ODA throughout the post-World War II period. Asia has been the centrepiece Japan's political activism, as seen for example by the deployment of the Japanese Self Defense Forces (SDF) to Cambodia for UN-sponsored peace-keeping operations in 1992–93.

In recent decades Tokyo has attempted to strengthen and balance both its US and Asia linkages in conducting foreign policy. Soeya asserts that Japan has tried to take independent policy initiatives in Asia while at the same time promoting the fundamental principle of global co-operation with the United States, still Tokyo's key foreign policy and economic partner. According to Soeya, Japan's diplomacy has involved a balancing act between these two desires – taking independent policy initiatives in Asia but also strengthening US–Japan relations – and that Japan has attempted to strive for policy co-ordination to achieve both these goals.[16]

Managing a balancing act between these aspirations, however, becomes extremely difficult when one linkage – the US connection – imposes constraints on the other, Japan's Asia connection. If the constraints are insurmountable, Japan yields to US *gaiatsu*, sacrifices its regional aspiration, and follows the US lead in conducting its Asia policy. Soeya argues that an important condition for Tokyo's autonomous diplomacy in Asia is the absence of serious conflicts of interest with the United States and that should any major conflicts of interest with Washington arise, Japan would pull back from its pursuit of regional activism.[17]

Japan's policy toward the SRV presents an excellent example of the dual-linkage framework. Since the 1970s, Japan has pursued a balancing act between its own desire to conduct an independent policy toward Vietnam on the one hand and its obligation to maintain the fundamental framework of US–Japan co-operation on the other. The balancing act becomes difficult when the US–Japan relationship poses constraints on Japan's foreign policy toward the SRV. If the constraints are insurmountable, Japan gives up its own desire to pursue an active regional role in order to accommodate US needs.

Reactivism and proactivism

In Japan's policies toward the SRV, there has clearly been a combination of reactivism and proactivism. Here proactivism means that 'Japan has its own ideas, interests, and policy objectives … Its policies are not based solely on the expectations foreign countries nor in response to direct foreign pressure'.[18] The hybrid model of reactivism and proactivism does not discount the principle features of the reactivist model, such as the prominent role of *gaiatsu* in Japanese policymaking, the centrality of the United States in Japanese foreign policy, or the 'coping' manner of diplomacy. Rather, this model clarifies the definition of Japan's reactiveness, expands the reactivist model to include proactivism, and links Japan's diplomatic behaviour to its dual relationship with Asia and the United States. With this hybrid model, we can make several propositions about Japan's foreign policy behaviour and Japan's relations with Vietnam in particular.

First, the hybrid model of reactivism and proactivism has a number of variations depending on time, location, and issue. In some situations, Japan may simultaneously exhibit both reactive and proactive policies toward the same country or region over different issues. For example, Tokyo is proactive on issue X toward country A but reactive towards the same country on issue Y. Another pattern of the hybrid model would be that Tokyo alternates between reactivism and proactivism toward the same country or region over an extended period of time. For example, Tokyo may be reactive toward country A during a certain period of time on issue X but may shift to proactivism in that country on the same issue at another time. It is also conceivable that Japan's policy in country A is reactive at one time not only over issue X but also over most issues involved in the bilateral relationship and that Japanese general policy toward A switches to activism at another time. Another pattern would be that Japan's reactivism in one country or region can be coincided with its proactivism in another country/region. For instance, Japan's reactivism toward country A may simultaneously take place with its proactivism in country B. In this case, the Japanese policies toward A and B can be either linked or unrelated to each other.

Japan's relations with the SRV have alternated between reactivism and proactivism toward Hanoi over an extended period of time. During the reactive period, mainly due to US *gaiatsu*, Japan gave up its aspiration to conduct autonomous diplomacy in Asia and followed American policies in the region. During the proactive period, Japan has acted relatively free of constraints of US–Japan relations and has searched for greater political and economic influence in Vietnam by formulating new doctrines, taking aid initiatives, and promoting regional integration policies. Japan's reactivism and proactivism in its policy toward Vietnam are not limited to a single issue, but affect the overall nature of relations between the two nations in given time periods. Although it is possible to identify distinct periods of activism and reactivism, it should be noted that Japanese policies toward Vietnam were never *exclusively* reactive or proactive at any period.

Second, there are two faces of *gaiatsu*: one pressuring Japan to *act* and the other pressuring it *not to act*. As we have seen, the example of the Gulf War illustrates a case in which the United States pressured a passive Japan to act when it did not want to. By contrast, I argue that Japan has all along hoped to take a proactive policy toward Vietnam since the end of the Vietnam War and that US pressure was exerted on Japan not to act when it in fact wanted to. The role of this type of *gaiatsu* is significant in Japan–Vietnam relations, for the reduction of *gaiatsu* contributed to Japan's more proactive stance toward the SRV. Japan has taken a reactive stance during periods of intense US *gaiatsu* and a proactive stance when US *gaiatsu* eases. Since Japan has continuously hoped to pursue activism in the SRV, one can argue that Tokyo has switched its *modus operandi* to reactivism unwillingly and has converted to proactivism voluntarily.

Third, Japan is susceptible to a *synergistic linkage* strategy. According to Schoppa, linkage refers to 'cases where a nation seeks to take advantage of its power advantage in one area by linking it to an issue area in which it has fewer power resources'.[19] The United States, for example, sought to influence Japan's SRV policy in the 1980s by linking it to American security interests in Southeast Asia and to US–Japan bilateral trade relations. Given America's advantageous position over Japan in security (i.e., Japan's need for a US security umbrella) and trade (i.e., Japan's need for an open US market), Tokyo became vulnerable to American *gaiatsu* to isolate communist Vietnam in the 1980s.

Fourth, *gaiatsu* can affect Japan through domestic politics, especially when the foreign government succeeds in changing the perceptions of various Japanese actors about the cost of no compliance. For example, during the 1980s, when the United States exerted a great deal of pressure on Japan to comply with US policy of containing Hanoi, many Japanese policy leaders – politicians, bureaucrats, and business leaders alike – resented American pressure and would have preferred to strengthen economic and political ties with Hanoi. Yet, they eventually yielded to the *gaiatsu* because they realised that the cost of non-compliance was higher than that of compliance. Here, Schoppa's synergistic linkage applies. Japanese policymakers reluctantly accepted American demands in the end because they linked it to Japan's other relations with the United States. Specifically, Japanese bureaucrats (particularly in the Ministry of Foreign Affairs, or MFA) and politicians yielded to US demands because they did not want to risk overall US–Japan security and economic relations; Japanese business leaders, likewise, withdrew their opposition to *gaiatsu* because they did not want to lose access to the American market.[20] In this way, *gaiatsu* works in combination with Japanese domestic politics. Unlike the reactivist model that simply singles out the role of *gaiatsu* in moving Japan, I argue that foreign pressure works well when it changes the perspectives of policymakers by relating a given issue to their broader concerns and interests.

Fifth, Japan's proactivism does not necessarily mean that Japan aggressively or high-handedly imposes its proactive policies. Japan's proactivism is constrained by the anti-Japanese sentiment shared by many Asian countries. Their antipathy toward Japan's military aggression during World War II has been a formidable challenge to Japan's leadership role in Asia, as they continue to see Tokyo as not having come to proper terms with its past. While anti-Japanese feelings have recently become subdued in some areas in Asia and increasing numbers of Asian leaders have begun to positively see Japan's economic activities and even its military presence in their region,[21] Japan still has to take its World War II legacy into consideration in conducting its foreign policy. Thus even during proactive periods, Tokyo takes a cautious approach, carefully calculating the international situation to its advantage and minimising risks.

Sixth, Japan's restricted military capacity and its continued reliance on US military protection have greatly affected Tokyo's diplomatic course, forcing it to resort to what Baldwin calls 'economic statecraft',[22] or more specifically what Wan calls 'spending strategies' such as ODA.[23] While economic statecraft or spending strategies can be quite effective when the international environment is peaceful and stable, they are less effective during times of crisis or war.[24] Japan thus places extraordinary emphasis on maintaining peace and stability in the international order as it would lose its leverage in situations of conflict and crisis. Although in recent years Japan has begun to develop the military means to increase its presence in the world, with Tokyo now sending its SDF to conflict regions, Tokyo's use of military means is still an anomaly. This is seen for example in Japan–SRV relations, with Japan relying principally on economic means to gain both economic and political influence during periods of proactivism.

In summary, this section proposes a reactive/proactive model with six propositions:

1　there are various patterns of reactivism and proactivism and Japan's relations with the SRV takes the form of alternation between the two;
2　there are two types of *gaiatsu* on Japan, one pressuring Japan to act and the other pressuring it not to act, and the second type of *gaiatsu* applies to Japan's relations with the SRV;
3　*gaiatsu* works well through a synergistic linkage;
4　*gaiatsu* is intertwined with domestic politics *and* is effective when it changes the perspectives of Japanese domestic actors;
5　Japan's manner of proactivism is not aggressive but cautious; and
6　Japan relies on spending strategies to implement its proactive policies.

Background: Japan and two Vietnams

Japan's policy toward the two Vietnams prior to the establishment of the SRV was strongly influenced by Tokyo's defeat in World War II and the subsequent American domination of Japanese foreign policy. During the early post-war era Japan adhered closely to the anti-Communist political and military policies of the United States. Japan did not seek an independent political role in Southeast Asia and maintained a low profile in regional affairs.

Japan had limited contact with Vietnam before occupying Indochina during World War II. The lack of interaction largely stemmed from trade restrictions imposed by Japan under the Tokugawa Shogunate from the seventeenth to the nineteenth century and by France, the colonial power in Indochina from the mid-nineteenth century to the 1930s. Japan's direct contact with Vietnam began with Japanese troops stepping in to control northern Vietnam in 1940. In the following year Japan stationed its forces throughout all of French Indochina and gained free access to all ports, bases, and airfields in the region. In March 1945, Japan carried out a coup d'etat against France and recognised the nominal independence of Vietnam, while virtually taking over the colonial function from its predecessor. Japan's harsh five-year rule over Vietnam (1940–45) ruined the local economy and sparked widespread Vietnamese nationalism. In 1944–45, nearly two million people in northern Vietnam died of starvation. The Viet Minh, an anti-foreign nationalist group formed by Ho Chi Minh in 1941, demanded independence from both France and Japan. To the Vietnamese, Japanese rule was no better than that of the French. Many Vietnamese blamed the Japanese for substituting a new imperialism and exploiting natural resources in Indochina. Japanese control of the region ended in August 1945, when Japan surrendered to the Allied Forces.[25]

Japan's first direct post-war contact with Indochina began in 1951, when Tokyo signed a peace treaty with 48 nations, including the French-sponsored State of Vietnam (SOV) under Bao Dai in Saigon.[26] The peace treaty did not include the Democratic Republic of Vietnam (DRV), a government in Hanoi established by Ho Chi Minh in 1945. Japan, having been defeated in World War II by the United States and just emerging from American occupation, was careful to follow the American lead in its post-war Asia policy and did not recognise the DRV. In 1959 Japan agreed to provide war reparations ($39 million), aid loans ($7.5 million), and private loans ($9.1 million) to the newly established government of Vietnam in Saigon under Ngo Dinh Diem. By contrast, Japan denied any financial assistance to the DRV, with which it lacked diplomatic relations.[27] Japan's refusal to pay reparations to the DRV was a bitter irony, as north Vietnam had suffered more from Japan's rule during World War II than their southern counterparts. The reparations to Saigon were not paid in cash but in Japanese goods and services, thus paying the way for Japanese products to penetrate into South Vietnam as in many other parts of Asia.

During the Vietnam War, the Japanese government firmly supported US policy toward Hanoi. Under the US–Japan Security Treaty (signed in 1951 and renewed in 1960), the United States was entitled to maintain American military bases in Japan for use in preparing ground and air operations in Vietnam. Though the Vietnam War was generally unpopular in Japan, with citizens' groups, trade unions, and leftist politicians protesting the American bombings raids, the Japanese government backed Washington's war efforts primarily for pragmatic reasons. Japan provided goods and services to both US and South Vietnamese forces, and the Japanese economy profited substantially from that collaboration. In addition, Tokyo also hoped that in exchange for Japanese backing in the Vietnam War, the US would return control over the islands of Okinawa to Japan. Regaining sovereign control over Okinawa was one of the foremost important issues in Japan's relations with the United States in the 1960s and early 1970s. Japan's proving that it was a loyal US ally was a critical prerequisite for the retrocession of the southern islands.[28]

According to Havens, what the Vietnam War meant to the Japanese was 'fire across the sea', or *taigan no kaji*.[29] It was an American war in Asia and Japan was not directly involved. Japan did not send any military personnel to the region due to constitutional restrictions. Japan's policy in Indochina was in line with Yoshida Doctrine, which emphasised non-involvement in regional conflicts in order to concentrate on its own economic growth.

After the completion of war reparation payments in 1965, Japan's bilateral financial assistance to South Vietnam was halted for a few years due to the escalation of the Vietnam War. After the announcement of President Richard Nixon's Guam Doctrine in 1969, which stated that the United States would expect its allies to take more responsibility for containing communism in Asia, Japan renewed its ODA to Saigon.[30]

While Japan recognised only the Saigon government, Tokyo dealt privately with the DRV through the Japan–Vietnam Trade Association (JVTA), a non-governmental pro-Hanoi organisation established in 1955.[31] Trade with Hanoi was based on Prime Minister Ikeda Hayato's pragmatic policy for relations with communist nations: 'the separation of politics and economics' (*sei kei bunri*). The most valuable export from Hanoi was Hongay coal, which the Japanese had been purchasing since the French colonial era. Once the United States entered the war in full force in March 1965, however, trade with Hanoi became extremely difficult. Goods had to be shipped between the DRV and Japan in third-country vessels. The Japanese government banned the export of items which could bolster North Vietnam militarily. From 1965 until the signing of a Paris Peace Accord in 1973, political and economic contacts with the DRV fell to a minimum.[32]

Initial pursuit of activism in the SRV (the early 1970s to 1979)

Toward diplomatic normalisation with Vietnam

The situation in Indochina changed rapidly in the early 1970s as US influence in the region declined. The weakening of US influence was signalled by the withdrawal of American forces from Vietnam following the 1973 Paris Peace Accord as well by the collapse of US-led anti-Communist organisations. For example, the Southeast Asia Treaty Organization (SEATO), established in 1954 at American initiative, stopped its military functions in 1973 and dissolved in 1975. Similarly, the Asia and Pacific Council (ASPAC), established through South Korean initiatives, died out in 1973. The liberation of Saigon in 1975 was the final blow effectively ending US dominance of Vietnam.

The 1970s saw an emergence of new thinking among Japanese foreign policy-makers who tried to take a policy stance that was independent of the United States. A significant incident that prompted Japan to search for a more independent role was the 1971 Sino–US Communiqué announcing President Nixon's forthcoming visit to the People's Republic of China (PRC). The communiqué caught Japan by surprise, and Japanese leaders were annoyed that they had not been consulted prior to its announcement. This was evidence that the United States could not be always relied upon to take Tokyo's views into consideration before making major policy changes. The decision by the Japanese leaders to take more independent policy initiatives was also influenced by increasing confidence in Japan's rapid economic development in the 1960s and early 1970s. With the successful economic growth, Japanese leaders came to believe that Tokyo could and should play an independent role in international affairs. An early indication of Tokyo's greater foreign policy independence came in 1973 when Japan, heavily dependent on Middle Eastern oil, broke ranks with the US and declared its support for the right to Palestinian self-determination.[33]

US withdrawal from Southeast Asia and America's declining influence in the region also confirmed to Japanese policymakers that they could no longer depend on US political-strategic leadership in Asia. They welcomed the changing political climate in Southeast Asia, finding new opportunities to have a freer hand to implement an independent policy in the region for the first time since World War II.[34] In their thinking, anti-Communist ideology mattered little, particularly after the announcement of Nixon's visit to China and the diplomatic normalisation between Japan and China in the same year. Japan became eager to strengthen its political and economic ties with communist Indochina. With a policy often characterised as 'omni-directional diplomacy' (*zenhoi gaiko*), Tokyo tried in the 1970s to improve relations with Hanoi while maintaining its alliance with the United States and other Western countries.

Vietnam offered both economic and political opportunities to the Japanese leadership. Tokyo's economic goal was to help bring about the reconstruction of Vietnam's war-damaged economy and promote the incorporation of Indochina into the market economies of Asia. Japanese leaders were convinced that when integrated into the capitalist economies, Vietnam would provide impressive economic opportunities for Japanese firms seeking to expand trade and investment, extract natural resources, and establish offshore manufacturing in Indochina. Japan's political goal, was to induce Vietnam to loosen its ties with the communist bloc and become 'a Socialist country of the Yugoslav type, open to the Western world'.[35] Japan was particularly interested in contributing to the creation of a new equilibrium between ASEAN and Vietnam to promote peace and stability in Southeast Asia.

Japan began taking independent initiatives to reach these goals well before the 1975 liberation of Saigon. In 1970, the Director General of the First Southeast Asia Division of the Ministry of Foreign Affairs, Miyake Kazusuke, contacted North Vietnamese officials in France to explore possibilities of rapprochement with Hanoi. In 1971, the Japanese embassy in Paris continued these discussions and offered to send Miyake to Hanoi in order to negotiate normalisation of ties between Japan and Vietnam. In February 1972, Miyake visited Hanoi for the first time to advance the negotiations[36] and in May 1973, four months after the signing of the Paris Peace Accord, revisited Vietnam to finalise normalisation talks. In September 1973, Japan and the DRV formally established diplomatic relations.[37]

After diplomatic normalisation, rapprochement accelerated between Japan and the DRV.[38] Communications between the two countries increased and even conservative Diet members started contacting elected officials in Hanoi. In 1974, Japanese and Vietnamese politicians established the League for Japan–Vietnam Friendship to promote mutual understanding and friendship. The Japanese members included Diet members not only from the pro-Hanoi Socialist and Communist parties, but also from traditionally anti-Communist parties, such as the Liberal Democratic Party (LDP) and the Democratic Socialist Party (DSP). The LDP Secretary General, Sakurauchi Yoshio, was appointed as chairman.[39]

The liberation of Saigon in April 1975 encouraged Japanese leaders to take more initiatives in Indochina. In June 1975, Japanese Foreign Minister Miyazawa Yoshio indicated Japan's readiness to play an active political role in Southeast Asia:

Japan is now a huge economic power and is politically stabilized. It is very necessary that Japan should keep a relationship of mutual understanding with all of the countries in Southeast Asia, in order to maintain peace and stability in Asia, where there exist various unstable factors and a fluctuating situation. Japan can contribute to the stabilization of the area by promoting mutual understanding and keeping friendly relations with all the countries, even though some of them have a different political system from ours.[40]

Miyazawa's statement confirmed Japan's omni-directional diplomacy and showed its strong interest in maintaining regional stability and peace, necessary conditions for Japan's exercise of economic power in the region.

Proactivism through aid

Japan's main means for gaining influence in Vietnam was through spending, particularly through the disbursement of ODA. Without waiting for the United States to start its own relief programme, Tokyo provided the newly unified SRV with $28 million in grant aid for FY 1975 and $17 million in grant aid for FY 1976.[41] Japan did not agree to any further assistance in FY 1977 due to a disagreement over the debt incurred by the Saigon government; Japan claimed the SRV should assume responsibility for the debt of about $50 million owed by the Saigon government to Japan.[42] In December 1978, Japan resolved the dispute by announcing that it would provide $55 million in grant for FY 1979 in exchange for Hanoi's payment of the South Vietnamese government's leftover debts.[43]

The beginning of ODA to Hanoi had an important impact on the Japanese private sector. Japanese exports increased rapidly and Tokyo immediately became Vietnam's second largest trading partner after the Soviet Union. Japanese goods such as steel, machinery, and fertilisers were exported to Vietnam for its urgent post-war reconstruction. In return Japan imported maize and petroleum from Hanoi. In 1976, Japan's exports to Vietnam reached $167 million, while Japanese imports from Vietnam totalled $49 million.[44] The Japanese private sector was so eager to do business in Vietnam that it came up with a solution to Vietnam's mounting trade deficit with Tokyo; Japanese city banks provided commercial loans to the Vietnamese government in 1977 and 1978 so that Hanoi could continue to purchase Japanese goods.[45]

Fukuda Doctrine

The zenith of Japanese proactivism in the 1970s was Prime Minister Fukuda's speech (known as 'the Fukuda Doctrine') in Manila in August 1977. Only two years after the end of the Vietnam War and merely one year after the unification of Vietnam, Fukuda's speech revealed that for the first time in the post-World War II era the Japanese government was willing to play an active role in Southeast Asian affairs, 'without depending on military imperatives and in such a way as to make military considerations less prominent'.[46] Soeya calls Fukuda's Manila speech the 'basic tenor of Japan's Indochina policy'.[47] The speech consisted of three principles:

1 rejection of the role of a military power;
2 consolidation of the relationship of mutual confidence and trust based on 'heart-to-heart' understanding; and
3 equal partnership with the ASEAN for building peace and prosperity throughout Southeast Asia.[48]

The most significant point in the speech was the third principle which indicated that the Japanese government was willing to act as a political mediator between the ASEAN and Indochina to bring about a peaceful co-existence between the two blocs.[49] It was the first statement in the post-World War II era that explicitly expressed Tokyo's political intentions in Indochina. In Tokyo's strategic thinking, Vietnam was the focal point; the ultimate goal for Japan was to play a role in neutralising Vietnam so that all Indochina would become open to the Western world.

The first and second principles of Fukuda's speech were also significant, indicating Japan's attempt to improve the prevalent image of Japan as a potential military threat and economic aggressor in Southeast Asia. In particular, these two points were designed to reduce resentment, which had arisen toward Japanese business activities in the region due to the rapid penetration of Japanese goods into Southeast Asia since the end of World War II. The 1974 anti-Japanese riots occasioned by Prime Minister Tanaka's trip to Jakarta and Bangkok had alarmed Japanese leaders. They felt they had to articulate Japan's policy stance toward the region in order to soften opposition to the Japanese economic presence. Fukuda's speech, an attempt to forge friendly relations with Southeast Asian countries, reveals Japan's caution in taking initiative in the region, due to the historical legacy of Japanese military aggression and the emerging fear of Japanese economic activities.

Another important aspect of Fukuda's 'doctrine' was the way it was created. Unlike previous policies, Japanese officials in MFA took the initiative in developing the Fukuda doctrine without consulting the United States prior to its announcement in Manila. Fukuda's speech was primarily the brainchild of an informally organised MFA group consisting of four policy co-ordinators in the Asian Affairs Bureau.[50] Soeya observes that Fukuda's speech 'reflected Japan's aspiration for a larger role in areas where there was no major conflict of interest with the United States'.[51] Since Washington did not oppose the Fukuda Doctrine, Tokyo was able to proceed to implement it immediately after the Manila announcement.

Retreat from activism in the SRV (the 1980s)

Vietnam's occupation of Cambodia

Japan's proactive policy in Vietnam did not last long. Cold War geopolitical struggle intensified in Indochina at the end of the 1970s and Japan could not resist international pressure, particularly from the United States, to act in concert with the West to isolate Soviet-backed Indochina. The third principle of the Fukuda Doctrine that stressed Japan's role as a mediator between the ASEAN and Indochina was thus stalled, along with the more general notion of omni-directional diplomacy. The 1980s saw a retreat of Tokyo's independent, proactive policymaking in Vietnam.

A series of events triggered Cold War conflicts in Indochina in the late 1970s, polarising the region into Soviet and China/US blocs. First, Pol Pot's Democratic Kampuchea (DK) and the SRV began intensive fighting along their border, which became intertwined with Cold-War conflicts at a global level: DK strengthened ties with China while the SRV drew closer to the Soviet Union. As tensions intensified in the region, Vietnam broke its formal equidistance between the USSR and the PRC by joining the Soviet-led Council for Mutual Economic Assistance (CMEA) in June 1978. A month later, the PRC completely stopped aid to Vietnam, and in November of the same year, Hanoi signed a Treaty of Friendship and Cooperation with Moscow. A month later, the United States and China officially normalised diplomatic relations. The US–PRC rapprochement effectively severed US–Vietnam relations as Washington stopped negotiating with Hanoi for diplomatic normalisation in order to finalise agreement with China.[52]

Tokyo did not want to sacrifice its improved ties with Hanoi, but the signing of a Sino–Japanese Peace and Friendship Treaty in August 1978 aggravated Japan–SRV relations. The conclusion of the treaty caused serious contention between Japan and the Soviet Union as it included an 'anti-hegemony' clause seemingly targeted at Moscow. Japan–Vietnam relations further worsened as a result of the establishment of the Soviet–Vietnam friendship treaty in 1978 that clarified Hanoi's stance on the Sino–Soviet conflict.

Tensions reached a peak in December 1978–January 1979, when the People's Army of Vietnam (PAVN) entered Cambodia and forced out of power Pol Pot's DK, installing Heng Samrin's People's Republic of Kampuchea (PRK). With the Khmer Rouge escaping to rural areas, a proxy war developed as the PRC, the ASEAN, and the United States backed the deposed Pol Pot regime, while the Soviet Union and Vietnam supported the Heng Samrin government. The situation in Indochina further deteriorated in February 1979, when the PRC attacked Vietnam to reprimand the PAVN's earlier invasion of Cambodia.

Suspension of foreign aid

When Vietnam occupied Cambodia in January 1979, Japanese foreign policy-makers were initially hopeful that the PAVN would soon withdraw. Tokyo responded ambiguously to the Vietnamese occupation of Cambodia. At first, Tokyo avoided using the term 'invasion' to refer to the entry of Vietnamese forces into Cambodia. And while Japan officially postponed the disbursement of promised FY 1979 ODA to Vietnam, Tokyo avoided making an official decision as to whether aid should be continued or ended.[53]

Tokyo had various reasons for not wanting to terminate its aid agreement with the SRV. First, Japan's MFA hoped to maintain lines of communication with the SRV to pursue the Fukuda Doctrine and to maintain its influence in the country and in Indochina as a whole. MFA officials believed that Japan should continue to offer a carrot (i.e., ODA) to Hanoi rather than a stick (i.e., the suspension of ODA). Foreign Minister Sonoda Sunao explained why Japan's ODA to Hanoi should not be stopped:

> Our country is one of very few (non-communist) countries which can communi-
> cate with Vietnam.… I believe that it was not wise to discontinue the aid. The
> reason was that we had to maintain a communication channel with Vietnam.
> In order to invite Vietnam's self-restraint, I judged it much more effective in
> the long run to tell Vietnam what we should require through this communica-
> tion route than to suspend our economic assistance of 14 billion yen per year.[54]

Second, MFA wanted to avoid public acknowledgement of its failure to have accurately assessed Vietnam's intention to invade Cambodia.[55] The occupation of Phnom Penh by the PAVN took place only two weeks after Tokyo and Hanoi had signed a $55 million grant aid agreement for FY 1979. Rather than admit to the Japanese public that it had misjudged Vietnam's intentions in Cambodia, MFA laid its hopes on the chance that the SRV would soon withdraw its troops from Cambodia.[56]

Third, many members of the Japanese Diet, particularly those in the League for Japan–Vietnam Friendship such as Sakurauchi Yoshio and Kimura Takeo, were adamantly opposed to the suspension of the aid to SRV. In 1979, the League sent a delegation consisting of two LDP (Sakurauchi and Kimura), three Socialist, and two Communist members to Hanoi to improve Japan–Vietnam relations. Upon his return to Tokyo, Kimura issued a statement that the SRV hoped for a peaceful environment for its post-Vietnam War economic reconstruction and thus that the Japanese government should keep open communications channels with Hanoi by providing aid.[57]

Fourth, Japanese business leaders opposed the suspension of Japanese ODA to Vietnam as detrimental to their interests. The suspension of Japanese ODA was accompanied by termination of government loan guarantees, export insurance, and funds from the Japan Import–Export Bank for Japanese companies. Japanese companies who chose to remain in Vietnam would have to operate without govern-ment guarantees or support. Bilateral trade relations between Japan and Vietnam had improved since the early 1970s and the Japanese business community hoped to continue to expand trade with Hanoi. Japanese companies with vested interests in Vietnam lobbied for liberalising bilateral relations and demanded that the Japanese government not suspend ODA.

As the Cambodian conflict progressed, *gaiatsu* on the Japanese government to suspend aid to Vietnam mounted especially from the United States but also from the PRC and the ASEAN members. For example, at the ASEAN Ministerial Conference in Bali in July 1979, the United States and ASEAN exerted strong pressure on the Japanese government to freeze ODA to Vietnam. Japan tried to deflect *gaiatsu* and defend its position by saying that Tokyo could maintain more influence over Vietnam by keeping open communication channels with Hanoi rather than by discontinuing aid.[58]

Of all the *gaiatsu* on the Japanese government from a number of allies, US pressure had the most significant impact. While Japanese policymakers – MFA officials, politicians, and business leaders – wanted to continue the ODA, they were concerned that they would be seen by Washington as having legitimised the Vietnamese invasion of Cambodia and that security and economic relations between the United States and Japan would deteriorate as a result.

Furthermore, the Japanese aid decision could not be taken in isolation from other issues of US–Japan relations around the globe. The US–Japan relationship underwent a serious test in November 1979 when the Iran hostage crisis broke out. In retaliation against the taking of more than 50 American hostages by Iranian militants in Tehran, the US asked its allies to support US economic sanctions against Iran. Defying US calls for economic sanctions, Japanese firms covertly bought large amounts of Iranian oil at escalated prices in late November of 1979. US policymakers were outraged when they learned of these purchases and US Secretary of State Cyrus Vance expressed his strong criticism to Japanese Foreign Minister Okita Saburo. Following this incident, the Japanese government realised that it had to regain the trust of the Carter administration or risk serious deterioration of bilateral relations with the United States. Similarly, Japanese business leaders realised that a serious rift was developing in US–Japan relations and were concerned that if they continued to oppose American policy in Southeast Asia, they risked losing the US market for Japanese products.[59]

When US–Soviet Cold War rivalry reached its peak following the deployment of Soviet troops to Afghanistan in late December 1979, Japan could no longer refrain from taking a clear stance on its aid to Hanoi. Tokyo was compelled to follow the lead of the United States, the ASEAN, and China in working to isolate Soviet-backed Indochina from the rest of Asia. Following the Soviet invasion in Afghanistan, Tokyo officially suspended the aid to Hanoi as a punishment for supporting Russia's incursion in Afghanistan. Japan announced that Japanese ODA to the SRV would not be released until the PAVN withdrew from Cambodia.[60] This announcement of Japan's aid decision finally proved Tokyo's allegiance to the United States and demonstrated Japanese support for the American effort to deter Soviet influence in Southeast Asia. The official aid postponement also indicated that Tokyo would not hesitate to sacrifice its relations with other countries if the United States pressured Tokyo to do so. As illustrated by Tokyo's aid decision following the Soviet invasion into Afghanistan, Japan's main concern was with how its reaction to the Afghan crisis would affect future US–Japan relations.

Throughout the 1980s, Japan did not recognise the Heng Samrin government in Cambodia. For two years from 1979, it followed the United States, the ASEAN, and the PRC in supporting the Pol Pot's DK as the legitimate Cambodian government at the UN. In 1982, Tokyo, along with its allies, gave support to the Coalition Government of Democratic Kampuchea (CGDK), a Cambodian tripartite coalition in exile consisting of the Front Uni National pour Cambodge Indépendent, Neutre, Pacifique et Coopératif (FUNCINPEC), the Khmer People's National

Liberation Front (KPNLF), and the Party of Democratic Kampuchea (PDK). These parties were led by Prince Norodom Sihanouk, Son Sann, and Pol Pot respectively. Consequently, Japan provided relief aid to the CGDK, not to the Phnom Penh government which was in more dire straits.

While Japan did not completely abandon the Fukuda Doctrine to play a regional role in mediating between the ASEAN and Indochina in the 1980s, there was little Tokyo could do to achieve this goal. Japan began to provide small-scale human-itarian relief aid to Vietnam in 1982 in a hope to draw Hanoi closer to the capitalist world in Southeast Asia. Nevertheless, Tokyo's attempt was minuscule and did not bring any positive diplomatic results. In most of the 1980s, Japan kept a low profile in Indochina and failed to play a mediator role in Indochina.

PRESERVING US–JAPAN ECONOMIC TIES

Japan's compliance with US *gaiatsu* over the SRV throughout the 1980s was also related to bilateral trade disputes between the United States and Japan over Tokyo's swelling trade surplus. Anti-Japanese sentiment heightened in the United States in the second-half of the 1980s, particularly in the spring of 1987 when it was revealed that Toshiba Machine Co. had sold sophisticated milling equipment for submarines to the USSR in violation of CoCom (Coordinating Committee for Export Control) restrictions.[61] After the incident, the Japanese government and business community were more mindful of rising anti-Japanese sentiment, in the US and elsewhere, over Japanese business practices.

During most of the 1980s all major Japanese general trading firms (*sogo-shosha*) established dummy firms in Vietnam to carry out business activities under disguised names to keep a low profile in the country. Unlike the United States, Japan did not impose trade sanctions on the SRV as a reprisal for the overthrow of Pol Pot's government and thus trade between Tokyo and Hanoi continued. However, Japanese trading firms were afraid that if they openly engaged in trade with Vietnam, their business activities in the United States would be adversely affected by possible retaliatory measures by the US Congress. For example, Mitsui Co., one of the largest Japanese *sogo-shosha*, created a shadow company named Shinwa Co. to continue trade with Vietnam.[62] Fear of American retaliation reached a peak in September 1987, when the US Senate passed the Kasten Resolution, condemning Japanese economic activities in Vietnam and urging the Japanese government to persuade firms to refrain from trading with Vietnam. The Kasten Resolution singled out Japanese business activities in Vietnam and ignored those of other countries, such as France, Malaysia, and Thailand. As such, it created resentment among the Japanese business community, which perceived the resolution as a part of 'Japan-bashing' exercise rather than as a reflection of genuine concerns over the presence of Vietnamese forces in Cambodia.[63] However, Japanese firms could not ignore this resolution. Honda Motors, for example, voluntarily abandoned its plan for a motorcycle assembly plant in Ho Chi Minh City for fear of risking its US market.

For the ten years following the 1979 Vietnamese invasion of Cambodia, Japan reacted passively to political developments in Indochina. While Japan never abandoned the idea of taking a leadership role in Indochina throughout the 1980s, there was little Tokyo could do other than adjust itself to the rapidly changing international environment. Political developments in the world, and specifically in Indochina, were beyond Japan's control. Despite the lack of legal restrictions on Japanese firms, Japan refrained from openly seeking an economic role in Vietnam. American pressure kept Japan self-contained politically and economically in the region.

Revival of pursuit of activism toward the SRV (1989– present)

Cambodian peace process and aftermath

With the end of the Cold War, the political situation in Indochina rapidly changed in the late 1980s. The largest factor for the change was that with the demise of the Soviet bloc, Vietnam no longer appeared a threat to the capitalist Southeast Asia. Hanoi completely withdrew the PAVN from Cambodia in 1989 and tried to concentrate on its own economic development through a national policy of *doi moi* (renovation) adopted in 1986. The changing political climate in Southeast Asia was perhaps best expressed by Thailand's Prime Minister Chatichai Choonhavan, who stated in August 1988 that Indochina should be transformed 'from a battlefield to a trading market'. Chatichai's statement indicated Thailand's changing attitude from hard-line to moderation toward the SRV and the Phnom Penh government now led by Hun Sen. The international environment was becoming favourable to a settlement of the Cambodian conflict. In September 1988, peace negotiations began in Indonesia among Cambodia's four warring factions: Hun Sen's Kampuchean People's Revolutionary Party (KPRP), Prince Sihanouk's FUNCINPEC, Son Sann's KPNLF, and Pol Pot's PDK.

The end of the Cold War had another profound impact on Japanese policy toward Indochina. Washington's interest in the Cambodian conflict declined as the issue had little meaning to Washington in the post-Cold War era. With the demise of the Soviet Union, the United States was less worried about possible communist expansion in Southeast Asia. The new US attitude toward Cambodia set Tokyo free from previous constraints on its policies. Given the declining US influence in the region, Japanese leaders began to seek ways to act independently of the United States in pursuit of Tokyo's own political and economic interests.

The Cambodian peace negotiations from the late 1980s to the early 1990s became Tokyo's first litmus test for political activism in Indochina in the post-Cold War era. Also, a settlement of the Cambodian conflict was a necessary condition for improved relations between Japan and the SRV. From the late 1980s Tokyo tried to establish itself as a legitimate participant in the Cambodian peace process along with the ASEAN countries, Australia,[64] and the five permanent members of the UN Security Council ('Perm Five'). Japan first indicated its interest in the

Cambodian peace process in August 1988, when it invited Prince Sihanouk to Tokyo as a national guest to discuss peace resolution for Cambodia. In May 1989, Prime Minister Takeshita Noboru stated during his ASEAN tour that Japan was willing to offer assistance in resolving the Cambodian conflict. At the Paris Peace Conference in July 1989, the Japanese delegation lobbied for a greater role for Japan and accepted co-chairmanship of the Standing Commission on Cambodian Reconstruction and Refugees. In February 1990, Japan's MFA unofficially sent its diplomat, Kono Masaharu in the Southeast Asia Division, to Phnom Penh to meet with Hun Sen and other government officials. Kono's visit to Cambodia represented Tokyo's first contact with the Phnom Penh government since its establishment in 1979. Kono's mission signalled to Hun Sen that Tokyo was moving towards a recognition of Phnom Penh as the *de facto* government of Cambodia. After Kono's meeting with Hun Sen, Tokyo ended its support for the anti-Hun Sen tripartite coalition of FUNCINPEC, KPNLF, and PDK[65] and launched diplomatic efforts to seek a peaceful solution in Cambodia. These efforts included:

1 co-hosting a conference with Thailand for the four rival Cambodian factions in June 1990;
2 offering a new proposal to the Cambodian factions in March 1991 to complement the comprehensive peace plan developed the previous year by the Perm Five;
3 sending the SDF in the PKO of UNTAC from September 1992 to May 1993;
4 providing the world's largest financial contribution for the operations of UNTAC in March 1992–May 1993; and
5 convening a Ministerial Conference on the Rehabilitation and Reconstruction of Cambodia in June 1992 to co-ordinate international economic assistance for the war-torn society.

Of these five Japanese achievements in the Cambodian peace process in the early 1990s, the first and the third – hosting the Tokyo Conference and sending the SDF to Cambodia – were especially significant in Tokyo's Indochina policy. These measures did not represent the usual Japanese 'chequebook diplomacy' and they thus helped Tokyo gain political capital for its peacemaking role.[66] At the Tokyo Conference on the Cambodian Settlement in June 1990, the Japanese government demonstrated that it would not only finance the reconstruction of war-torn Cambodia but also participate actively in helping promote and guide the peace process. The conference had been proposed by Thailand's Prime Minister Chatichai to Japanese Prime Minister Kaifu Toshiki in April 1990 to invite the Cambodian factions to negotiate for a peaceful settlement. Although Khmer Rouge spokesperson Khieu Samphan boycotted the conference,[67] Prince Sihanouk and Hun Sen participated and decided that the tripartite coalition (FUNCINPEC, KPNLF, and PDK) and the Phnom Penh government (KPRP) would share equal representation in the Supreme National Council (SNC).[68] The decision on the two party representation at the SNC was significant, as it became the basic framework of the SNC throughout the years of UNTAC's rule in Cambodia.[69]

The deployment of the SDF to Cambodia marked a milestone in Japanese foreign policy, as it became the first dispatch of Japanese military forces overseas in the post-World War II era, making an important precedent for further military participation by Tokyo in international conflicts. The Japanese Diet passed a PKO bill in June 1992 to allow Japanese SDF to provide logistical support to UNTAC, an operation headed by a Japanese UN diplomat, Akashi Yasushi. Although the issue of sending SDF overseas incited the Japanese left to organise large demonstrations, the deployment proceeded anyway and the Japanese government showed that Japan was willing to join in international peace-making efforts by sending its own troops to the world's conflict zones. At the same time, the Japanese use of military forces was limited because of the strict application of the PKO bill. This bill limited SDF missions to traditional peace keeping operations (e.g., use of weapons only for self-defence) and humanitarian assistance. These limitations on military deployment indicated that military strategies were not replacing Japan's spending strategies.

Tokyo's participation in the Cambodian peace process was not free from international criticism. Some Western observers accused Japan of being more interested in enhancing its political standing rather than resolving a stalemate between the Cambodian government and opposition factions. They claimed that Tokyo hastily joined the peace process to compensate for its diplomatic blunder in its response to the Gulf War and to gain approval for its membership of the UN Security Council.[70]

In fact, though, Japan did not act hastily or aggressively. When Japan started testing the international waters in search of its appropriate role in the Cambodian peace process, Tokyo acted cautiously rather than taking abrupt or bold steps to overturn the current established state of affairs in Indochina. According to Cronin, 'after years of avoiding the political limelight, Japan is moving cautiously but steadily to play a political and diplomatic role more commensurate with its economic strength'.[71] This cautious approach is reflected in Japan's desire not to stir suspicion that Tokyo might have military intentions in Southeast Asia.

Since the 1993 UNTAC-sponsored general elections in Cambodia, Japan has continued to play an important diplomatic role in that country. When the political climate in Cambodia grew volatile in June 1997, with the two prime ministers – First Prime Minister Prince Norodom Ranariddh (FUNCINPEC) and Second Prime Minister Hun Sen (the Cambodian People's Party or the CPP) – in conflict, Tokyo immediately sent Sachio Imagawa, former Japanese ambassador to Cambodia and Japan's top advisor on the country, to Phnom Penh to represent the Group of Seven (G–7) nations. Following Hun Sen's coup d'etat and ouster of Prince Ranariddh in July 1997, Tokyo has been trying to broker a settlement between Hun Sen's government and the prince. Japan has become an active member of a Friends of Cambodia group consisting of several aid donor countries in Cambodia such as the United States, France, and Australia. In January 1998, Japan proposed a peace plan to Hun Sen and Ranariddh to end fighting in Cambodia and to pave a way towards the expected general elections in July 1998.[72] The international community, including the Friends of Cambodia and ASEAN, has fully supported the Japanese peace plan and has pressured Hun Sen and Ranariddh to accept the deal, to which they eventually agreed. The Japanese plan has provided an important step toward a peaceful settlement in Cambodia and stability in Southeast Asia.

Resumption of ODA

The progress of the Cambodian peace process served to thaw the freeze on Japanese bilateral aid to Vietnam. In 1992, Japan resumed its ODA to Vietnam after a series of negotiations with the United States. Due to unresolved MIA (Missing in Action) problems between Washington and Hanoi, the United States had originally opposed Japanese aid resumption. It was only after Japanese Foreign Minister Watanabe Michio intervened directly in the US–Japan negotiations and also persuaded Vietnamese Foreign Minister Nguyen Manh Cam to move forward with the MIA issue that the United States finally gave tacit approval to the Japanese government to restart aid. As it was, the United States requested Japan to announce its ODA resumption plan after the 1992 US presidential election; Japan did so within a week after the election.[73] This case illustrates how Japan's relations with the SRV were influenced by US–Japan relations, particularly by US *gaiatsu* on Japan. As soon as the American *gaiatsu* declined, Japan moved rapidly toward proactivism.

The 1992 resumption of ODA to Hanoi illustrates how Japan has used its spending strategy to achieve its diplomatic goals in the second proactive period. Tokyo restarted full-scale bilateral ODA to Hanoi for the first time in 13 years with ¥45.5 billion ($275.81 million).[74] The amount of the 1992 ODA disbursement was roughly equivalent to the debts Tokyo claimed that the South Vietnamese government had owed to it prior to the unification of Vietnam in 1975. This financial aid was given in exchange for Hanoi's payment of South Vietnam's leftover debts. The aid resumption was highly political and a significant step toward proactivism because it indicated that Tokyo would improve bilateral relations with Hanoi at the time that the United States, Japan's strongest ally, still had an economic embargo against Vietnam. At the same time, the resumption sent a strong signal to the Japanese private sector to move forward with trade and investment in Vietnam. Since the 1992 resumption of ODA, Tokyo has become the largest aid donor to Vietnam. Japan's strong interest in the SRV was further demonstrated by the 'Miyazawa Initiative', an aid plan proposed by Finance Minister Miyazawa Kiichi to revitalise Southeast Asian economies hit by the 1997 Asian financial crisis. Although Vietnam was relatively unaffected by the crisis due to its underdeveloped market economy, Japan extended the Miyazawa Initiative to Vietnam and awarded the SRV about $160 million in loans in addition to regular ODA allotments.[75]

MULTILATERAL DEVELOPMENT PLANS

Japan's economic strategy has also been extended to multilateral arrangements in which Japan has wielded its spending power not only for narrow economic aims but also for wider political goals, such as gaining international prestige and recognition. In Cambodia, Japan has exerted leadership in organising a International Committee on the Reconstruction of Cambodia (ICORC) in order to co-ordinate foreign aid to Phnom Penh. ICORC was established at the Ministerial Conference on the Rehabilitation and Reconstruction of Cambodia in June 1992 to oversee the aid programme. Japan has served as chair since the first ICORC meeting in Paris in September 1993. In Vietnam, Japan worked with France in April 1993 in proposing granting Vietnam access to the IMF loans; the two countries eventually paid off Hanoi's debts to IMF in order to restart loans to Hanoi. Japan's interest in the economic reconstruction in Indochina was further underscored by its role in the Mekong River Commission (MRC), which was re-established in 1995 from its predecessor, the Mekong Committee (MC).[76] The MRC has been promoting the development of the Mekong River region since its establishment in 1995. Japan has been one of the main financial contributors to the organisation. The current chief executive officer of the MRC is a Japanese bureaucrat, Matoba Yasunobu, from the Ministry of Agriculture, Forestry and Fishery.

Recently, Japan's policy toward Indochina has merged with its ASEAN policy as the whole of Indochina is moving toward 'ASEANisation'. Vietnam joined the organisation in 1995, followed by Laos and Cambodia in 1997 and 1999, respectively. Japan's main goal in Southeast Asia has not changed since the 1970s: to accelerate the integration of Indochina into the ASEAN market. Tokyo welcomed the new membership of Vietnam and Laos in the ASEAN and hopes that Cambodia will soon follow their footsteps.

Of the three nations in Indochina, Vietnam is most involved in multilateral regionalism and has the most contacts with Japan. Along with Laos, Vietnam became a member of the ASEAN Regional Forum (ARF) upon the admission to the ASEAN. The ARF is a forum set up by the ASEAN in 1994 for discussing security in Asia and its members are the ASEAN, Japan, the United States, and China. Vietnam is also expected to participate in the Asia Pacific Economic Co-operation (APEC) in the end of 1998. Japan fully supports Hanoi's integration into these regional multilateral institutions.

The revival of the Fukuda Doctrine? Some observers of Japanese foreign policy believe there has been a revival of the principles of the Fukuda Doctrine in the 1990s, as Japan has once again pursued an active, independent role in Southeast Asian politics.[77] Japan's current policy goals are generally similar to those of its first proactive period of the 1970s. As before, Japan now hopes to accelerate the integration of Indochina into the rest of Southeast Asia, to maintain regional peace and stability in the region, and to increase Japan's economic and political influence in the region predominantly by means of spending strategies. To achieve these goals, Tokyo also tries to ensure its Asian neighbours that it will not become a military power in the region.

According to Soeya, the revival of the Fukuda Doctrine was first signalled by Prime Minister Kaifu during his ASEAN tour in May 1991.[78] In a speech in Singapore Kaifu expressed Japan's strong interest in assuming a greater political role in Asia. He stated that there was considerable expectation, in the international community, for Japan to make greater contributions in the Asian region, not only in the economic sphere but also in the political sphere. Kaifu stressed Japan's role in searching for a solution to the conflict in Cambodia as an appropriate role for Japan in the political sphere,.[79] At the same time, Kaifu apologised to the ASEAN audience for the Imperial Japanese Army's actions during World War II by expressing 'sincere contrition at Japanese past actions which inflicted unbearable suffering on a great many people of the Asia Pacific region'.[80] The timing for such a speech was appropriate. Responding to the diplomatic debacle in the Gulf War, the Japanese government decided in April 1991, a few weeks before Kaifu's speech, to dispatch SDF mine-sweepers to the Gulf region, the first operational mission beyond Japanese territorial waters since the end of World War II.[81] The content and tone of Kaifu's speech were basically the same as those of Fukuda's 1977 statement. Kaifu reiterated two of the principles of the Fukuda Doctrine of 1977: Japan would take on a political role in contributing to regional stability in Asia, particularly in Indochina, and Japan vowed never again to become a military power. According to a Singaporean diplomat, Kaifu's statement represented a cautious, step-by-step approach to gaining Asian support for Japan's larger political role.[82]

The Japanese government issued another similar statement in January 1993, when Prime Minister Miyazawa Kiichi visited Bangkok during his ASEAN tour. Miyazawa indicated Japan's interest in promoting the integration of Indochina into the ASEAN-led market and proposed that Japan and ASEAN cooperate together in the economic reconstruction of Indochina. The regional co-operation would include such areas as transport and communications and developing human resources. In the speech Miyazawa proposed the establishment of a Forum for Comprehensive Development of Indochina (known as 'the Indochina Forum'), including ASEAN members and other countries in an effort to bring economic prosperity to the war ravaged Indochina. Miyazawa's statement on Japan's role in Indochina, however, was intentionally kept low-key, as Tokyo was aware of uneasiness felt by some Asian leaders toward the resurgence of Japanese power in the region.[83]

In January 1997, Prime Minister Hashimoto Ryutaro tried to further reinforce Japan's role in Indochina during his visit to Southeast Asia. He made a speech in Singapore, again reminiscent of Fukuda's doctrine of 20 years before. Hashimoto reiterated that the 'heart-to-heart' co-operation between Japan and the ASEAN for the last twenty years had built the foundation of Southeast Asia's rapid economic growth and called for further intense co-operation with ASEAN into the twenty-first century.[84] Hashimoto went on to propose that Japan–ASEAN relations be elevated via a summit-level forum that would regularly discuss security, trade, and investment. Hashimoto's proposal indicated that Japan would plan to be a much more vigorous foreign policy actor in Asia. At the same time, Hashimoto emphasised that the US–Japan alliance would remain the core of Japanese foreign policy and that Japan's commitment to the US role in Asia had not changed in the post-Cold War era.[85] Hashimoto's speech revealed Tokyo's long-standing aspirations of taking initiatives in Asia and also cementing the foundation of co-operation with the United States.

Whether Japan succeeds in pursuing initiatives to contribute to Southeast Asia's stability and development while accommodating American policy in the region is yet to be determined. The Fukuda Doctrine withered in the 1980s due to US pressure on Japan to curtail contacts with the SRV in the midst of heightened Cold War tensions. Is Japan's current regionalism destined to follow the same fate? The answer to this depends on how Tokyo manages its dual relations with Asia and the United States. Japan needs to conduct a balancing act between its own desire to play an independent role in Asia and its obligation to maintain the fundamental framework of US–Japan co-operation in Asia.[86] The balancing act becomes especially difficult when the United States poses *gaiatsu* on Japan's pursuit of an active foreign policy. If the constraints are insurmountable, Japan gives up its own desire in order to accommodate US needs. The balancing act becomes easier when US *gaiatsu* is at a minimum. With the end of the Cold War, we may expect US *gaiatsu* to decline but the reality is that there are a host of other bilateral and international issues that could result in increased US pressure in the future.

Conclusion

This analysis of Japan–Vietnam relations shows the difference between reactivist perspectives and a hybrid reactivist/proactivist perspective. Reactivist and hybrid approaches share in common the recognition of the key role of US *gaiatsu* in influencing Japanese foreign policy; indeed, the focus on the impact of US *gaiatsu* is the main strength of the reactivist perspective.

Yet these two views differ in their analysis of what happens during periods of limited US *gaiatsu*. The reactivist school would have us believe that in the absence of *gaiatsu* Japan takes no initiatives on its own. Yet an analysis of Japan–Vietnam relations shows that this is not the case. Japan has consistently sought to take a proactive policy toward the SRV, making definite (albeit cautious) efforts to pursue its economic and political interests through foreign policy during periods of limited *gaiatsu*. It is only during periods of intense US *gaiatsu* that Japan has reverted to a reactive stance. Japanese foreign policy toward the SRV is thus characterised by an alternation between reactivism and proactivism rather than a simple reactivism.

The hybrid model of reactivism and proactivism takes place within the framework of Japan's dual relations with the United States and Asia. In the case of Japan–SRV relations, Japan pursued an active policy toward Vietnam when the United States did not exert strong pressure on Tokyo not to do so. When serious conflicts of interest arose between Japan and the United States, Washington exerted strong *gaiatsu* on Japan and Japan gave up its independent policy in the SRV. The dual linkages of Japan with Asia and the United States requires Tokyo to take a careful balancing act between the two and Tokyo's active regional policy occurs when the balance is maintained.

This hybrid approach toward understanding Japan–Vietnam relations still leaves many questions unanswered – for example, the relationship between the intended policies, implemented policies, and impact of Japanese proactivism toward Vietnam – but recognising the coexistence of reactivism and proactivism is a necessary first step toward addressing these broader questions. At the same time, further study is required to indicate whether and to what extent this hybrid reactivist/proactivist model also holds true in Japan's foreign policy in other regions of the world.

Notes

This chpater is a revised version of an articel published as 'Japan as a reactive state? Analysing relations with the Socialist Republic of Vietnam', *Japanese Studies*, vol. 18, no. 2, 1988.

1 See for example, Calder, K., 'Japanese Foreign Economic Policy Formation: Explaining the Reactive State', *World Politics*, vol. 40, July 1988; Lincoln, Edward J., *Japan's New Global Role*, The Brookings Institution, Washington, DC 1993; Hellmann, D., 'Japanese Politics and Foreign Policy: Elitist Democracy Within An American Green House', in Takashi Inoguchi and Daniel I. Okimoto (eds), *The Political Economy of Japan: vol. 2: The Changing International Context*, Stanford University Press, Berkeley, CA, 1988; Hellmann, D., 'The Confrontation with Realpolitik', in James Morley (ed.), *Forecast for Japan: Security in the 1970s* Princeton University Press, Princeton, NJ, 1972; Blaker, M 'Evaluating Japan's diplomatic performance', in Gerald L. Curtis (ed.), *Japan's Foreign Policy After the Cold War: Coping with Change*, M.E. Sharpe, Armonk, NY, 1993.

2 See Yasutomo, D., *The New Multilateralism in Japan's Foreign Policy*, St. Martin's Press, New York, 1995, chapter 2. Yasutomo discusses four main tenets of the reactivist approach:

(1) the external origin of reactivity;
(2) the United States as the primary locus of reactivity;
(3) the immobile domestic policymaking process as the fundamental causes of reactivity; and
(4) the scope of reactiveness as both foreign economic policy and political-strategic diplomacy.

3 See Hellmann, 'The Confrontation with Realpolitik', 1972; Blaker, 'Evaluating Japan's diplomatic performance', 1993.

4 Lincoln, *Japan's New Global Role*, 1993.

5 Hellmann, 'Japanese Politics and Foreign Policy', 1988.

6 Hellmann, 'Japanese Politics and Foreign Policy', 1988, p. 358.

7 Funabashi, Y., 'Japan and the New World Order', *Foreign Affairs*, vol. 70, no. 5, Winter 1991–92, p. 61.

8 Calder, 'Japanese Foreign Economic Policy Formation', 1988, p. 519.

9 Calder, 'Japanese Foreign Economic Policy Formation', 1988, p. 520.

10 Calder, 'Japanese Foreign Economic Policy Formation', 1988.

11 Blaker, 'Evaluating Japan's diplomatic performance', 1993, p. 3.

12 Calder, 'Japanese Foreign Economic Policy Formation', 1988, p. 519.

13 Blaker, 'Evaluating Japan's diplomatic performance', 1993, p. 4.

14 Lincoln, *Japan's New Global Role*, 1993. Failing to recognise how serious the crisis was, Japan initially hesitated to contribute financially to the allied forces. In August 1990 Tokyo pledged a mere $1 billion. In September of the same year, following intense US pressure, Japan reluctantly announced that it would provide an additional $3 billion. It was only in March 1992, well after the actual end of the war, that the Japanese Diet passed a bill authorising a $9 billion contribution for the Desert Storm Operations.

15 See for example, Yasutomo, D., *The Manner of Giving: Strategic Aid and Japanese Foreign Policy*, Lexington Books, Lexington, MA, 1986.

16 Soeya, Y., 'Jishu Gaiko in Action', *The Woodrow Wilson Center Asia Programme Occasional Paper*, no. 64, 8 June 1994.

17 Soeya, 'Jishu Gaiko in Action, 1994.

18 Yasutomo, *The New Multilateralism in Japan's Foreign Policy*, 1995, p. 57.

19 Schoppa, Leonard J., *Bargaining with Japan: What American Pressure Can and Cannot Do*, Columbia University Press, New York, 1997, p. 36.

20 See Nakatomi, H., *Jikkan Betonamu Keizai*, Nihon Hyoronsha, Tokyo, 1995; and Nakahara, M., *Betonamu e no Michi*, Shakai shisosha, Tokyo, 1995.

21 Morrison, C., 'Southeast Asia and US–Japan Relations', in Gerald Curtis (ed.), *The United States, Japan, and Asia: Challenges for US Policy* , New York: W. W. Norton & Company, 1994.

22 Baldwin, David A., *Economic Statecraft*, Princeton University Press, Princeton, NJ, 1985. Baldwin explains that statecraft refers to the selection of means for the pursuit of foreign policy. Economic statecraft has negative and positive sanctions. The negative sanctions include embargo, boycott and tariff increase. The positive sanctions include tariff reduction and granting 'most-favoured-nation' treatment. Economic strategies can be used to pursue various goals of a state. They can be used to pursue only economic ends, or for other purposes such as political, psychological, and military goals.

23 Wan, M., *Spending Strategies in World Politics: How Japan Used Its Economic Power 1952–1992*, unpublished doctoral dissertation, Harvard University, 1993. Wan distinguishes spending from earning strategies. He refers to spending as a means to influence other nations with wealth, whereas earning aims at accumulating wealth.

24 See for example, Lincoln, *Japan's New Global Role*, 1993, chapter 6. Lincoln points out the limits of Japan's economic power particularly at a time of crises. '(N)ot all of the world's problems are economic, and the nation (Japan) still faces a major question: how to participate more fully in solving international political problems or crises' (p. 201).

25 Havens, Thomas R.H., *Fire Across the Sea: The Vietnam War and Japan 1965–1975*, Princeton University Press, Princeton, NJ, 1987.

26 Shiraishi, M., *Japanese Relations with Vietnam*, Cornell University Press, New York, 1990, p. 4.

27 Havens, *Fire Across the Sea*, 1987.

28 Havens, *Fire Across the Sea*, 1987.

29 Havens, *Fire Across the Sea*, 1987.

30 Shiraishi, *Japanese Relations with Vietnam*, 1990.

31 The JVTA was established in 1955 by Nakahara Mitsunobu and his associates, who had fought in World War II as Japanese soldiers in Vietnam, and then remained in Vietnam and fought in the First Indochina War as Viet Minh soldiers. Interview, General Manager of Representative in Hanoi, JVTA, May 1997; Nakahara, *Betonamu e no Michi*, 1995.

32 Nakahara, *Betonamu e no Michi*, 1995.

33 Kuroda, Y., 'Japan and the Israeli–Palestinian Conflict', in Edward Lincoln (ed.), *Japan and the Middle East*, The Middle East Institute, Washington, DC, 1990, pp. 40–9.

34 Tomoda, S., *Nyumon Gendai Nihon Gaiko: Nitchu Kokko Seijoka Igo*, Chuo shinsho, Tokyo, 1988.

35 Shiraishi, *Japanese Relations with Vietnam*, 1990, p. 72.

36 Tomoda, S., 'Taietsu Enjo Saikai no Keii to Haikei', *Asia University Asia Research Project Report*, March 1997.

37 Shiraishi, *Japanese Relations with Vietnam*, 1990.

38 Between 1973 and 1975, Japan had diplomatic relations with two Vietnams: DRV in the North and the Republic of Vietnam (ROV) in the South.

39 Shiraishi, *Japanese Relations with Vietnam*, 1990.

40 Miyazawa, K., 'Saikin no Kokusai josei to Nihon no Gaiko: Indoshinahanto no Kyuhen o Chushin ni', *Asia Jiho*, September 1975, p. 7, translated and cited in Shiraishi, *Japanese Relations with Vietnam*, 1990, pp. 70–1.

41 Shiraishi, *Japanese Relations with Vietnam*, 1990, p. 55.

42 Shiraishi, *Japanese Relations with Vietnam*, 1990.

43 Shiraishi, *Japanese Relations with Vietnam*, 1990.

44 Shiraishi, *Japanese Relations with Vietnam*, 1990, p. 53.

45 Shiraishi, *Japanese Relations with Vietnam*, 1990, p. 55.

46 Soeya, 'Vietnam in Japan's Regional Policy', in James W. Morley and Masashi Nishihara (eds), *Vietnam Joins the World*, M.E. Sharpe, New York, 1997, p. 179.

47 Soeya, 'Jishu Gaiko in Action', 1994, p. 1.

48 Sudo, S., *The Fukuda Doctrine and ASEAN: New Dimensions in Japanese Foreign Policy*, Institute of Southeast Asian Studies, Singapore, 1992.

49   *Japan Times*, 19 August 1977, p. 14.
50   Sudo, *The Fukuda Doctrine and ASEAN*, 1992.
51   Soeya, 'Vietnam in Japan's Regional Policy', 1997, p. 180.
52   Tomoda, *Nyumon Gendai Nihon Gaiko*, 1988. For a detailed account of US decision-making of the normalisation with the SRV under the Carter administration, see Chanda, N., *Brother Enemy: The War After the War*, Collier Books, New York, 1986. Chanda delineates conflicts between the State Department and the National Security Council over Vietnam policy.
53   Tomoda, 'Taietsu Enjo Saikai no Keii to Haikei', 1997.
54   Sonoda, S., 'Nihon Gaiko no Tenkan o Kokoromite', *Chuo Koron Keiei Mondai*, March 1980, translated and cited in Shiraishi, *Japanese Relations with Vietnam*, 1990, p. 71.
55   Some MFA officials felt they had been betrayed by Vietnamese officials. In December 1978 they had asked Vietnamese officials for a peaceful resolution of the Cambodian conflict because there was a rumour that Vietnamese forces were planning an attack on Cambodia. In reply Vietnamese officials had promised the Japanese government that Vietnamese forces would not enter Cambodia. Two weeks later their 'promise' was broken. See Tomoda, 'Taietsu Enjo Saikai no Keii to Haikei', 1997.
56   Tomoda, *Nyumon Gendai Nihon Gaiko*, 1988.
57   *The Asahi Shimbun*, 2, 16, 17, 22, 23 August 1979, cited in Shiraishi, *Japanese Relations with Vietnam*, 1990.
58   Tomoda, 'Taietsu Enjo Saikai no Keii to Haikei', 1997.
59   Tomoda, *Nyumon Gendai Nihon Gaiko*; 1988; Komori, Y., 'Okoreru Amerika to 'Kiku to Katana'', *Bungei Shunju*, February 1980, pp. 114–23.
60   Shiraishi, *Japanese Relations with Vietnam*, 1990.
61   Tomoda, *Nyumon Gendai Nihon Gaiko*, 1988.
62   These trading houses quietly conducted business activities in Vietnam via the JVTA, which had close ties with the SRV. Interview, General Manager of Representative in Hanoi, JVTA, May 1997.
63   Awanohara, S., and Charles Morrison, 'Looking Beyond Cambodia: Japan and Vietnam', *Indochina Issues*, August 1989.
64   Australian Foreign Minister Gareth Evans played a significant role in making a proposal for creating an international peacekeeping operation in Cambodia, a model on which UNTAC was based.
65   Ikeda, T., 'Kanbojia Wahei e no Michi: Tai to no Kyodo Sagyo', *Gaiko Forum*, no. 81, January 1995, pp. 88–95; Tomoda, S., 'Japan's Search for a Political Role in Asia: The Cambodian Peace Settlement', *Japan Review of International Affairs*, vol. 6, no. 1, September 1992, pp. 43–60.
66   Japan's proposed peace plan provided for step-by-step monitoring of a cease-fire, the rejection of participation in the 1993 elections by any faction violating the Paris Agreement of 1991, and the establishment of a special body to investigate human rights violations during the Pol Pot's rule in 1975–78. However, the proposal failed as none of the Cambodian factions supported it. See Tomoda, 'Japan's Search for a Political Role in Asia', 1992.
67   Khieu Samphan boycotted the conference because the Khmer Rouge opposed the two-party representation at the SNC. The Khmer Rouge insisted that each of the four factions should have an equal representation at the SNC. Khieu Samphan was vice-president of the CGDK, and Sihanouk was president. The Prince broke ranks with the Khmer Rouge and participated in the Tokyo Conference as a private citizen. See Tomoda, 'Japan's Search for a Political Role in Asia', 1992.
68   Tomiyama, Y., *Kanbojia Senki*, Chuko shinsho, Tokyo, 1992.
69   Zagoria, Donald S., 'The Great Powers and Indochina', in Dick Clark (ed.), *The Challenge of Indochina: An Examination of the US Role*, The Aspen Institute, Queenstown, MD, 19–21 April 1991, pp. 34–5.
70   Hiebert, M., and Louise do Rosario, 'Japan Poised to Play Role in Reviving Indochina: Waiting in the Wings', *Far Eastern Economic Review*, 30 May 1991, pp. 68–9.
71   Cronin, Richard P., *Japan, the United States, and Prospects for the Asia–Pacific Century: Three Scenarios for the Future*, St. Martin's Press, New York, p. 57.

72 The peace proposal consisted of four principles: (1) the renunciation by FUNCINPEC of any ties with the Khmer Rouge; (2) a cease-fire between Hun Sen's and Ranariddh's troops and the reintegration of the latter into the former; (3) the conclusion of a trial in absentia of Ranariddh and a royal pardon granted by Sihanouk that would allow his son Ranariddh to participate in the elections; and (4) the safety of Ranariddh's return and full participation of opposition parties in the political activities for the elections. *The Japan Times Weekly International Edition*, 9–15 February 1998, p. 3.

73 Tomoda, 'Taietsu Enjo Saikai no Keii to Haikei', 1997.

74 The Ministry of Foreign Affairs, *Japan's ODA Annual Report: 1995*, The Association for the Promotion of International Cooperation, Tokyo, 1996, p. 42.

75 'Japan Includes Vietnam in Asian Aid Initiative', *The Nikkei Weekly*, 24 May 1999.

76 The MC was established in 1957 by Thailand, Vietnam, Cambodia, and Laos under the auspices of UN's regional body, the Economic Commission for Asia and the Far East (ESCAP). The current MRC has the same original members of the MC. See OECF, *OECF Newsletter*, August 1996.

77 Soeya 'Jishu Gaiko in Action', 1994; Tomoda, 'Japan's Search for a Political Role in Asia', 1992.

78 Soeya 'Jishu Gaiko in Action', 1994.

79 Vatikiotis, M., 'The Gentle Giant: Kaifu Soothes Fears Over Japan's Political Plans', *Far Eastern Economic Review*, 16 May 1991, pp. 11–12.

80 Vatikiotis, 'The Gentle Giant', 1991, p. 11.

81 Delfs, R., 'To the Gulf, at Last', *Far Eastern Economic Review*, 9 May 1991, p. 19.

82 Vatikiotis, 'The Gentle Giant', 1991.

83 Delfs, R. and Michael Vatikiotis, 'Low Key Diplomacy: Miyazawa Treads Delicate Path in Region', *Far Eastern Economic Review*, 14 January 1993, pp. 11, 14.

84 'Heart to Heart: First Clean Your Own House', *Asia Times*, 14 January 1997, p. 8.

85 Kato, C., 'Nichibei Ampo Taisei o Chushi', *The Asahi Shimbun*, 30 April 1997.

86 Soeya, 'Jishu Gaiko in Action', 1994.

7 Japan's diplomatic initiatives in Southeast Asia

Lam Peng Er

Despite a desire to play a more active role in international affairs commensurate with its economic superpower status, many analysts have labelled Japan as a passive and reactive state.[1] This image stems from a constellation of factors: the stereotype that Japan is essentially a merchant state which avoids entanglements in areas of potential armed conflict; that it is an incomplete superpower which heavily depends on the US for its security; persistent regional allergy to Tokyo's leadership role due to its burden of history; that it is not a permanent member of the United Nations Security Council; and the considerable domestic hurdles to an active stance in regional affairs. These internal obstacles include constitutional constraint (Article 9, the no-war clause of the constitution), mass pacifism, a critical news media, the paralysis of an unstable coalition government, vociferous opposition parties, the weak office of the Prime Minister, a poor crisis management system, and the national malaise that grips the country's political, social and economic systems.

The impediments are formidable but, I argue, that Japan has still been able to undertake diplomatic initiatives to address politico-strategic instability in Southeast Asia. It neither adopts a low profile nor confines itself exclusively to economic interests in that region. Driven by its desire for status and security, Tokyo is increasingly seeking a higher political profile in Southeast Asia. In January 1997, at the end of a five-nation visit to Southeast Asia, Prime Minister Hashimoto Ryutaro articulated the so-called Hashimoto Doctrine in Singapore. He emphasised that Japan was prepared to co-operate with the ASEAN countries on a wide spectrum of issues beyond economics, such as issues of environmental protection, anti-terrorism, intellectual and cultural exchanges, and the AIDs problem. The message was that Japan was shedding its traditional allergy to strategic and military issues. Hashimoto not only proposed a regular political summit between Japan and ASEAN countries but also bilateral discussions about security matters. In the same month, Murata Naoaki, Administrative Vice Minister of the JDA (Japan Defense Agency), visited several regional countries and secured agreements with the governments of Indonesia, Thailand and Singapore to hold periodic bilateral security dialogues.[2] In December, the first Japan–ASEAN summit of top political leaders was held in Kuala Lumpur. This flurry of activity in Southeast Asia demonstrated Tokyo's keenness to be seen as assuming a higher political and strategic profile in this region.

Of course, the Japanese government has not neglected economic diplomacy. In the wake of the East Asian financial crisis and currency meltdown in 1997–98, in South Korea, Thailand and Indonesia, Foreign Minister Obuchi Keizo committed Japan to extending an unprecedented financial aid package of US$42 billion.[3] Winding up his three nation tour to Thailand, Malaysia and Singapore, Obuchi, in his May 1998 speech titled 'Japan and East Asia: Outlook for the New Millennium' delivered in Singapore, said:

> Geography and history have linked Japan and the rest of East Asia closely. We have developed increasingly interdependent relations in the recent years. I decided to make this trip in the hope that we can all join hands to deal successfully with the currency and financial turmoil and the difficulties that beset this region … As the largest economy in Asia, Japan feels a responsibility, despite its own very difficult situation, to do everything it can to help its East Asian friends through this time of economic trial. To date, we have contributed, both in international efforts led by IMF and in bilateral programmes, a total of about 37 billion dollars – a sum that far exceeds the assistance from any extra-regional country. We will continue to exercise the leadership to support the East Asian countries in co-operation with the international community. We also intend to tailor our efforts to address the needs of the region's less developed countries hit by the economic difficulties … These economic measures also include an additional 700 billion yen or about 5.4 billion dollars in support for the Asian economies. Among them are the Export–Import Bank financing to facilitate trade financing, ODA loans to support economic reform, technical assistance for human resources development, and assistance in food and medical supplies to Indonesia and elsewhere.[4]

Foreign Minister Obuchi's commitments in Southeast Asia went beyond economics and ODA. He expressed Japan's desire to promote regional stability through the US–Japan Alliance and the ASEAN Regional Forum, assisting and ensuring free and fair election in Cambodia, and by addressing regional environmental problems. Obuchi proposed an environmental and intellectual leadership role in the region for Japan:

> The forest fires and the haze problem that are raging in this region aggravated by El Nino, are another cause of concern, as they have an averse impact on the health and lives of a vast number of people and the ecological system in the region. In order to establish new systems of fire risk management and anti-smoke measures, I am proposing a seminar of experts from the countries concerned as well as the relevant international organisations so that we can better draw on abundant experience and knowledge. Also in this vein, I would like to encourage the International Tropical Timber Organization (ITTO) to dispatch missions on fire-management.[5]

Hashimoto and Obuchi's diplomatic forays in the region signal Japan's intent to be more than just a merchant state. This chapter raises the following questions: Why is Tokyo playing a more active political role in Southeast Asia? Where and in which areas does the Japanese government seem likely to play a more active role? What is Tokyo's style of diplomacy in this region? What are the major impediments to Japan's regional role?

Even though Japan engaged in sporadic and tentative diplomatic initiatives in Southeast Asia during the Cold War, the end of the Cold War and the outbreak of the Gulf War were catalysts that propelled Japan to play a larger international role. This chapter examines four case studies that reflect Tokyo's new activism in addressing regional instability, real or potential. They are: the Cambodian conflict, human rights and democracy in Myanmar, the Spratlys dispute in the South China Sea, and the formation of the ASEAN Regional Forum (ARF). Distilled from these case studies, the Japanese style of diplomatic initiatives displays the following features: an emphasis on playing a 'bridging role' between antagonists, a preference for multilateralism and consensus diplomacy, a willingness to be involved in domestic politics of Southeast Asian countries when that is deemed necessary for regional stability, a reliance on Official Development Aid (ODA) to induce good behaviour from recalcitrant groups, and a pragmatic 'realist approach' to domestic politics in the region despite the idealistic rhetoric of democracy and human rights in its foreign policy. Each of these features are not uniquely Japanese but as a whole there is, arguably, a distinctive Japanese diplomatic style which is shaped by the nation's history, culture and capabilities.

Although Japan has adopted a higher political profile in Southeast Asia in the post-Cold War era, certain constraints to its activism still remain. Its diplomatic successes are to a certain extent contingent on the support of the ASEAN countries, China and the United States, and the consent and co-operation of the target states or groups. Moreover, its initiatives are over-reliant on ODA at a time when Japan is scaling back its ODA because of financial constraints; the country is unwilling and unable to underpin its diplomacy with military power.

The Cold War

Japan's diplomatic initiatives in Southeast Asia

Even during the Cold War, Japan was involved in a few nascent and tentative attempts to address regional conflict. For instance, the Japanese government did try to act as a bridge between Malaysia, Indonesia and the Philippines in 1964 to resolve their differences over the formation of Malaysia. Later, in 1970, Japan also sought to address the Cambodian imbroglio at a conference on Cambodia held in Jarkarta.[6] However, these were exceptions to the norm of concentrating on economics and seeking refuge behind the US–Japan Alliance.

Japan's articulation of the Fukuda Doctrine in 1977 was a first step in becoming more active in Southeast Asia.[7] In the wake of US withdrawal from Vietnam, Japan hoped to avoid a polarisation between communist and non-communist Southeast Asia which might lead to regional instability. Despite the new doctrine of activism, there was virtually no progress in reconciling the non-communist ASEAN countries and communist Indochina. The attempts to use ODA (Official Development Assistance) to lure Vietnam out of the Soviet orbit were complete failures.[8] Vietnam remained more concerned with obtaining the support of a superpower ally as an insurance policy against the Chinese threat. Moreover, Hanoi did not view Tokyo as an honest broker because of its security partnership with the US. The failure of Japanese diplomacy was clearly demonstrated when Vietnam invaded Cambodia in 1979. Japan reluctantly joined the united front forged between China, the US and ASEAN, which objected to Vietnam's invasion of Cambodia and the alliance between Moscow and Hanoi.

Catalysts to Japan's diplomatic initiatives: the end of the Cold War and the Gulf War

Many Japanese analysts believe that the end of the global Cold War heralds a period of greater regional uncertainty. This is because vestiges of the Cold War still remain in the Korean peninsula and, despite Washington's commitments to retain a 100,000 troops and a strengthening of the US–Japan Alliance, it is not unthinkable that the US will downsize its presence in the future. Also China is seen as a long-term threat even if most Japanese politicians, bureaucrats and analysts are too polite and unwilling to annoy China by stating that openly. The Japanese push to strengthen its relations with the Southeast Asian countries is, in part, to counter-balance China's rising influence as a great economic, strategic and political power in the region.

Even if the consequences of the end of the Cold War are not altogether benign, the termination of US–Soviet rivalry and Moscow's retreat from the region have created space for Tokyo to adopt a more expansive role. If such a role is appreciated by most of the Southeast Asian states, Tokyo hopes to translate this into regional support for its quest to obtain a permanent seat in the United Nations Security Council (UNSC). Gaining a permanent seat would satisfy Japan's ambitions for status within the international community and influence in the management of global strategic issues which may impact on Japan's security interests.

One positive outcome of the collapse of the Soviet Union was that it deprived Vietnam of Soviet patronage. That, and the crippling economic and diplomatic cost of occupying its neighbour, forced Vietnam to withdraw from Cambodia in 1989. Consequently, the PRC also lost its incentive to support the Khmer Rouge against Vietnam and its Cambodian clients. Abandoned by their erstwhile patrons and desperate for economic assistance, the Cambodian factions were more receptive to Japanese overtures to play a 'bridging role'. At the 1990 Tokyo Conference, the host country invited the Cambodian factions for talks and offered them significant ODA to reconstruct their country upon cessation of the civil war. The Tokyo Conference paved the way for the Paris Peace Talks, which resulted in agreement between the Cambodian factions to hold a national election under the supervision of the United Nations.

Ironically, barely a year after Japan's commendable activism over Cambodia, its response during the Gulf War was just the opposite: reactive, piecemeal, incoherent and timid. It was simply not prepared to be embroiled in a major interstate conflict that was taking place in a distant theatre. In the case of Cambodia, the conflict was in Japan's backyard, had become intermittent and localised and appeared to demand only diplomatic and financial resources with no danger of dragging Japan into actual conflict.

The 1991 Gulf War exposed the inadequacies of Tokyo's crisis management system. Even though the country depended on the US to protect its sea lanes and oil supply from the Middle East, Japanese leaders dithered about the appropriate contributions to the UN-sanctioned multinational forces arrayed against Iraqi occupation of Kuwait. It avoided manpower contributions but, under US pressure promised financial contributions of US$13 billion toward the multilateral effort. The external and domestic criticisms that Japan could only engage in chequebook diplomacy, prompted the Japanese government to tackle the task of legal-institutional reforms to deal with future international crises.

After protracted negotiations between the ruling Liberal Democratic Party (LDP) and the non-communist opposition parties, the Japanese legislature finally passed the Peacekeeping Operations (PKO) Bill in 1992 permitting the country to despatch troops under the aegis of the UN for non-combatant roles. For its first PKO exercise, Tokyo picked Cambodia, a country where it had made substantial diplomatic investments. Besides the contribution of Japanese troops to the UN Peacekeeping Force, Japan was a key financier of UNTAC (United Nations Transitional Authority in Cambodia). Not surprisingly, the UN picked Akashi Yasushi, a Japanese national, to head UNTAC. This can be interpreted as a shrewd move by the UN to ensure continued Japanese support for the mission in Cambodia and future UN missions elsewhere. Although the experiences of Somalia and Bosnia may indicate otherwise, the UN may well emerge as a suitable vehicle for Japan to adopt a higher profile in international affairs. A multilateral approach is less likely to arouse domestic and regional suspicions of Tokyo's intentions. Indeed, Japan had made positive contributions to PKO in Mozambique, Zaire and the Golan Heights. Such involvement in Southeast Asia, Africa and the Middle East were probably unthinkable, let alone acceptable to the Japanese and their neighbours barely a decade ago.

The convening of the Forum for Comprehensive Development of Indochina in Tokyo may be viewed as another attempt by Japan to influence development in that region.[9] In addition, it also specifically advocated the Mekong Basin project to spearhead regional developments that could benefit Vietnam, Cambodia, Laos, Thailand and China.[10] Besides the potential economic benefits Japan might gain from this project, it also appears that it is keen to promote its vision of regional order and stability, by responding to common economic interest of the Indochinese countries and instigating a positive-sum game to reduce the possibility of future conflicts.

Hun Sen's 1997 coup d'etat and the Japanese peace plan in Cambodia

Despite Japan's hope to reconcile the warring Cambodian factions and foster peace in the war torn country, civil war erupted once again in 1997. The renewal of violence demonstrated the limits for external powers, Japan, the US, ASEAN and the UN, in addressing the seemingly intractable domestic conflict. Japan, the UN and even the NGOs (Non-Governmental Organizations) had poured in substantial resources to rebuild the country but these efforts appeared to be of little avail.[11]

The immediate cause of the renewed conflict in Cambodia is murky. Cambodia had a hydra-headed government of two coexisting but rival Prime Ministers, Prince Ranariddh and Hun Sen. Although Prince Ranariddh and his royalist FUNCINPEC (National United Front for an Independent, Peaceful, Neutral and Co-operative Cambodia) coalition had won UN-supervised elections, the Prince had no choice but to share power with Hun Sen and his party, the former communist Cambodian People's Party (CPP). It was not a marriage between equals; the Hun Sen group had de facto control of the army and bureaucracy, the two institutions that still functioned in Cambodia. Without the inclusion of Hun Sen, the Prince would have been unable to exercise power even though he had won at the ballot box. The power sharing arrangement was an untidy compromise but was endorsed by the international community including the UN, ASEAN and Japan.

The international community, including Japan, faced a dilemma. It could have supported the democratic ideal that Prince Ranariddh become the sole Prime Minister because he had won the election but the constraint was that Hun Sen controlled the army and the state bureaucracy. The latter could derail the peace process if he were excluded from power. Thus, even though Tokyo's ODA Charter clearly stated that foreign aid disbursement was predicated upon the recipient regime's respect for human rights and democracy, it adopted a pragmatic approach in addressing the Cambodian conflict.

The power sharing arrangement in Cambodia was marked by suspicions and rivalries right from the very start but came undone when the Prince allied himself with the Khmer Rouge against Hun Sen and his Vietnamese backers. Hun Sen alleged that Ranariddh was guilty of smuggling arms to reinforce FUNCINPEC forces in Phnom Penh and forging an unholy alliance with the remnants of the Khmer Rouge but if true Ranariddh was probably doing these out of desperation to bolster his weak position in response to Hun Sen's relentless pressure to marginalise him. Hun Sen was gradually but surely undermining and weakening his rival's position: he succeeded in attracting large numbers of disgruntled Khmer Rouge troops to defect from the Pol Pot leadership and join his army; he also sought to create dissension and defection from Ranariddh's FUNCINPEC coalition. The simmering conflict exploded in July 1997.

Earlier, anticipating the deterioration in Cambodian politics, the G–8 countries at the June 1997 Denver Summit delegated the task of addressing Cambodia's instability to Japan and France. Tokyo sent envoys to the Cambodian factions to urge a peaceful resolution of the tension between them. Despite promises of good and peaceful behaviour from both camps to the Japanese emissaries, the coup occurred shortly after this Japanese initiative.[12]

The July 1997 coup was a one-sided affair; Hun Sen's troops easily crushed the weak forces of Ranariddh. In reprisals against Ranariddh's supporters, the Hun Sen group committed serious violations of human rights but Japan, continued to deal with Hun Sen because he was probably the only strongman who could restore political stability to Cambodia.

The entire episode was particularly embarrassing to ASEAN which had hoped to crown its 30th Anniversary with an enlarged ASEAN 10 that would include the new members of Vietnam, Burma and Cambodia. The organisation hoped that a more inclusive ASEAN would lead to a more stable Southeast Asia and translate into greater diplomatic clout in international affairs. In the end, ASEAN rejected Cambodian membership because of domestic violence and problems of governability.

Japan had supported ASEAN's initiative to promote regional solidarity, peace and stability because it perceived that its strategic and economic interests were intertwined with Southeast Asia. When the Hun Sen forced Prince Ranariddh and some of his supporters into exile, Japan promptly suspended ODA to Cambodia. ODA is exceptionally important to Phnom Penh because about 40 per cent of Cambodia's $780 million budget in 1997 depended on it; in 1996, Tokyo had pledged between $98 million and $123.3 million in economic aid to Cambodia.[13] Tokyo hoped to exercise some leverage over the Hun Sen regime because of its excessive dependence on foreign aid.[14]

Japan's approach to the coup had a different nuance from those of the US and some of the ASEAN members. Washington quickly condemned Hun Sen's coup as a breach of the 1993 election and a violation of human rights. In the case of Singapore, the city-state stated clearly that it was in principle against any unconstitutional and violent seizure of power. Tokyo's response was much more muted. While deploring the violence and the abuse of human rights in Cambodia, Tokyo avoided calling it a coup and did not withdraw its recognition of the Hun Sen government despite supplications from Prince Ranariddh. However, it made any resumption of ODA contingent upon the holding of a clean and fair election in Cambodia in 1998.[15] But barely a month after it froze its ODA to the Hun Sen government, Japan resumed its aid even though other major donors including the US, Germany and Australia continued suspending their aid to Cambodia.[16] Because of Japan's importance as an aid donor, both Hun Sen and Ranariddh sought to visit and to court Tokyo. Ranariddh's request was denied by Tokyo but Hun Sen was permitted a 'private' visit ostensibly for medical reasons.[17]

In the midst of anarchy within Cambodia, the Japanese government had to consider evacuating its nationals from Phnom Penh. Unlike some ASEAN countries, which sent military planes to the Cambodian capital to rescue their nationals, the Japanese response was a symbolic attempt to break new ground. Sensitivities within the coalition government and potential negative public sentiments towards the despatch of military aircraft to a danger zone prevented any bold move but the Japanese government still took the opportunity to depart from another post-war taboo by sending military aircraft overseas, even though most of its nationals had already been evacuated by commercial planes. It was bizarre, however, that the destination for aircraft was Bangkok and not Phnom Penh. No doubt this was to avoid negative public reaction.

In 1998, after consultations with the ASEAN countries and the Friends of Cambodia (another group of countries that is interested in the Cambodian conflict), Tokyo proposed a peace plan that would pave the way for national elections later that year. According to the Japanese-brokered peace plan, Prince Ranariddh would stand trial for weapon smuggling and collusion with the Khmer Rouge and, upon conviction by Hun Sen's kangaroo court, would receive a royal pardon from his father, King Sihanouk. Ranariddh also agreed to give up further dealings with the Khmer Rouge and his remaining FUNCINPEC troops were to merge with the national army. In turn, the Prince would be permitted to compete 'freely' in the proposed July national elections.

Japan's involvement in Cambodia reveals the following pattern: a 'bridging' role between the G8, ASEAN, the Friends of Cambodia and the Cambodian factions to address the crisis even if it meant entanglement in the domestic politics of a Southeast Asian country; the use of ODA to purchase good behaviour from target groups, and a pragmatic preference for order rather than the abstract principles of democracy. The Japanese-brokered peace proposal in Cambodia was hardly neutral: its terms favoured Hun Sen rather than Ranariddh. The conditions that the Prince give up dealings with the Khmer Rouge and amalgamate the remnants of his forces with the army clearly favoured Hun Sen. Ironically, Hun Sen was an ex-Khmer Rouge who also sought to encourage Khmer Rouge forces to join the army. That Ranariddh was to be found guilty in a dubious court also obviously damaged the Prince's prestige.

It appears that Japan is keen for the national elections to be held so that the likely winner, Hun Sen, is properly legitimised in the eyes of the international community, and then restores order in Cambodia. If Hun Sen is shunned by the international community, it is possible that the Cambodian government may move closer to Beijing to avoid isolation. Apparently, Beijing is annoyed by Rannaridh's alleged good ties with Taiwan and will work with any strongman including Hun Sen who respects its sensitivities towards the Taiwan question. It is probable that Japan and the US, along with some of the other regional countries, would prefer Cambodia not to be too closely tied to China. In the ideal scenario, a national election in Cambodia in 1998 will permit a resumption of foreign aid especially from Japan, the repair of national monuments like the Angkor Wat, restoration of tourism, progress in mine-clearing and the start of the Mekong Basin project. The alternative is bleak: more killing fields despite the best intentions of the international community, including Japan.

Japanese diplomacy in Burma

Besides Cambodia, Tokyo also sought to play a role in the domestic conflict in Burma. While the Japanese government has maintained cordial relations with Burma and its military rulers, there is also substantial good will within Japan, especially in the mass media, for Aung San Suu Kyi, the Nobel Peace Laureate, the symbol of Burma's democratic movement and the nemesis of the military junta. After the military disregarded Aung San Suu Kyi's electoral victory in 1990,

Japan suspended ODA to Burma and made its resumption contingent on the release of Aung San Suu Kyi from house arrest, progress in Burma's democratisation and respect for human rights. Since Japan was the largest foreign aid donor to Burma,[18] the military junta could not ignore their key donor if they did not desire their country to fall further behind the rest of the ASEAN economies.

On 10 June 1995, the junta first informed the Japanese embassy in Yangon before releasing elsewhere the news about its decision to free Aung San Suu Kyi from house arrest. Japan had calibrated its ODA disbursement to Burma dependent on the junta's conduct: more aid if there was political relaxation and the reduction or freezing of aid if there was a crackdown on the democratic movement.[19] The Japanese ambassador to Burma is also known to have tried a bridging role between the military junta and Ang San Suu Kyi and has urged them to talk and seek national reconciliation.[20] Thus far, these attempts have not borne fruits. To the military junta, the most critical issue is to maintain political control and order rather than to appease Japan or grant political space to Aung San Suu Kyi and the democratic movement even at the cost of losing its foreign aid.

Similar to its approach in Cambodia, Tokyo is less critical of the military junta than Washington. Unlike its American ally, Japan does not impose trade embargo and economic sanctions against new investments by Japanese companies in Burma because of the junta's abuse of human rights. While Prime Minister Hashimoto said that Burma's membership in ASEAN should not be used as a camouflage for human rights abuse, Japan did not oppose its membership in ASEAN. According to *Asiaweek*:

> The Japanese are also offering a carrot to ASEAN's newest member, Myanmar (Burma). Fresh aid from Tokyo will come in the form of $20 million to upgrade Yangon International Airport. Publicly, Japan insists the money by no means represents support for Mayamar's military regime, only an emergency loan to ensure aviation safety. But Foreign Ministry officials in Tokyo hint that they want to maintain engagement with the junta to nudge it toward a measure of democracy. The US prefers to leave Yangon out in the cold, and apparently objected in private to Japan's unilateral move. Japanese companies, however are eager to get into Myanmar. And the Japanese do not want the country to turn even more toward the Chinese, who already supply most of its military hardware.[21]

There are also persistent rumours that Burma has permitted China to set up listening posts in its territory for surveillance of ships traversing the Indian Ocean and into the Straits of Malacca. Although denied by the Chinese and Burmese, such suspicions give further justification to Japan's attempts to befriend Burma and prevent it from drifting too closely into the Chinese orbit. In dealings with Burma, we can again detect a familiar pattern of Japanese diplomacy: seek a 'bridging' role, offer foreign aid incentives, pursue a softer line towards authoritarian regimes than Washington and a willingness to work with them in consideration of the 'China factor'.

Japan and the Spratlys dispute

Although Japan is not a claimant state, it is concerned about the Spratlys dispute in the South China Sea because around 70 per cent of its oil supplies are transported by tankers through the atolls' vicinity. Since the Peoples Republic of China (PRC), Vietnam, Malaysia, Brunei, Taiwan and the Philippines claim part or all of the Spratlys and indeed China and Vietnam had engaged in naval skirmishes over some of the islands, there is a potential danger that any escalation of tension over the issue of sovereignty and suspected reserves of oil and minerals will destabilise the region. The Spratlys dispute is a potential a flashpoint in East Asia along with the other two in the Korean peninsula and the Taiwan Straits. Since I have already written in detail about Tokyo's attempts to address the conflict in the South China Sea, only a few points will be highlighted in this chapter.[22]

First, when the Philippines approached Japan to intercede with the PRC over the 1995 Mischief Reef Incident[23], it responded positively; then Prime Minister Murayama Tomiichi urged the PRC to act with restraint in the South China Sea. Japan also offered to host and fund annual semi-official workshops on the South China Sea in Tokyo. These actions on the part of Japan can be understood as the country's new found willingness to be involved in sensitive strategic issues. In the case of Japan and the Spratlys dispute, the country seeks to perform the roles which it is comfortable with: that of being a 'bridge' between disputants and providing financial support for dispute resolution. Similar to Japanese initiatives in Cambodia and Myanmar, Tokyo is not oblivious to the China factor in the South China Sea dispute.

Tokyo and the ASEAN Regional Forum

Arguably, more successful than its involvement in Cambodia was Tokyo's contribution to establishing the ASEAN Regional Forum (ARF). With the end of Cold War and its polarisation of the region, it became feasible for Japan to envisage and propose a multilateral organisation in Southeast Asia that could serve as a regular platform to discuss political and security issues, promote confidence building, increase military transparency, and enhance regional order. Potentially, the ARF might evolve into a regional mechanism that helps to pre-empt regional conflict.

When foreign Minister Nakayama Taro floated his proposal for a Southeast Asian forum to discuss security issues, it startled the ASEAN countries because there was no precedence of Japan initiating ideas concerning regional security. Moreover, some of the ASEAN countries were initially sensitive to the manner in which the proposals were made; Nakayama did not engage in prior consultation or secure a prior understanding with the ASEAN countries before he officially floated his trial balloon. This appeared odd especially because it came from Japan, a country whose culture places a premium on consensus-building.

Two clarifications about Japan and the ARF need to be made at this juncture. First, even though Japan has claimed credit for the intellectual underpinnings for the ARF, ASEAN–ISIS, an organisation comprising regional think-tanks had also made similar proposals about an ARF-type organisation around the same time. Thus while Japan did indeed provide some impetus to the formation of the ARF, its proposals were by no means original. According to some ASEAN–ISIS insiders, a top Japanese foreign ministry official, Satoh Yukio, had attended an ASEAN–ISIS meeting where nascent ideas about the formation of the ARF were articulated. Apparently Satoh informed his ministry about the discussions and it was refined and repackaged as 'Nakayama's Initiative'. Second, proposals from Tokyo about the ARF should be more accurately known as 'Satoh's Initiatives'[24]; Nakayama merely articulated ideas that have been already formulated by Satoh and his Ministry of Foreign Affairs.

Just how substantial is Japan's vision of an ARF as a multilateral organisation that could possibly address regional instability? In reality, it is simply too early to tell. The ARF has held regular summits that draws the participation of top leaders beyond the region including the US, Japan and the PRC. A forum that provides an opportunity for nations to seek clarifications and to build confidence and relationships is obviously better than none. However, critics have pointed out that the real underpinning of regional stability is the traditional balance of power; the ARF may end up just a talk-shop without the capacity to address the real hot spots in Pacific-Asia: the divided Korean peninsula, the Taiwan Straits and the Spratlys dispute. [25] Even though Japan hopes that the ARF will help to socialise China to become a more co-operative and transparent state that is more at ease with its neighbours, China adamantly refuses to discuss any issues which may impinge on its sovereignty. These include the Spratlys dispute and the Taiwan Straits. Although Japan was one of the intellectual leaders to set up the ARF, certain Japanese officials have expressed their concerns about the limits of the ARF as a multilateral organisation to underpin regional stability. A key dissatisfaction in the perception that the ASEAN states are setting the agenda for the ARF while non-ASEAN participants including Japan do not. A corollary of an ASEAN-driven organisation is a tendency that regional attention is centred narrowly on Southeast Asia while neglecting developments in the Korean peninsula.[26] While certain Japanese analysts appreciate the ARF's confidence building measures (CBMs), they also note its present limitations: an evolutionary approach and decision-making by consensus which implies that the 'ARF would not be able to effectively respond to regional contingencies'.[27]

These analysts have also pointed out that the ARF has yet to develop beyond CBMs to constructing mechanisms of preventive diplomacy and crisis management. Thus, to Japan, the US–Japan alliance remains the linchpin of their security policy and nascent multilateral organisations, like the ARF, are at best, merely a supplement to the alliance to maintain regional stability.

Problems and prospects

Japan is likely to adopt a higher politico-strategic profile in the region whenever an opportunity presents itself. To address the emergence of China as a great economic and strategic power in the twenty-first century, and to further cement

US–Japanese relations after the 1995 Okinawa Incident, Japan adopted the New Defense Guidelines whereby it will assist the US in 'situations in areas surrounding Japan'. Some Japanese analysts have interpreted the ambiguous phrase as encompassing not only the Korean peninsula and the Taiwan Straits but also the South China Sea, the Straits of Malacca and as far as the Gulf region. To avoid further annoying Beijing, Tokyo has purposefully kept its explanation ambiguous and even contradictory: the phrase 'situations in areas surrounding Japan' is a 'situational rather than a geographical concept'.[28]

In August 1997, the Japanese government held a meeting on the Guidelines with the ASEAN country ambassadors. Some of the ASEAN countries requested clarification of the term 'situations in areas surrounding Japan' but Tokyo insists that there is no intention to define a geographical range.[29] If the US were to commit itself to keeping the sea lanes open in the South China Sea in the event of a regional conflict, Japan is most likely to be obliged to provide logistical support to the US even if it eschews direct military involvement in any armed conflict. beyond defending its immediate territory.

Another instance of Japan seeking to play a more active regional role was when the Indonesian political crisis erupted in May 1998. Tokyo despatched six C–130 military transport planes to Singapore and two maritime safety vessels to the vicinity of Indonesian waters in case they were needed to evacuate Japanese nationals. However, many Japanese critics argued that commercial flights were already adequate to bring their nationals to safety and that the crisis merely provided the Japanese government an opportunity to test the political waters, give an inter-national role to its armed forces, and to reduce domestic and international allergy to Japanese military despatched abroad.[30]

Although Japan has embarked on a more active political role in Southeast Asia in the 1990s, it has to operate within the constraints of the US–Japan Alliance. Not underpinned by autonomous military power, Tokyo has to rely on the ODA carrot as a key instrument of its foreign policy. Even though it has demonstrated some degree of autonomy from the US with regards to addressing authoritarian regimes in Cambodia and Burma, it is able to do so insofar that the independence of its foreign policy does not impinge on the core strategic interests of the US.

A case in point is Tokyo's reluctance to support an ASEAN initiative to sign a Southeast Asia Nuclear Weapon Free Zone Treaty (SEANWFZ). Since it is the only country that had suffered from a nuclear catastrophe, had rejected the acquisition of nuclear devices as a foreign policy principle, and had criticised China's nuclear testing, it is perhaps surprising that Japan does not support the SEANWFZ. The US and the PRC do not support the SEANWFZ for different reasons. In the case of Washington, it is concerned that the Treaty may compromise the freedom of navigation of its ships with nuclear capability in Southeast Asian waters. As for the PRC, it is afraid that recognition of the SEANWFZ may compromise its territorial claims in the South China Sea. The key reason why Japan does not support the SEANWFZ is simply because its American ally rejects the proposal.[31] Japan's softer line towards Burma and Cambodia does not affect core American strategic interests but if it had supported ASEAN's SEANWFZ, the US would have interpreted it as compromising American security interest. In addition, because Tokyo operates within the framework of the US–Japan Alliance and the Western camp of capitalism and liberal democracy; some East Asian countries are unlikely to view Japan as neutral and 'autonomous', but matter as one which is often closely aligned to US strategic and ideological interests.

Another challenge to an active Japanese foreign policy in Southeast Asia is the reduction of its ODA. Since its economy has been in the doldrums, ODA is no longer a sacred cow safe from the sharp knives of the Ministry of Finance. Can Japan hope to strengthen its international role while cutting back on ODA? Last but not least is the weakness in Japan's crisis management system. The Gulf War, the Peruvian hostage crisis and the Cambodian civil war have, time and time again, caught the Japanese decision-makers flat-footed. Unless Japan can improve its crisis management system within the Prime Minister's office, the Cabinet, the Ministry of Foreign Affairs and the Defence Agency, it will be difficult for the country to act decisively in international affairs.

Notes

1 See for example, Curtis, Gerald L. (ed.), *Japan's Foreign Policy after the Cold War: Coping with Change*, M.E. Sharpe, Armonk, NY, 1993.
2 *East Asian Strategic Review: 1997–1998*, National Institute for Defense Studies, Tokyo, 1998, p. 206.
3 The statistics were released by the Japanese embassy in Singapore on 4 May 1998 to coincide with Obuchi's keynote speech.
4 Obuchi, K, 'Japan and East Asia: Outlook for the New Millenium', 4 May 1998. Transcript of speech was released by the Japanese embassy in Singapore.
5 Obuchi, 'Japan and East Asia', 1998.
6 Sudo, S., *Southeast Asia in Japanese Security Policy*, Pacific Strategic Papers, no. 3, Institute of Southeast Asian Studies, Singapore, 1991, p. 21.
7 Sudo, S., *The Fukuda Doctrine and ASEAN: New Dimensions in Japanese Foreign Policy*, Institute of Southeast Asian Studies, Singapore, 1992).
8 Shiraishi, M., *Japanese Relations with Vietnam: 1951–1987*, Southeast Asia Programme, Cornell University, Ithaca, 1990.
9 Soeya, Y, 'Vietnam in Japan's Regional Policy', Economic and Politics Series, East–West Center Working Papers, no. 6, May 1995. See also Ronald Bruce St John, 'Japan's Moment in Indochina: Washington Initiative … Tokyo Success', *Asian Survey*, vol. 35, no. 7, July 1995.
10 A detailed explanation on Japan's support for the Mekong River Basin Development is found in the Japanese Ministry of Foreign Affairs (MFA) web page: *http://www.mofa.go.jp/asean/dimension*.
11 Japan disbursed US$ 152.04 of bilateral assistance to Cambodia in 1995. See Ministry of Foreign Affairs, Japan's Official Development Assistance 1996, Association for Promotion of International Cooperation, Tokyo, 1997, p. 84.
12 On 18 June 1997, the military factions of Ranariddh and Hun Sen exchanged gunfire in Phnom Penh. During the Denver Summit (20–22 June), it was agreed that special envoys would be sent to Cambodia from Japan and France and a special statement was adopted which called for political stability, restoration of order and confirmation of the schedule for holding a general election in 1998. On 26 June Japanese special envoy Imagawa Yukio met separately with Hun Sen and Ranariddh. Both Prime Ministers promised to end the conflict and hold the general elections on schedule. However, on 5 July, Hun Sen's troops attacked Ranariddh's forces in Phnom Penh and fighting broke out across Cambodia.
13 *The New Paper* (Singapore), 7 August 1997.

14 Prince Ranariddh argued that Japan could play a more positive and active role in Cambodia by sending a strong message to Hun Sen through the withdrawal of its ODA to Phnom Penh. Author's interview, Singapore, August 1997.

15 On the resumption of ODA, the MFA stated that Japan asked the Cambodian government to observe the following four basic principles: observation of the Paris Peace Accords; maintenance of the present Constitution and political system; respect for basic human rights, and the implementation of free and fair elections in May 1998. Press Conference by the Japan MFA Press secretary, 25 July 1997, *http://www.mofa.jo.jp/press/1997/7/725.html*

16 Tokyo was also the first to resume its aid to the PRC after the Tiananmen Incident and also to the Burmese regime after its crackdown on the democratic movement. Perhaps Tokyo hopes that this gesture of goodwill will provide an incentive for these regimes to be less recalcitrant, suspicious and more appreciative of the positive rewards of good behaviour and an increase in ODA.

17 According to an informed Japanese source, Hun Sen was allowed to visit Tokyo for the ostensible reason of fixing his artificial, glass eye which was made in Japan. Hun Sen took advantage of his 'private visit' to hold consultations with the Japanese government. In contrast, the Japanese government discouraged the exiled Prince Ranariddh from visiting Tokyo to lobby for support. Thus Tokyo did not adopt an even-handed approach but leaned towards the person who held the reins of power in Cambodia.

18 Japan disbursed US$114.23 of bilateral assistance to Myanmar in 1995. See, *Japan's Official Development Assistance 1996*, 1997, p. 84.

19 For a Japanese view on Tokyo–Yangon relations and the issues of ODA, human rights and democracy, see Uchida, I., 'Embracing the Future: Japan must rethink its Myanmar Policy', *Burma Debate*, vol. 2, no. 4, August/ September 1995.

20 See 'Japan trying to mediate a political pact in Myanmar', *The Business Times*, 27 August 1996, 'Can Tokyo do anything to influence Events in Myanmar?', BBC London (English), Newshour, 2,100 hours, 10 June 1996, 'Burma: Japanese Ambassador 'Mediator' between SLORC, Suu Kyi', FBIS–ES–96–099, 21 May 1996. For another example of Japan's 'bridging role': 'She (Suu Kyi) met with Ambassador Yoichii Yamaguchi on 17 and 20 May just before the latest mass arrests of NLD members elected in the 1990 elections and of other activists, and NLD sources said she asked the envoy to convey to the junta some of the requests of Myanmar's democratic movement', FBIS–EAS–96–106, 31 May 1996.

21 Editorial, 'Helping Hands: Tokyo's active role in Cambodia and Myanmar is welcomed', *Asiaweek*, 20 March 1998, p. 16.

22 Lam, P.E., 'Japan and the Spratlys Dispute', *Asian Survey*, vol. 36, no. 10, October 1996.

23 When the Philippines discovered Chinese territorial markers, structures and personnel on Mischief Reef in the South China Sea, it protested vigorously to the PRC. The Incident also alarmed the ASEAN states who were afraid that the PRC is becoming more assertive about their territorial claims.

24 Tsutomu, K., *APEC: Ajia taiheiyo shinjitsujo no mosaku* (APEC: The search for a Asia–Pacific New Order), Nihon kokusai mondai kenkyujo, Tokyo, 1995, pp. 264–73.

25 Leifer, M., 'The ASEAN Regional Forum', *Adelphi Paper*, no. 302 (London: International Institute of International Affairs, 1996).

26 Kondo, S., 'The ARF and Its Future: A Japanese Perspective', Institute of Defence and Strategic Studies, Seminar on the Future of the ARF, 27–28 April, 1998, Singapore, p. 3.

27 Kondo, 1998, p. 2.

28 *East Asian Strategic Review: 1997–1998*, 1998, p. 55.

29 *East Asian Strategic Review: 1997–1998*, 1998, p. 213.

30 See Kwan Weng Kin, 'Tokyo under fire for sending military planes', *Straits Times*, 23 May 1998.

31 According to Ambassador-at-large Nobuo Matsunaga, it is simply not practical for Japan to support the SEANWFZ if the US is against it. Author's conversation with Ambassador Matsunaga at Japan Institute of International Affairs, Tokyo, December 1995.

8 Conclusion

S. Javed Maswood

Contributors to this volume have focused on the nature and effectiveness of Japan's regional diplomacy. In this brief conclusion, I will draw on some of the main findings to present a broad outline of Japan's regional engagement. Such an exercise runs the inevitable risk of distorting individual contributions and I may succeed only in doing considerable injustice to the rich variety and detail presented in each of the chapters. The richness and contrast is greatest in the chapters on environment and human rights, where the authors present a divergent conclusion on the effectiveness of Japan's regional diplomacy. At the same time, in terms of understanding the dynamics of contemporary Japanese regional foreign policy objectives, the contributors generally agree that the Japanese government has progressively shifted to, or is searching for, a more active role. Evidence of activism can be found in Japanese willingness, for instance, to participate in a search for solutions to regional conflicts. There is no suggestion, however, that the Japanese government will develop a leadership role in defining and imposing solutions to regional issues.

For several decades, it was obvious that Japanese economic power had not translated into political power and influence, either on a regional or a global scale. Despite its status as the second largest economy in the world, the Japanese government maintained a low political profile and its modest diplomatic presence was even more pronounced in a regional context. The constraints to a larger regional role and influence could be traced both to the regional countries and to competing Japanese national interests. Within the region there was unease about Japanese involvement in regional affairs as a result of wartime experiences. The Japanese government, for its part, emphasised its security and economic linkages with the United States and adopted a foreign policy posture of following American initiatives. Within Japan, bureaucratic dominance of policy making structures also contributed to relative foreign policy inactivism. The more powerful and larger domestic ministries swamped any latent activist desires within the Ministry of Foreign Affairs in Japan to be more active on the international stage. According to Kent Calder, Japanese foreign policy is best described as reactive.

Kent Calder formulated the reactive state thesis, in the late 1980s to delineate a foreign policy that was driven less by independently formulated foreign policy objectives than by foreign pressure.[1] In particular, he argued that Japanese foreign policy was more susceptible to American pressure than is the case for most other countries. Subsequent refinements of this foreign policy model have included a role for domestic interest groups within Japan. Thus, Frances Rosenbluth[2], and Dennis Encarnation and Mark Mason[3] argued that financial and economic liberalisation in Japan, as demanded by the US, was only realised with the active support of similarly inclined domestic pressure groups.

Borrowing on Eric Nordlinger's work on democratic states[4], the difference between an active and a reactive foreign policy can be shown as in Figure 8.1.

A reactive foreign policy can be identified in situations where the US and Japan disagree and the Japanese government acts on American interests, while activism might be described as behaviour that can be classified in one of the following two categories:

1 where US and Japan disagree and Japan acts on its interests, and
2 where US and Japan agree and Japan acts on its interests.

Terms like activism and reactivism are broad categories and their usage should not be interpreted as implying that periods of Japanese foreign policy can be exclusively identified as being either reactive or active. Moreover, the idea of a reactive foreign policy was largely used to explain foreign economic policies, particularly trade relations with the United States. Japanese behaviour appeared to be highly sensitive to US pressure and the explanation had a good fit to episodic trade disputation between Japan and the United States. The model, however, has also been used to explain Japanese foreign policy behaviour in a broad range of issue areas.

However, if recent Japanese foreign policy was largely reactive there were also instances of activism. The Japanese government, for example, was active in early negotiations to establish the Asia Pacific Economic Cooperation (APEC) forum, which has become an important mechanism for promoting freer trade among regional members. Examples of activism can be found even in more politically charged regional issues. In June 1990 the Japanese government convened a meeting

		Japanese and American Interests	
		Convergent	Divergent
Japanese and American Policy Responses	Convergent	Proactive	Reactive
	Divergent	N.A.	Proactive

Figure 8.1 Proactive and reactive Japanese foreign politics

in Tokyo in which the four warring factions in Cambodia agreed to a cease-fire. In the absence of enforcement mechanisms this was largely a symbolic agreement but important, nonetheless, in ending deadlock at the Paris conference to find a solution to the Cambodian conflict. By the late 1990s, as documented by Lam Peng Er, Japan's involvement in a Cambodian solution was both more intensive and effective.

Japan was never completely reactive and passive but, in recent years, there has been a shift to a more activist foreign policy stance. This is because of changes in the underlying factors that supported a reactive foreign policy. There is considerably less regional antipathy toward Japan and within Japan the bureaucratic dominance of policy making is also changing as a result of many factors, including political reforms. There is also a better understanding and recognition among political leaders that Japan has to use its considerable economic strength to contribute to regional stability. However, if the Japanese government seems ready to play a larger regional role, it still must balance that with its wider roles and responsibilities. In other words, as Pempel argues, the Japanese government has to balance the tensions between regionalism and internationalism.

The reality is that Japan has dual citizenship, as a regional powerhouse and as a member of the western bloc, and has not found it easy to balance its commitments. The US dominates the latter grouping and Japan's security and economic relations with the US enhance its sensitivity to American interests even more. Thus, even though it is not unusual for states to enjoy dual citizenship, problems for the Japanese government have arisen at times, as a result of discordant Japanese and American interests in the Asia Pacific region. However, even if the Japanese government defines its regional interests differently from the United States, it cannot afford to antagonise the US. Japanese policy initiatives seemingly have to clear the hurdle of American acquiescence or support and where this has not been forthcoming the Japanese government is inclined to wait for more favourable circumstances.

Maintaining good relations with the United States remains a primary Japanese foreign policy objective but demands of good regional citizenship also require Japan to be more active and to expand its regional presence. The dilemma for Japanese political leaders is that American interests do not always coincide with those of Japan and the two countries do not necessarily agree on common regional objectives. Disagreements between Japan and the US can be found in the field of human rights and democratic reforms in Asia, regional integration and regionalism, to economic management. Consequently, Japan is forced to walk a fine line and this balancing act has not proved easy.

To the extent that we can identify divergent Japanese interests in pursuing an increased regional role, it is necessary to further modify the reactive state thesis to suit the new conditions. Recognising that the Japanese government has ambitions of an expanded presence within the region, it still must balance these with the important objective of maintaining close links with the US. In that context, it is appropriate to depict emerging Japanese regional diplomacy as 'active but constrained'. It is certain that activism will continue to be constrained by demands of an American alliance. Japanese foreign policy, as Hirata states, is a hybrid and the balance between activism and reactivism is shifting in favour of the former.

As already indicated, since the end of the Second World War, Japan and the United States have developed very strong and close relations based on economic and security interdependencies. However much Japan wishes to play a regional role it cannot afford to jeopardise those trans-Pacific connections. Moreover, given that America's regional agenda is often at odds with some of the key East Asian countries, the US is a real constraint on Japanese foreign policy. The primacy of the Japan–US relationship means that Japan cannot afford to ignore American interest. Consequently, any attempt by Japan to assume a role within the region can only be achieved by implicitly or explicitly securing American acceptance of such a role. The Japanese government would not be prepared to chart an independent course if as a consequence relations with the US were to deteriorate. To the extent, therefore, that Japan can pull the United States along, we can expect to see a more prominent regional role by Japan. It is less certain whether the Japanese government can also overcome American resistance in its pursuit of regional activism, or whether it must wait for the US to come around to Japanese position on specific issues.

An opportunity for Japan to demonstrate a capacity for a larger and constructive regional role presented itself during the Asian financial and currency crisis. The financial crisis in 1997 was a result of a complex mix of endogenous and exogenous factors but the trigger to the crisis was a sudden and large scale withdrawal of foreign capital from several Southeast Asian countries. The ensuing crisis in the real economy reversed many of the gains of previous decades. Shortly before the crisis, the World Bank had identified these as 'miracle economies' for their success in achieving high growth with equity and yet it did not take long to descend to the depths of an economic meltdown.

The crisis had important consequences for the regional countries but it was also an opportunity for countries, like Japan and China, to step into the breech, play a responsible role in crisis management, and consequently emerge with an enhanced regional standing. The Chinese government was deft at 'exploiting' the crisis. It immediately reassured the crisis countries that it would not devalue the Yuan in line with falling regional currencies to ensure that its exports were not handicapped by the sudden and dramatic improvement of trade competitiveness of regional countries. This commitment was not necessarily risky, in the immediate future, because of the real economic crisis in Southeast Asia and their inability to exploit their trade advantage. Nonetheless, it created the image of China as a responsible country, willing to suffer hardship in order to facilitate early economic recovery in the crisis countries.

The crisis also created considerable expectation that Japan would use its economic prowess to assist regional countries, not only by providing immediate financial assistance but also by providing a large market for regional exports. The Japanese response was generous. This was not unusual, as Japan had earned a well-deserved reputation for chequebook diplomacy as a way of avoiding responsibility. For example in the Gulf crisis of the early 1990s, Japan was the largest single source of financial assistance but refused direct participation in the allied military operation. This time, however, in a marked departure from established diplomatic pattern, the Japanese government also proposed Asian Monetary Fund (AMF) to deal with similar crises in the future.

Japanese interests in establishing a regional monetary fund were partly to assist the regional countries and partly to secure a larger role and influence for itself. The proposal for an AMF was not simply an extension of chequebook diplomacy because it also entailed the establishment of a new institutional structure to prevent a recurrence of financial crisis. Regional countries could benefit by gaining access to emergency funds to fend off speculative attacks on local currencies and sudden capital flight. At the same time, the AMF could also become the building block for Japan's regional influence and profile. It would inevitably lead to greater regional influence for Japan since it, by providing the funds, would dominate the AMF and through it gain influence over regional economic issues.

The idea of a regional monetary institution was welcomed by regional countries but strongly criticised by the United States as unnecessarily diluting the role and importance of the International Monetary Fund and that of the United States, which dominated the IMF. The US argued that the IMF had the resources and the expertise to manage global financial crises and that while Japan might have had the resources, it lacked the expertise to deal with crises of such magnitude and might even exacerbate them by recklessly lending to countries without requiring structural reforms.

Confronted with swift and unequivocal American rejection of AMF, the Japanese government abandoned the idea. For all practical purposes, this seemed to be a replay of Japanese involvement in the 1970s Law of the Seas negotiations, and a reconfirmation of the reactive state thesis.[5] According to Michael Blaker, in the Law of the Seas negotiations, the Japanese government initially indicated its preference to retain the existing three-mile limit on territorial seas and economic zones. As a large maritime country, this was clearly in Japanese interests but the government failed to win support of other participating countries and decided to go along with the dominant view in favour of extending territorial seas and exclusive economic zones. Surprisingly, it chose not to lobby or negotiate hard to win concessions from other countries. Blaker labelled this as a 'coping' strategy, of accepting prevailing views rather persevering with its own objectives.

The Japanese abandonment of the AMF may also be interpreted as confirmation of a reactive foreign policy and of capitulation to western, especially American, pressure. However, the Japanese government did not altogether abandon the idea of a regional monetary institution. Without pushing for a formal institutional structure, a similar objective was achieved through the Miyazawa initiative, which initially provided US$30 billion in soft aid to regional countries, without the more onerous conditions required by the IMF in return for IMF aid. Moreover, in early 1999, the Japanese government established a task force to study and refine the proposal for an AMF and submit recommendations to the government. Finally, in November 1999, a meeting of Japanese and ASEAN deputy finance ministers produced an agreement to establish a 'standby facility' to provide concessional loans to countries in crisis. This agreement marked the realisation, by stealth, of the AMF that had earlier been vetoed by the US and confirmed also a determination of the Japanese government to assume a larger regional role. The important question, however, is whether the Japanese government is prepared to defy US pressure to pursue its own interests in the region.

The establishment of the standby facility did not provoke the same American reaction as had the AMF in 1997 and this more subdued response was not because the American government had been won over by the Japanese. Indeed, the US reaction was subdued not because of anything that the Japanese government had done in the intervening two years but rather because of the highly publicised criticisms of the IMF among policy analysts and suggestions that an institution like the AMF would have done a superior task of alleviating the crisis. When Japan in 1997 seemingly abandoned the proposed AMF, regional countries had no option but to turn to the IMF for assistance and to submit to harsh conditionality. IMF intervention in the crisis countries with strict restructuring requirements have been criticised as being largely irrelevant and even detrimental to economic recovery rather than being beneficial. For instance, the IMF required the Indonesian government to forcibly close some of the weaker financial institutions but instead of restoring confidence in the banking sector it created panic and did more damage to the Indonesian currency and exchange rate. The IMF has also been criticised for a formulaic approach to crisis management and inappropriate policy recommendations.

It is instructive that before the November agreement on standby loans, the Japanese government had opted to wait patiently for conditions that would make it harder for the US to overtly criticise and reject the initiative. The widespread criticisms of the IMF in policy circles and favourable reviews of the proposed AMF meant that this time, the US could not mount the same criticisms as before, even if it was displeased by the initiative. But what the episode really demonstrates is that while Japan is keen to pursue its interests, it is not prepared to do so regardless of costs and is prepared to wait for favourable international circumstances before pressing ahead. The US consequently remains an important constraint but where one might have expected Japan to abandon entirely the idea of an AMF or other similar institution, Japan was prepared to persevere and wait for more propitious circumstances.

At the same time, however, aspects of Japanese foreign policy also demonstrate a more cautious approach. This caution was evident in the East Timor crisis of 1999 and the on going struggle for democratisation in Southeast Asia. The Japanese government has not actively supported the push for democracy, which is perceived by ruling elites as part of an orchestrated western campaign to undermine regime stability. It is interesting that Japan is the largest and most stable regional democracy and yet is reticent about aggressively pursuing the democratic agenda. In the Indonesian democracy movement and in the struggle for East Timor, the Japanese government remained on the sidelines and unprepared to risk its relationship with the Indonesian government. Within the region, preserving good relations with Indonesia is a long-standing Japanese priority dating back to the Sukarno period and can be explained by Indonesia geo-strategic location on the sea-lanes of communication and trade, and by its importance as a source of oil imports. Throughout the post-war period, the Japanese government has carefully avoided upsetting close links with the Indonesian government and has been generally successful, even as Indonesia aligned itself with one or the other great powers, US, the Soviet Union, or China. This explains why the Japanese government avoided entanglement in the East Timor crisis, preferring to ensure that long term relations with Indonesia remained stable. This might be interpreted as an example of unprincipled foreign policy behaviour but might equally be explained as a result of material and pragmatic interests.

As well as balancing tensions between regionalism and internationalism, the Japanese government is careful also to avoid regional activism that might be confused by regional countries as evidence of assertive leadership. It wants a larger role but does not want to be seen as dictating solutions. It is constrained, as mentioned above, by residual antipathy within the region, and within policy circles in Japan by a lack of a clearly defined vision and programme of action. The issue of trust is not simply a hangover of wartime experiences but also of some post-war experiences, which have created a perception of Japan as an undesirable partner. As Peter Dauvergne points out there is a perception within the region of Japan behaving as an environmental predator despite also being a source of considerable environmental aid. Perceptions, such as this, are a product of accumulated history and emphasis on self-serving economic exchange between Japan and regional countries. The negatives preclude the possibility of Japan assuming a leadership mantle and explain its preference also to act through multilateral fora to gain greater political voice.

Notes

1 Calder, K., 'Japanese Foreign Economic Policy Formation: Explaining the Reactive State', *World Politics*, vol. 40, July 1988.
2 Rosenbluth, Frances M., *Financial Politics in Contemporary Japan*, Cornell University Press, Ithaca, NY, 1989.
3 Encarnation, Dennis J. and Mark Mason, 'Neither MITI No America: The Political Economy of Capital Liberalization in Japan', *International Organization*, vol. 44, no. 1, Winter 1990.
4 Nordlinger, Eric A., *On the Autonomy of the Democratic State*, Harvard University Press, Cambridge, MA, and London, 1981.
5 See Blaker, M., 'Evaluating Japanese Diplomatic Performance', in Curtis, G., *Japan's Foreign Policy After the Cold War: Coping with Change*, M.E. Sharpe, Armonk, NY, 1993.

Index